100 THINGS
BEATLES FANS
SHOULD KNOW & DO
BEFORE THEY DIE

Gillian G. Gaar

TRIUMPH
BOOKS

Copyright © 2013 by Gillian G. Gaar

Library of Congress Cataloging-in-Publication Data

Gaar, Gillian G., 1959–
  100 things Beatles fans should know & do before they die / Gillian G. Gaar.
     pages cm
  ISBN 978-1-60078-799-7
  1. Beatles—Miscellanea. I. Title. II. Title: One hundred things Beatles fans should know & do before they die.
  ML421.B4G33 2013
  782.42166092'2—dc23

                                        2012051424

This book is available in quantity at special discounts for your group or organization. For further information, contact:

Triumph Books LLC
814 North Franklin Street
Chicago, Illinois 60610
(312) 337-0747
www.triumphbooks.com

Printed in U.S.A.
ISBN: 978-1-60078-799-7
Design by Patricia Frey
Photos courtesy of Getty Images unless otherwise indicated

To Bob Wooler, who saw it all happen.
Thanks for sharing your stories with me.

Contents

1 In Which We Meet the Leading Players of Our Story

So, who were the Beatles? Even newbies most likely know the names of the band members: John, Paul, George, and Ringo. They probably also know that the Beatles were from Liverpool, England. But a Beatle fan should know a little more background info about who the band members were before they became the Fab Four.

John Winston Lennon was born on October 9, 1940, at Liverpool's Oxford Street Maternity Hospital to Alfred and Julia Lennon. Alf was a merchant seaman, and his frequent absences meant that the couple's marriage eventually foundered. In 1945, Julia gave birth to another man's child (the baby, a girl, was put up for adoption), and by 1946 she'd moved in with John "Bobby" Dykins, with whom she had two more daughters, Julia and Jacqui. At age five, John was asked who he wished to live with, his father or his mother, an agonizing choice no child should be forced to make. John chose to stay with his mother. But Julia was unable to get a divorce from Alf and legally marry Bobby. So her sister Mary Smith, known as Mimi, was able to wrest John away, insisting that he live with her and her husband, George, to spare John the indignity of being raised by a woman "living in sin."

Julia was forced to agree, but was able to see John on a regular basis as he grew up (though he would not see his father again until 1964). When John was bitten by the rock 'n' roll bug in 1956, it was Julia who bought him his first guitar. Julia also taught him to play the instrument, teaching him banjo chords, as that was the instrument she knew how to play. John then started his own group, the Quarrymen. Unlike his aunt Mimi, Julia encouraged John's interest in music. He was devastated by her death on July

15, 1958, when she was hit by a car while walking to the bus stop, after a visit with Mimi.

James Paul McCartney was born on June 18, 1942, at Walton Hospital in Liverpool to James and Mary McCartney; he would always be known by his middle name, Paul. James was a cotton salesman, while Mary worked as a nurse and midwife. James also had a keen interest in music, playing piano and trumpet, and had been the leader of a semi-pro dance band, initially called the Masked Melody Makers and later Jim Mac's Jazz Band. When Paul became interested in music, his father first gave him a trumpet, but as rock 'n' roll became a greater interest, Paul traded it in for a guitar.

The family grew to four when Peter Michael McCartney (like Paul, known by his middle name, Mike) was born in 1944. But the happy home was shattered when Mary died of breast cancer on October 31, 1956. Paul worked out his grief by spending more time practicing guitar. The following July he was taken to a church fair by his friend Ivan Vaughan to see a band whose members Ivan was friendly with—the Quarrymen.

George Harrison was born to Harold and Louise Harrison at the family's home, 12 Arnold Grove, in Liverpool, on February 25, 1944 (there's some confusion over the date of his birth; a report later stated that "family records" indicated he was born on February 24, but his birth certificate, as well as the recollections of family members and his second wife, Olivia, confirm that it was the 25th). George was the youngest of four siblings: Louise, Harry, and Peter. His father worked as a ship's steward, but gave up life at sea to become a bus driver; his mother worked as a shop assistant. The family was close; of the four Beatles, George family's was the only one to have no disruptions. Like John and Paul, when he discovered rock 'n' roll he was anxious to get a guitar. His mother gave him the money to buy his first guitar, and later helped him buy his first electric guitar. His first (short-lived) band was the Rebels, who only played a single show. He soon found another position with the Les Stewart Quartet, and regularly played with other musicians as well. One of those other musicians was Paul, who attended the same school as George. In 1958, Paul, now a member of the Quarrymen, started bringing George to the band's shows, and George eventually became a member of the band himself.

Ringo Starr was born Richard "Ritchie" Starkey on July 7, 1940, at the home of his parents, Richard and Elsie Starkey, at 9 Madryn Street, in the Dingle, one of Liverpool's poorest neighborhoods. Richard worked as a baker, and after the couple's divorce (when Ritchie was three), Elsie returned to her former occupation, tending bar in neighborhood pubs. When he was six, a burst appendix sent Ritchie to the hospital for several months; at age 13 he developed pleurisy and spent a further two years in the hospital. His education suffered, but it was during his second stay in the hospital that he first played drums, as part of a hospital band organized to occupy the young patients.

Ritchie's mother married Harry Graves in 1953, and he helped Ritchie get a job as an apprentice at a company that made gymnasium equipment. When rock 'n' roll hit the UK, Ritchie and a fellow apprentice founded the Eddie Miles Band, later renamed the Eddie Clayton Skiffle Group, in 1957. His stepfather bought him his first (secondhand) drum kit; when his paternal grandfather helped him buy a brand new kit in 1959, he moved into one of Liverpool's top acts, the Raving Texans, soon renamed Rory Storm and the Hurricanes. Ritchie's penchant for wearing jewelry led to the nickname "Rings," which then became "Ringo"—and then "Ringo Starr," so that his solo spots during the Hurricanes' sets could be called "Ringo Starr-time." Ringo was still playing with Rory Storm in 1962 when he was asked to join the band the Quarrymen had become: the Beatles.

2 The Band That Became The Beatles

The Beatles had their roots in John Lennon's skiffle group the Quarrymen, "skiffle" being a lively blend of jazz, blues, and American folk music. It was George Lee, a fellow student with John at Quarry Bank High School, who first suggested they start a skiffle group with another student, Eric Griffiths, who, like John, played guitar. John liked the idea, but decided to form his group with Griffiths, not Lee, later inviting Quarry Bank students Rod Davis and Bill Smith to join on banjo and washtub bass, respectively. John's best friend, Pete Shotton, was drafted in to play washboard (an "instrument" played by strumming the washboard with thimble-capped fingers).

The group was initially known as the Blackjacks for about a week; some accounts say there was already a band in Liverpool with the same name, while the book *John Lennon: The Life* says John's friend Pete Shotton suggested a name change to something "more in tune with the skiffling ethos of hoboes and chain gangs." Either way, the Quarrymen was a reasonable choice, given that the band's founding members all attended Quarry Bank; the school anthem, "Song of the Quarry," also features the lines "Quarrymen, old before our birth/straining muscle and sinew."

As is typical of many bands, there were various lineup changes during the early days. Smith soon stopped showing up for rehearsals, so John simply took the washtub bass from Smith's garage one day, and the role of bassist passed between Quarry Bank student Nigel Whalley (who later took over as the group's manager), Ivan Vaughan, and eventually Len Garry, both of whom attended another local high school, the Liverpool Institute. Rod and Eric also managed to rustle up a drummer, asking a friend of theirs, Colin

Hanton, if he'd join the band. Hanton was the oldest member of the group, having already left school and working as an apprentice upholsterer. His presence gave the Quarrymen a real boost, as there weren't many people who could afford an entire drum kit.

There's some uncertainty as to when the group actually formed. Rod Davis told me he thinks the group got together in early 1956; Colin Hanton has said it was the summer of that year, while Pete Shotton told Rod Davis it must've been later, as "That was the summer John and I discovered girls." Early shows were mostly at local parties, and no one bothered to keep a record of the dates. "It's so long ago," Rod says. "And it was obviously totally unimportant to us then."

The Quarrymen's early repertoire featured "just about every skiffle number Lonnie Donegan had ever recorded," says Rod, who recalls songs like "Rock Island Line," "John Henry," and "Bring a Little Water, Sylvie" in the band's setlist, adding there were also "quite a few old Carter Family numbers which had been recycled by Lonnie Donegan, such as 'My Dixie Darling,' and 'Worried Man Blues.' And then gradually people realized that the same chords that worked for skiffle also worked for rock 'n' roll. And whilst Donegan was pretty good, he wasn't anything like as sexy and glamorous as Elvis. So most people were knocked sideways by Elvis, and wanted to be Elvis and play rock 'n' roll."

Certainly that was John's ambition. But the Quarrymen's career progressed in fits and starts. On June 9, 1957, the group boldly entered the Liverpool heat for the talent contest show *TV Star Search*, but failed to qualify. Nigel Whalley managed to get the group booked at a new club in Liverpool's city center, the Cavern, but the band's tendency to veer from straight skiffle into rock 'n' roll brought complaints from the management; on one occasion, the band received a note from owner Alan Sytner saying, "Cut out the bloody rock 'n' roll!"

The band's most important show, though no one knew it at the time, was undoubtedly July 6, 1957, the legendary day John Met Paul. By the fall of 1957, Paul had joined the band, making his debut at a show at the New Clubmoor Hall on October 18, 1957. By then, Rod Davis and Pete Shotton had both left. Neither was replaced; without a banjo and washboard, the Quarrymen could now leave skiffle behind for good and become a full-fledged rock 'n' roll group. In 1958, Paul introduced George, another student at the Liverpool Institute, to the band. George was only 14 and John was hesitant about having such a youngster in his group, but, according to legend, George impressed John with a skillful performance of the classic rock instrumental "Raunchy," and he was in.

There was no need for three guitarists in the band, and Eric Griffiths was summarily dropped. Len Garry left the group when he contracted meningitis the same year. The Quarrymen were occasionally joined by another school friend of Paul's, John "Duff" Lowe, who played piano when the band had a gig at a venue that actually had a piano. It was this lineup—John, Paul, George, John Lowe, and Colin Hanton—that made one of the first known recordings of the nascent Beatles at a private studio in Liverpool.

Colin Hanton left the band in 1959, due to an argument that followed a less than impressive club date, which the band members had ruined by drinking too much during their break. Gigs petered out at this point, until August 29, 1959, when John, Paul, and George joined guitarist Ken Brown in a reformed Quarrymen that played a few dates at Liverpool's Casbah Club. But this lineup had split up by the end of October, and when John, Paul, and George entered another *TV Star Search* contest at the end of the month, they did so under the name Johnny and the Moondogs. The trio made it to the finals in Manchester on November 15, but had no money to stay overnight and thus missed appearing at the end of the show, when the winners were chosen.

George Harrison, John Lennon, and Paul McCartney stand outside of Paul's Liverpool home in 1960.

The Quarrymen name was then seemingly retired for good—until the Quarrymen decided to reform for a show commemorating the July 6, 1957, gig when John and Paul met, held on July 5, 1997, at the same location as the original show, St. Peter's Church in Liverpool. The lineup featured Eric Griffiths, Rod Davis, Len Garry, Pete Shotton, and Colin Hanton, and the show proved to be so successful, the group decided to stay together. They released their first album, *Get Back—Together* later that same year. Though Pete Shotton retired from the group in 2000, and Eric Griffiths died in 2005, the rest of the band, now joined by John Lowe, continue to play the occasional show. "We don't go out actively searching for gigs very much," Rod Davis admits. "We just wait for them to come to us on the Internet. And if they're interesting and they fit in with our otherwise hectic lifestyles then we do them." Rod also maintains the band's website www.originalquarrymen.co.uk. As the website states, though the band's name has sometimes been spelled as "Quarry Men," the proper spelling is as one word: Quarrymen.

Further reading: *The Quarrymen* (Hunter Davies), *John Lennon: In My Life* (Pete Shotton and Nicholas Schaffner), *John, Paul and Me: Before The Beatles* (Len Garry)

3 When John Met Paul

The Quarrymen, and John Lennon, might well have faded into obscurity if they hadn't agreed to play the Woolton Parish Church Garden Fête on July 6, 1957. For it was at this event that John met his future songwriting partner, Paul McCartney.

Woolton was the Liverpool neighborhood where John lived, and St. Peter's Church regularly hosted a garden fête (party) in the summer. The Quarrymen made their first appearance of the day playing on the back of a flatbed truck in the procession that led up to the church. The band played two sets in the afternoon, then shared the billing at the dance held that evening in the church hall with the George Edwards Band.

Paul had been brought to the fête by his friend Ivan Vaughan, who had briefly played bass with the Quarrymen and went to school with Paul at the Liverpool Institute. Paul was especially impressed with the band's performance of the Del Vikings' "Come Go With Me," noting that John sang with confidence even though he didn't know all the words and was making up his own; "I just thought, 'Well, he looks good, he's singing well and he seems like a great lead singer to me,'" Paul later recalled to *Record Collector*.

Before the evening performance, Ivan introduced Paul to the band. Paul was soon demonstrating his skill on the guitar; unlike the others, he actually knew how to tune the instrument. In short order, he ran through Eddie Cochran's "Twenty Flight Rock," Gene Vincent's "Be-Bop-A-Lula," and a medley of Little Richard songs, later graciously writing out the words to "Twenty Flight Rock" for the Quarrymen. A further bond was formed when John told Paul "Twenty Flight Rock" was one of his favorite songs; "That's when I knew he was a connoisseur," Paul told Beatles biographer Hunter Davies.

John didn't ask Paul to join the Quarrymen right away. He'd been the acknowledged leader of the band, and feared that getting a capable musician like Paul into the group might lead to Paul eventually challenging his authority. But he soon decided that it was better to let Paul in and make the group stronger, and about two weeks after the fête, when Pete Shotton ran into Paul cycling around the neighborhood, he asked him if he'd be interested in joining the Quarrymen. Paul said yes.

A fellow Quarry Bank student, Bob Molyneux, recorded part of the Quarrymen's evening performance on a Grundig TK8 portable reel-to-reel tape recorder. When the tape was up for auction in 1994, two short clips of Lonnie Donegan's "Puttin' on the Style" and Elvis Presley's "Baby Let's Play House" were made public; though the sound quality is poor, John's distinctive voice comes through, giving the listener some idea of what Paul experienced when he first saw the Quarrymen.

As John aptly put it, "That was the day, the day that I met Paul, that it started moving."

4 What's In a Name?

As 1960 began, the Quarrymen were down to three members: John, Paul, and George—who all played guitar. Not only did they need band members who played different instruments, they also decided they needed a new name.

John was by then attending the Liverpool College of Art, and had struck up a friendship with a fellow student, Stuart Sutcliffe. Though a promising painter, Stuart had an interest in rock 'n' roll as well, and eventually joined John's group. Stuart is credited with thinking up the name "Beetles," inspired by the name of Buddy Holly's group the Crickets. Some have noted that the name is the same one used by the female members of a motorcycle gang in the Marlon Brando film *The Wild Ones* (about motorcycle gangs wreaking havoc in a small town), though others have pointed out that the film was banned in Britain at the time. But in the 2005 edition of Philip Norman's Beatles biography *Shout!*, he confidently states that "pop culture-vultures like Stu and his circle would undoubtedly have known all about [the film]." In any case, Stu and John played around with the name, Stu spelling it "Beat-als" (as in "beat all the competition"), while John spelled it "Beatles," in reference to beat music. But none of their contemporaries liked the name, urging them to add something else to it. The group eventually agreed to amend the name to the Silver Beetles.

Posters and newspaper articles show that the name was variously spelled as the Silver Beetles or the Silver Beats. But over the summer of 1960, the group was increasingly referred to in print as the Beatles. And by the time the band left for Germany in August, "the Beatles" had become the final name—and spelling.

Brian Epstein: The Beatles' Manager

Brian Epstein was more than just the Beatles' manager. He was instrumental in the group's transformation from the scrappy rock 'n' roll band they were in Liverpool to becoming national—and then international—stars.

Brian Samuel Epstein was born in Liverpool on September 19, 1934, the eldest son of Harry and Malka "Queenie" Epstein (a brother, Clive, was born in 1936). Harry worked at the furniture shop owned by his father, Isaac; originally called Epstein's, later amended to I. Epstein's & Sons, after Isaac's sons joined the firm. Compared to the Beatles, Brian's upbringing was decidedly upper middle class. He was sent to private schools, but failed to do well, eventually leaving school without graduating. But when he was put to work in the family business, he proved to have a natural flair for sales.

He was then conscripted into the army, but was discharged before his two-year stint was completed; he later hinted the discharge was due to his homosexuality. Homosexual acts, even between consenting adults, were illegal in Britain at the time, and Brian would find himself facing legal difficulties and blackmail attempts because of his sexuality on more than one occasion. His studies at London's Royal Academy of Dramatic Art, which he attended after his time in the army, were curtailed when he was arrested by an undercover police officer for "importuning" (unlawfully soliciting for sex).

As a result, Brian returned to work in Liverpool. Epstein's & Sons had expanded into a new business, North End Music Stores (NEMS), which initially carried pianos and sheet music, then began stocking radios and record players. Brian was put in charge of the music department, first running a store on Great Charlotte Street, then managing one in the heart of Liverpool on Whitechapel. Brian made it a company policy that the record department would carry any record that was commercially available. So in October 1961, when a request came in for a record NEMS didn't have in stock, called "My Bonnie" and recorded by a group he wasn't familiar with named the Beatles, Brian was intrigued. He may well have seen the Beatles' name in the Liverpool music paper *Mersey Beat*, which was sold at NEMS and that Brian wrote an occasional column for. But at the time he was not especially interested in rock 'n' roll, beyond keeping up on current releases for his shop.

Brian soon learned that the Beatles played at a club called the Cavern, which was less than a three-minute walk from NEMS. On attending a lunchtime gig at the club, Brian learned the Beatles were actually only the backing group on "My Bonnie," which was credited to British guitarist Tony Sheridan. Brian quickly became fascinated by the Beatles and began attending more of their shows.

Some have said his interest in the group was simply because he was gay, and enjoyed watching the band frolicking on stage in their full leather outfits. That was undoubtedly part of the attraction. But the Beatles also had a charisma that transcended a simple sexual appeal. And by discovering the Beatles, Brian became increasingly immersed in Liverpool's booming rock scene, which he had largely been unaware of, and which must have been exciting to discover. Brian had also become bored by running the record shop, and was seeking some other outlet for his artistic ambitions.

Brian and the Beatles met a few more times, and by the end of the year, the group agreed to have Brian manage them. He moved quickly, getting higher fees for their public appearances, and smartening up their look by having them wear proper suits, knowing they could never rise to a national level while wearing leather jackets and trousers. Most importantly, by June 1962, he'd secured a recording contract for the group with Parlophone, a subsidiary label of EMI. He also started a management company, named NEMS Enterprises, and signed up other Liverpool acts, including Gerry and the Pacemakers, Cilla Black, and Billy J. Kramer and the Dakotas.

In future years, Brian's managerial skills would be criticized, as he didn't always get top dollar for his clients and was sometimes taken advantage of by others in the business. But he had another quality that was just as important in its own way—a genuine love for the Beatles, especially, above all the other acts he managed. Instead of seeing them simply as a vehicle to make money with, he respected the Beatles' talent, and while he polished their appearance, he left them in charge of their own artistic development. It was the best decision he could have made.

Further reading: *A Cellarful of Noise* (Brian Epstein); *The Man Who Made The Beatles* (Ray Coleman); *In My Life: The Brian Epstein Story* (Debbie Geller)

6 George Martin: The Man Behind the Mixing Board

You could say the Beatles were lucky that they were turned down by the first record companies Brian Epstein approached in the hopes of landing them a deal. For it meant they ended up working with producer George Martin at Parlophone, and he ended up playing a key role in helping to shape their career.

George Henry Martin was born on January 3, 1926, and grew up in London. At the age of six he began playing the family piano, later taking a few lessons, but primarily teaching himself. By 15, he was leading the Four Tune Tellers dance band (later George Martin and the Four Tune Tellers). World War II interrupted his budding musical career, and he joined the Fleet Air Arm of the Royal Navy in 1943. After the war, his veteran's grant enabled him to study music formally at London's Guildhall School of Music and Drama. He hoped to become a classical composer.

After leaving Guildhall, he worked briefly at the British Broadcasting Corporation (BBC), in their music library. Then a friend, music professor Sidney Harrison, recommended George to Oscar Preuss, head of Parlophone Records, who was looking for an assistant. George landed the job, and when Preuss retired in 1955, he became the head of Parlophone, a plum position for such a young man.

George quickly made his name as a producer of comedy records, working with Spike Milligan and Peter Sellers, both of whom had starred in the British radio program *The Goon Show*, as well as producing albums by Britain's Beyond the Fringe comedy troupe (which featured Dudley Moore in the cast). He also produced records by Australian Rolf Harris (of "Tie Me Kangaroo Down, Sport" fame),

Matt Monro (a Sinatra-esque crooner who would later cover the Beatles), the Temperance Seven jazz band (producing their No. 1 UK hit "You're Driving Me Crazy"), and Dick James (who recorded a hit version of "The Adventures of Robin Hood," theme of the British TV series of the same name, before becoming a music publisher, later taking on the Beatles as clients). In 1962, George also released his own record, an instrumental called "Time Beat," released under the pseudonym "Ray Cathode."

The Beatles pose with producer George Martin in April 1963.

But George was also interested in finding a rock act to work with, envious of Columbia Records' producer Norrie Paramor's success with Cliff Richard, Britain's answer to Elvis. So when he received a call from Sid Colman, a London music publisher, about a manager named Brian Epstein who was looking for a recording contract for a group he managed, George agreed to meet him. The two first met on February 13, 1962, where Brian played George a demo the Beatles had recorded the previous month for Decca Records. While George wasn't overly impressed, he didn't turn Brian down completely. At a second meeting on May 9, George agreed to arrange a recording session and sign the Beatles if he liked what he heard. In anticipation of this, George had a contract prepared, while Brian rushed off to send a telegram to the Beatles, then playing in Hamburg, Germany: "Congratulations boys. EMI request recording session. Please rehearse new material."

The recording session was held on June 6 at EMI Recording Studios in London. After hearing the Beatles play, George agreed to sign them, and the contract was signed, backdated to June 4. George initially wondered which singer he should put out front, a la Cliff Richard and the Shadows, but ultimately decided to leave them as they were. Though he did tell Brian he wanted to use a session drummer, and not the band's current drummer, Pete Best, for recordings—a move that spelled the end of Best's tenure in the group.

Other than that significant change, George was largely content to let the Beatles have their own way. Instead of insisting they record songs by professional songwriters—the standard practice at that time—he let them record their own material from the beginning. His suggestion of boosting the tempo of their second single, "Please Please Me," was an early indication of how valuable his suggestions regarding arrangements would become. After discovering how feedback could enhance a song while recording "I Feel Fine," Martin became just as open to experimenting with different sound and recording techniques as the Beatles, which eventually resulted in the group's elaborate productions of the psychedelic era. Instead of maintaining strict control over his charges, George respected the Beatles' innate talent, allowing them to develop and grow as musicians and songwriters.

George also frequently performed on the Beatles' records, often contributing a keyboard part. He arranged the instrumental scores for *A Hard Day's Night* and *Yellow Submarine*, and also released his own albums of instrumental versions of Beatles songs, including *Off the Beatle Track* and *George Martin Instrumentally Salutes the Beatle Girls*. After the Beatles broke up, he continued working on various Beatle-related projects, most notably the *Live at the BBC* and *Anthology* releases, as well as working with Ringo and Paul on various albums. In 1988, he was awarded a CBE (Commander of the Most Excellent Order of the British Empire). He then became a Knight Bachelor in 1996.

Further reading: *All You Need Is Ears* (George Martin, Jeremy Hornsby)

7 The First US Hit

"I Want to Hold Your Hand" was the single that broke the Beatles in America. It was their first single to top the US charts, as well as their first American million seller.

It wasn't the first Beatles single to be released in America. Capitol was a US subsidiary of EMI, but until "I Want to Hold Your Hand," the label had declined to release the Beatles' records in the states ("They're a bunch of long-haired kids. They're nothing," is how Dave Dexter, an A&R executive at Capitol dismissively

Die Beatles

In 1964, EMI's West German branch, Odeon, insisted they needed German-language records by the Beatles to sell in their country. The Beatles weren't enthusiastic about the idea, but George Martin convinced them. So while they were in the middle of their 19-day run at the Olympia Theatre in Paris, a recording session was set up on January 29, 1964, so they could record *"Komm, Gib Mir Deine Hand"* and *"Sie Liebt Dich."*

A new vocal was all that was needed for *"Komm, Gib Mir Deine Hand,"* but they had to record *"Sie Liebt Dich"* from scratch, as the two-track original of "She Loves You" had been destroyed (only the mono master remained). They were also able to start work on a new song, "Can't Buy Me Love."

"Komm Gib Mir Deine Hand"/ "Sie Liebt Dich" was released in Germany in March 1964. *"Sie Liebt Dich"* was first released in the US on May 21, 1964, on Swan, who believed, since they had first released "She Loves You," that they had the rights to the German language version of the song as well. Capitol thought otherwise and filed a suit, which was quickly settled, so the song barely had time to reach its peak of No. 97. *"Komm, Gib Mir Deine Hand"* was first released on Capitol's *Something New* album, released on July 20, 1964. Both songs are now on the *Past Masters* set.

described the Beatles to the label's president, Alan Livingston). So it was left to smaller labels to release the band's earlier singles in 1963—"Please Please Me," "From Me to You," and "She Loves You"—all achieving little success. But after Brian Epstein called Livingston and complained about Capitol's persistent neglect of the Beatles, Livingston agreed to give "I Want to Hold Your Hand" a US release.

"I Want to Hold Your Hand" has a bright buoyancy that's instantly appealing. The song's rising guitar intro builds the excitement, the backing handclaps provide an exciting rhythmic bounce, and when the Beatles' voices coalesce into a glorious falsetto as they sing the word "hand," it's a moment of pure joy. The single set a record in Britain for achieving advance orders of over a million copies before the record was even released, on November 29, 1963.

Its US release was originally scheduled for January 13, 1964. But then Carroll James, a DJ at Washington, D.C., station WWDC, got a hold of the British single and gave "I Want to Hold Your Hand" its first US airplay on December 17, 1963. The song was then picked up by other US stations across the country, and so Capitol moved the single's release date up to December 26. While the UK single featured the ballad "This Boy" on the B-side, Capitol opted to replace it with the classic rocker "I Saw Her Standing There."

The single flew up the charts during January 1964. The Beatles were on tour in France when they heard "I Want to Hold Your Hand" had topped the US charts, and spent the rest of the night in celebration; they'd finally conquered America, something no previous British music act had done. And with the Beatles scheduled to appear on *The Ed Sullivan Show* the following month, the timing of their breakthrough single couldn't have been better. "I Want to Hold Your Hand" was quickly certified gold, with sales of over a million copies. And on February 10, just six weeks after the single had been released in the US, the Beatles were given a gold record award for "I Want to Hold Your Hand" during their first triumphant visit to America.

Ruling the Airwaves

While the airplay "I Want to Hold Your Hand" received brought the Beatles to the attention of America's teenagers, their appearances on *The Ed Sullivan Show* in February 1964 introduced them to the vast nationwide audience that gathered every Sunday to watch the country's top-rated variety show.

Legend has it Ed Sullivan discovered the Beatles when he witnessed the mob scenes at London Airport when the Beatles returned to the UK after a short tour of Sweden in October 1963. In fact, as described in James Maguire's biography of Sullivan, *Impresario*, Sullivan had been tipped off about the Beatles by his London agent, Peter Pritchard (Sullivan later fabricated the "airport discovery" story himself). When Brian Epstein went to New York City in early November 1963, seeking to promote another act he managed (singer Billy J. Kramer, who accompanied Brian to New York), he also set up two meetings with Sullivan, on November 11 and 12. Though the Beatles had yet to have a hit in the US, Sullivan agreed to book them for two live appearances on February 9 and 16, as well as taping a third appearance for later broadcast.

By the time the Beatles arrived in New York on February 7, "I Want to Hold Your Hand" was No. 1 on the *Billboard* chart, the *Meet The Beatles* album was No. 3, and the Beatles were the hottest entertainment story in town. There had been 50,000 requests for tickets for a theater that held 728, and on February 9, the streets around CBS Studio 50 were thronged with fans and curiosity seekers. The Beatles actually performed three times on February 9. First came a dress rehearsal at 2:30. Afterward, the Beatles taped three songs for broadcast on February 23. The live broadcast began at 8:00 PM, with the Beatles opening the show with three songs: "All My Loving," "Till There Was You," and "She Loves You." They performed two more numbers later on in the show, "I Saw Her Standing There" and "I Want to Hold Your Hand." The excitement was palpable even to viewers at home; screams drowned out Sullivan's introductions, and teenage girls were shown shrieking with delight while the Beatles played.

The reviews were mixed (the *New York Herald-Tribune* described them as "Seventy-five percent publicity, twenty percent

On the set of The Ed Sullivan Show, *New York, February 9, 1964: Sullivan smiles while standing with his arms thrown around the young Mop Tops.*

haircut and five percent lilting lament," while the *New York Times* wrote them off as "incoherent"). But Sullivan's gamble had nonetheless paid off handsomely, as the show drew a viewing audience of over 73 million people, the highest ever for a television program at that time. In one night, the Beatles were seen by more people than on all their other live shows for the past seven years combined.

The February 16 show was broadcast from the Deauville Hotel in Miami, with the Beatles performing "She Loves You," "This Boy," "All My Loving," "I Saw Her Standing There," "From Me to You," and "I Want to Hold Your Hand"; the previously taped performance from February 9 that was broadcast on February 23 featured just three songs, "Twist and Shout," "Please Please Me," and "I Want to Hold Your Hand." The exposure paid off quite well for the Beatles; by the end of February they had four singles and two albums in the Top 40. And in years to come, countless musicians would talk about seeing the *Ed Sullivan* shows and being inspired to become musicians themselves. And they were now firmly installed at No. 1 in the hearts of America's youth.

9 Sgt. Pepper: A Psychedelic Masterpiece

It wasn't the Beatles' biggest-selling album, and today it's not even seen as their best album. But at the time of its release, *Sgt. Pepper's Lonely Hearts Club Band* was regarded as the Beatles' finest achievement.

After the stressful tours of the summer of 1966, the Beatles decided to stop touring. When no British tour was announced for the fall of '66, rumors began circulating that the Beatles were breaking up. The rumors were strengthened by the fact that the Beatles released only one album that year, *Revolver*. At the time, it was usual for groups to release a minimum of two, or even more, albums each year, and the Beatles had been no different. And no band had ever survived without making regular live appearances.

But the Beatles had decided to put all their energy into recording, and from November 1966 to April 1967, they spent over 700 hours in the studio. Paul is credited with suggesting that the Beatles create an alter-ego band. By throwing off the constraints of their identity as "The Beatles," they would be free to create whatever they wanted to. And they adopted a name reflecting the multi-titled monikers then being used by US bands, particularly on the West Coast: Sgt. Pepper's Lonely Hearts Club Band.

Sgt. Pepper is often described as the first "concept" album, though the alter-ego idea is really only present in the album's opening numbers, and the reprise of the title song toward the end. But if there's no conventional storyline, there is an underlying theme: each song becomes another act in Sgt. Pepper's show. The dazzling array of sounds and imagery is still impressive today. John's "Lucy in the Sky with Diamonds" glitters with surreal wordplay inspired by the world of *Alice in Wonderland*; "Being for the Benefit of Mr. Kite" creates a psychedelic carnival mood in sound with lyrics drawn verbatim from an antique poster; "Good Morning Good Morning" chronicles the hum-drum life of the everyday worker with the resigned admission "...but it's okay." Paul's songs were typically more optimistic, and brimming with the expectation of good times ahead, as can be seen in the titles "Getting Better" and "Fixing a Hole," and in his sprightly chat-up of a meter maid in "Lovely Rita." Even old age was cast in a whimsical light in the vaudevillian soft shuffle of "When I'm Sixty-Four." Though Paul did strike a poignant note in his tale of a teenage runaway, "She's Leaving Home" (which is slightly undermined by an instrumental score that's a bit too ornate; perhaps significantly, it wasn't by George Martin, who wasn't available at the time, but Mike Leander, a producer who'd previously worked with singer Marianne Faithfull).

George's Indian-influenced "Within You Without You" brought together Western and Eastern instruments in hitherto unimagined ways. And the homespun "With a Little Help From My Friends" became Ringo's signature song. But most remarkable was the closing track, "A Day In the Life," which combined John's world-weary observations with Paul's surreal look at the morning work day, the two sections linked by a stunning sweep of sound from an orchestra seemingly going crazy, and everything brought to a conclusion by the somber thud of a gigantic piano chord, which is allowed to fade away into eternity.

The Beatles also took considerable time in planning the cover shot, which had them posing in bright satin military-style outfits in front of a collage of their heroes, influences, and assorted pop culture personalities: Edgar Allen Poe, Bob Dylan, Marlene Dietrich, Lenny Bruce, Aldous Huxley, and Shirley Temple, to name a few. And in a first for a rock album, all the song lyrics were printed on the back cover. The gatefold sleeve also held a sheet of cardboard cutouts, featuring military medals, a postcard, and even a moustache.

When *Sgt. Pepper* was released on June 1, 1967, in the UK, June 2 in the US, it was met with astonishment and delight; London critic Kenneth Tynan even hailed it as "a decisive moment in the history of Western civilization" in *The Times*. The album easily topped the charts in the US and UK, and won Grammys for Album of the Year, Best Contemporary Album, Best Album Cover, and Best Engineered Recording.

Further reading: *With A Little Help From My Friends: The Making of Sgt. Pepper* (George Martin, William Pearson), *It Was Twenty Years Ago Today* (Derek Taylor)

10 A Dream of a Song

"Yesterday" is not only Paul's signature song, it's become the most played song on radio of all time. Over 2,000 cover versions of the song have been recorded as well.

The melody came to Paul in a dream; he'd awoken one morning with the tune running through his head, leading him to go straight to the piano next to his bed to formally work it out. Exactly when this happened is a little uncertain. Paul's authorized biography *Many Years From Now* says it happened in early May 1965, though at other times he's said his "dream" occurred in 1963. In any case, he didn't work on the lyrics immediately. Convinced he couldn't possibly have dreamed up an original melody, he was afraid he must've heard the tune somewhere before, and repeatedly played the tune for friends and fellow musicians, asking if they recognized it. John recalled the song being around for "months and months" before it was recorded, and that Paul's continual playing of the melody became a joke between them. Though the song had a working title of "Scrambled Eggs," George Martin, in the book *The Beatles Recording Sessions*, said that when he first heard the song in January 1964, Paul was already thinking about calling the song "Yesterday," though he'd wondered if it was "too corny." "I persuaded him that it was all right," said Martin.

Paul came up with a final lyric while on vacation in Portugal at the end of May 1965, and the song was recorded two weeks later, on June 14. The song's simplicity was such that after hearing Paul run through it, the other Beatles said they didn't think they could add anything to it instrumentally, and that Paul should just record it solo. Somewhat nervously, he agreed, recording two takes, accompanying himself on acoustic guitar (take two was released first, with take one later appearing on *Anthology 2*). Martin then suggested adding a string quartet to the track, and Paul agreed, as long as the arrangement was tasteful and clean, telling his producer, "I don't want any of that Mantovani rubbish." The two worked on the string arrangement together, and came up with music that was a perfect match for the song.

The narrative of "Yesterday" is straightforward; it's a sad look back at a relationship that's ended. But the song is also somewhat ambiguous; the singer doesn't know why the relationship is over and is left yearning for the better days of the past. It was the first song to feature just one Beatle—Paul—and the first Beatles song to feature string accompaniment. It was even suggested that Paul release it as a solo track, but he demurred; he didn't want to take precedence over the group. Nor did he want to put it out as a single in the UK, so "Yesterday" was initially only released as a single in other countries. In America, it was released on September 13, 1965, and soon went to No. 1. But it was eventually released as a single in the UK in 1976, when it reached No. 8.

Despite Paul being the only Beatle on the song, the band added "Yesterday" to their setlist, though at the time its delicacy was undermined by the audience's constant screaming during their shows. When you hear Paul perform it today, as he has at most of his post-Beatles concerts, there's generally a hush over the audience when he sings it—at least if the audience isn't singing along. "Yesterday" is said to have been played over 7 million times on the radio (so far) and was inducted into the Grammy Hall of Fame in 1997.

Further reading: *McCartney: Yesterday...and Today* (Ray Coleman)

11 See a Beatle In Concert

The last official concert by the Beatles was on August 29, 1966, at Candlestick Park in San Francisco. Their last live TV appearance came on June 25, 1967, when they premiered "All You Need Is Love," and they made an impromptu appearance on the roof of their Apple Corp. London headquarters on January 30, 1969, playing for a little less than 45 minutes before they were shut down by the police.

After that, nothing. The four Beatles never played in concert together ever again. But that doesn't mean you can't see *a* Beatle in concert. After a 10-year break beginning in 1979, Paul returned to full-scale touring in 1989. After 2005, the mammoth world-wide tours he used to do went by the wayside; Paul now generally tours in short bursts of a few weeks, takes a few months off, then returns to the road for another short stint. Which means you have a lot of chances to see him, especially if you're willing to travel. The personnel in Paul's touring bands has varied, but since 2002 he's toured with the same group of musicians (guitarists Rusty Anderson and Brian Ray, keyboardist Paul "Wix" Wickens, and drummer Abe Laboriel, Jr.), meaning he's played longer with them than he did with the Beatles.

Ringo also returned to regular touring in 1989, with what he calls his "All-Starr Band." The All-Starrs are a changing cast of characters, drawn from the large pool of musical luminaries who have had their own hits; past tours have included John Entwistle, Peter Frampton, Todd Rundgren, Edgar Winter, Sheila E., Hamish Stuart (who also toured with Paul), and Ringo's own son, Zak. Everyone does two or three songs, with Ringo doing around 10. The All-Starrs generally tour in the summer, and Ringo makes occasional live appearances during the rest of the year.

And don't forget Pete Best, who was the Beatles' drummer from 1960 to 1962. Though Pete left show business by the mid-'60s, he returned to performing in 1988, forming the Pete Best Band. The group occasionally tours, and also performs at Beatle Week in Liverpool.

12 Visit Liverpool

Every Beatles fan should take the opportunity to visit Liverpool if they can. There's simply no better way to get a real understanding of one of the Beatles' key influences—the city where they were born.

Liverpool is a few hours by train from London, or you can fly directly into Liverpool's John Lennon Airport, as Speke Airport was renamed in 2002 (you won't be using the same terminal the Beatles did, however; the Crowne Plaza Liverpool John Lennon Airport Hotel is now on the site where the original terminal stood). With a good travel guide at hand—*The Beatles Liverpool: The Complete Guide* by Ron Jones is especially recommended (as is his guide to US-related sites in Liverpool, *The American Connection*), for there are dozens of Beatle-related sites within walking distance of the city center. Ron's guide gives info for sites in other districts too, such as Strawberry Field and St. Peter's Church, where John and Paul first met.

If you don't want to do the legwork yourself, a number of tours are available. Cavern City Tours (CCT), which operates the Cavern, offers both bus tours and private tours (www.cavernclub.org). The National Trust offers tours of John's and Paul's homes, both of which have been designated historical landmarks (www.nationaltrust.org.uk/beatles). There are other vendors who offer tours as well. The Beatles Shop (located on Mathew Street) and The Beatles Story museum (located on Albert Dock) are good resources of information as well.

If you really want to go all out, consider visiting during Liverpool's annual International Beatle Week, hosted by CCT (their US agent for Beatle Week is International Tours and Events, www.toursandevents.com). Beatle Week is held every year over August Bank Holiday Weekend (the last weekend in August), beginning the Wednesday or Thursday before the weekend and continuing to the following Tuesday. Beatle tribute bands from all over the world appear; the Beatles Convention at the Adelphi Hotel brings

Mersey Beat

Bill Harry met John at art college; the two were part of a group called The Dissenters, four friends who were determined to make Liverpool famous: John in music, Bill in writing, and Stuart Sutcliffe and Rod Murray in painting (a plaque commemorating the Dissenters can be found in the pub where they used to drink, Ye Cracke).

Bill was interested in music as well as writing, and had published a newspaper called *Jazz*, about Liverpool's jazz scene. In 1961, he decided to launch a paper that covered Liverpool's growing rock scene, and the first issue of *Mersey Beat* was published on July 6, 1961.

As John was Bill's friend, the Beatles naturally came in for a lot of coverage in the paper. John even wrote a story for the first issue, "Being A Short Diversion On The Dubious Origins Of Beatles," a fanciful history that described how they got their name: "It came in a vision—a man appeared on a flaming pie and said unto them 'From this day on you are Beatles with an A.' Thank you Mister Man, they said, thanking him." John wrote other pieces for the paper under the pseudonym "Beatcomber," a play on the name of the *Daily Express* columnist, Beachcomber.

Mersey Beat was an immediate success. No one had previously grasped how large the Liverpool beat scene actually was, or that it commanded such a devoted audience. The paper enthusiastically charted the Beatles' progress, to the point that some readers grumbled it should be called "Mersey Beatles." After the Beatles became established stars, Brian suggested *Mersey Beat* transition into a national publication, and it was renamed *Music Echo*. Bill later resigned due to editorial disputes, and the paper became *Disc & Music Echo*. Bill went on to do publicity for numerous bands, and has written several books about the Beatles. The book *Mersey Beat: The Beginnings of The Beatles* has replica pages of the paper. There's also a website, www.triumphpc.com/mersey-beat.

in guests who knew or worked with the Beatles; on Bank Holiday Monday itself, the Mathew Street Festival takes over Liverpool's downtown area. It's a fantastic celebration of the Beatles and their legacy, a great excuse for a trip, and a fun way to make new friends.

Whether you go on your own or with a tour, after one trip to Liverpool you'll probably be thinking about how soon you can return.

Further reading: *Liddypool: Birthplace of The Beatles* (David Bedford); *The Beatles In Liverpool* (Spencer Leigh)

Revolver: Inventive and Imaginative

Revolver was a breathtaking achievement for the Beatles. Though it was *Sgt. Pepper* that captured most of the kudos during the '60s, it's now more often *Revolver* that is considered to be the band's best work.

Revolver is the album where the Beatles really began to stretch themselves as songwriters, as musicians, and as recording artists. It was the first time the Beatles released an album that wasn't dominated by love songs, as the single that preceded *Revolver*, "Paperback Writer"/"Rain" (released May 30, 1966, in the US, June 10 in the UK), was the first single where neither side was a love song. Indeed, *Revolver* marked the first time the Beatles addressed purely adult concerns, opening the album with George's "Taxman"; what teenager thinks about paying taxes? John's "Doctor Robert" was a not-so-subtle depiction of a physician who dispenses pharmaceuticals for reasons other than medicinal. The bubbly "Yellow Submarine" was a novelty number, written especially for Ringo, about—well, living in a yellow submarine.

What was equally impressive was not just the subject matter of the album's songs; it was how they sounded. Paul's "Eleanor Rigby," a sad tale of two lonely people, was set against a stark backdrop of strings that have the brittle sharpness of Bernard Herrmann's score for *Psycho*. John's languid "I'm Only Sleeping" heightens the mood with a sped-up Lennon vocal and backward guitar. George created raga rock with his first fully Indian-inspired song "Love You To." The greatest extravagances came on the closing track, John's "Tomorrow Never Knows," lyrically inspired by *The Tibetan Book of the Dead*, a nightmarish collage of sounds drawn from numerous tape loops (a loop of recording tape featuring a particular sound, distorted or otherwise), topped by an eerie, wailing Lennon vocal, an effect created by sending the vocal through a revolving Leslie speaker inside a Hammond organ.

The more conventional tracks were just as outstanding. Paul's exquisite "Here, There and Everywhere" features superb harmonizing by the Beatles that's only rivaled by their work on "This Boy" and "Because." His Motown-inspired "Got to Get You Into My Life" is positively giddy, while "Good Day Sunshine" has equally bright spirits, in sharp contrast to "For No One," a variation of the theme of "Yesterday," complemented by a French horn solo. John was typically more cynical, on the dreamy, edgy "She Said She Said," inspired by a cryptic remark he heard from actor Peter Fonda, while the Beatles were acid tripping at a party during their 1965 American tour, and in the stinging resentment of "And Your Bird Can Sing," with its thickly layered guitars. George was given an unprecedented three tracks on the album, rounded off by "I Want to Tell You," which zeroed in on the sometimes awkward, tentative nature of relationships, against a backdrop of more gorgeous harmonies.

The black and white cover, designed by Klaus Voorman, a friend the Beatles had met in Hamburg, gave no hint of the elaborately crafted music within. Released on August 5, 1966, in the UK, August 8 in the US, *Revolver* topped the charts in both countries. The music proved too complex to be performed live; the Beatles' summer tour that year featured not a single song from the album. The songs clearly pointed ahead to the Beatles' next level of musical experimentation. A Capitol Records ad for the album neatly summed up its impact in a single word: "Bang!"

Fabs On Film No. 1: A Hard Day's Night

United Artists had no other goal in mind when making the Beatles' first movie than in securing the rights to the film's soundtrack, thus securing a financial windfall at the height of Beatlemania. What they got was a film destined to become a classic; not just one of the best rock movies of all time, but a film that won numerous unexpected critical kudos as well, as when one critic dubbed it "the *Citizen Kane* of jukebox musicals."

Recognizing that the Beatles weren't natural actors, screenwriter Alun Owen, himself a Liverpudlian, wrote a script in which the Beatles essentially played themselves, traveling by train to appear in a London television show, while facing demands from all sides: from their managers, from the media, and from their rabid fans, who are seen chasing the Fabs at every opportunity. In short, shown as prisoners of their own success.

Richard Lester proved to be the perfect director for the Beatles. He already had their respect, having previously worked with one of their idols, Peter Sellers, and he was patient with the novice actors, even allowing them the occasional ad lib. The camera work is impressive, especially in the musical sequences, swooping and gliding around the band, creating a real sense of energy. The first "Can't Buy Me Love" sequence (the song is played twice in the

The Beatles have their hair combed by stylists on the set of A Hard Day's Night *(George is having his hair brushed by his future wife Pattie Boyd).* (AP Images)

movie), which showed the Beatles cavorting in an empty field, is a proto-music video (and a clear inspiration for the antics in *The Monkees* TV series). The film was shot in black and white for budgetary reasons, though it actually ended up enhancing the *cinema verité* feeling of the movie. Each Beatle also got a solo scene; unfortunately for Paul, his scene was determined not to be strong enough, and it was cut (even more unfortunately, all the film's outtakes were destroyed, so the scene only survives in the original script). Ringo had the biggest role, and was at the center of the story's biggest crisis, when hours before the climactic show he decides to walk out on the group. Will he be found in time? Suffice to say, the film does have a happy ending.

After considering various options, *A Hard Day's Night*, an off-hand expression of Ringo's, was chosen as the film's title. The UK album, released July 10, 1964, was the first Beatles record to feature all original material, and the first Beatles album consisting solely of Lennon-McCartney songs, side one featuring songs from the

Beatle Shorts

By the mid-'60s, the Beatles were tired of making television appearances to promote their records. So they began making what were then called promotional film clips.

The first Beatles promo films were straightforward performance clips of "I Feel Fine," "Ticket to Ride," "Help!," "We Can Work It Out," and "Day Tripper." The set was minimal; large tickets were used as a backdrop for "Ticket to Ride," while for "I Feel Fine" they played amongst an array of exercise equipment. They filmed similar studio clips for "Paperback Writer" and "Rain," but also shot more imaginative versions on the verdant grounds of Chiswick House in London.

The "Penny Lane" and "Strawberry Fields Forever" clips were the most creative, and featured no miming at all. Fans love the "Hello Goodbye" clip, which has the group performing in their *Sgt. Pepper* suits. "Lady Madonna" shows the group working in the studio. "Hey Jude" and "Revolution" were performance clips, the first in front of a studio audience (they also feature live vocals). "The Ballad of John and Yoko" used various contemporary clips of the two, while the *Let It Be* filming sessions were culled for clips for "Get Back," "Don't Let Me Down," "The Long and Winding Road," and "Let It Be." "Something" was the last clip, showing each Beatle with his wife.

An official DVD collection of all the Beatles' promo films would seem an obvious item, though one has yet to be released.

film, side two featuring six non-film songs. Standouts include not just the title track (with its memorable G suspended 4th chord that kicks off the number), but songs that also showed the Beatles' more contemplative side: "If I Fell," "And I Love Her," "Things We Said Today," and "I'll Be Back." The US version, released June 26, 1964, was more of a proper soundtrack, featuring the songs from the movie and incidental music from the film. Each album topped the charts in their respective countries, as did the accompanying single, which featured the title song.

A Hard Day's Night had its world premiere in London on July 6, 1964. Critics who expected another schlocky teen flick were surprised to find they liked the film, with Ringo singled out for special praise. It's a movie that doesn't condescend to its audience, bursts with the vigorous energy of youth, and captures all the zest and charm of the Beatles at the peak of Beatlemania.

15 A Worldwide Audience

The Beatles performed for their largest-ever audience on June 25, 1967, when their performance of "All You Need Is Love" was seen by over 400 million people.

In May 1967, it was announced that the Beatles would be participating in a program entitled *Our World*, the world's first live satellite television program, featuring contributions from 14 countries and broadcast throughout 31 nations. The Beatles were chosen to represent Britain. Just 14 days after the UK release of *Sgt. Pepper* on June 1, the Beatles were back in the studio working on "All You Need Is Love," which was John's song. The Beatles had been asked to keep the song simple, so that the message would translate more readily across the globe, and while the verses were somewhat elliptical, the song's message was neatly distilled in its title (which was also the song's chorus).

The Beatles' segment of the show showed the group at work on the song, then performing it in full, playing and singing live to their own pre-recorded backing track (with John only singing, and not playing guitar). Thirteen orchestra members (string and horn players), would also be playing live. The segment was shot at Abbey Road Studios' largest room, Studio One, which was colorfully decorated for the broadcast with balloons, streamers, and flowers (Paul also tucked a flower under his headphones). The Beatles were equally colorful, dressed in the height of psychedelic fashion, as were the many friends they'd invited to watch, including Mick Jagger and his girlfriend Marianne Faithfull, Eric Clapton, and Keith Moon, among other friends and family members. The orchestra men were more conventionally attired in formal evening wear.

The segment began with the camera swooping in to show the Beatles ostensibly working on the backing track. After an explanatory voice-over from announcer Steve Race, the Beatles then went into the song proper, the horns providing an opening flourish by playing a bit of "La Marseillaise," the French national anthem, emphasizing the international theme of the event (parts of the English ballad "Greensleeves" and Glenn Miller's "In the Mood" would be heard during the fade-out). Ringo sat behind his drum kit, with the other three Beatles in front sitting on high stools, John looking especially nonchalant, and apparently chewing gum as he sang. But the ebullient good spirits are unmistakable, especially given the inherent sing-along nature of the song, and by the end the mood is positively celebratory, with confetti cascading from the ceiling and a host of participants seen roaming around the studio wearing large sandwich boards, each bearing one word of the song's title translated into different languages. John, as always, provided a cheeky finishing touch by singing a bit of "She Loves You" during the fade-out.

The song was rush released in the UK on July 7, US release on July 17. Given that it had such an extravagant worldwide debut it was no surprise that the single topped the charts in both countries. "All You Need Is Love" fully reflected the Summer of Love ethos of the time, and remains one of the Beatles' proudest

The Beatles pose at a press conference one day before their performance of "All You Need Is Love" on satellite link-up for the Our World *program.*

accomplishments. As Paul put it in *The Beatles Anthology* book, "I'm really glad that most of the [Beatles] songs dealt with love, peace, understanding."

Further reading: *All You Need Is Love: The Beatles Dress Rehearsal* (Steve Turner)

16 The Longest Beatles Song

The anthemic "Hey Jude" is almost as much of a signature song for Paul as "Yesterday." The song's extended ending naturally lends itself to large-scale sing-alongs, with the result that it's a regular feature in Paul's live shows and at the numerous special events at which he appears.

The song's initial inspiration was simple and poignant. After John and his first wife, Cynthia, had separated in the summer of 1968, Paul drove out to Cynthia's home to visit her. On the way, he began composing a song of comfort for the couple's son, Julian, which he called "Hey Jules," before deciding that the name Jude sounded better.

But the song has a broader meaning than simply urging a child to cheer up. The song's narrator is also encouraging "Jude" to not be afraid of starting a new relationship. It's this element that led John to think Paul was subtly referring to John's own new relationship with Yoko Ono, telling *Playboy* magazine, "Subconsciously he was saying, 'Go ahead, leave me.' On a conscious level, he didn't want me to go ahead. The angel in him was saying 'Bless you.' The devil in him didn't like it all, because he didn't want to lose his partner." Yet when John suggested this interpretation to Paul, Paul said no, it referred to him.

"Check. We're both going through the same bit," John replied, knowing that Paul had also recently split from his longtime girlfriend Jane Asher. By that fall, Paul would be in a new relationship, with photographer Linda Eastman, and perhaps at this time he was urging himself to "go out and get her."

John also ended up giving a valuable suggestion to Paul regarding the song's lyrics. When first singing the song for John, Paul had explained that the lyric about the "movement you need is on your shoulder" was a filler line and would be changed. "You won't, you know," John told him. "That's the best line in it!" Which led Paul to reconsider, later recalling, "So of course you love that line twice as much because it's a little stray, it's a little mutt that you were about to put down and it was reprieved and so it's more beautiful than ever."

He had a little more difficulty in the studio with George, who wanted to put an answering guitar line after every line of lyric. Paul insisted he wanted to keep the main part of the song simple. And so the song is largely a piano-based ballad (with some nice harmonies at key points), until the midway point, when Paul takes the last word, "better," higher and higher up the scale until he erupts in a joyous scream. Now the song's coda begins, the band singing the mesmerizing "Na na na na-na-na na" line with Paul continuing to hit the upper register with his ad libs. A 36-piece orchestra rounded out the song, which ultimately ran to just over seven minutes (7:11). It was an extraordinary length for a single, but most radio stations played the song in its entirety because it was by the Beatles. A precedent for longer songs had also been set earlier in the year with Richard Harris' single "MacArthur Park," which ran 7:21.

"Hey Jude" was released on August 26, 1968, in the US, August 30 in the UK. It was the first record released on the Beatles' new Apple Records label, though as the Beatles were still signed with Capitol in the US and Parlophone in the UK, their records were still official Capitol/Parlophone releases, and given Capitol/

Parlophone catalogue numbers, though the actual records still featured Apple Records labels. The single topped the charts in both countries, and became the Beatles' most successful US single, remaining at No. 1 for nine weeks and selling over 4 million copies.

The Beatles also shot a wonderful promotional film for the song on September 4, 1968, the group seen performing for a seated studio audience, who then swarm excitedly around the band during the song's coda.

17 The Album That Renamed a Studio

Though it was released before the *Let It Be* album, *Abbey Road* was technically the last album the Beatles ever made. It became their biggest-selling album in America (selling over 12 million copies), and gave the studio where they recorded it a new name.

Though the *Let It Be* sessions, which had been held in January 1969, had no shortage of contentious moments, no sooner was the album completed than the band was back in the studio on February 22, 1969, working on new songs. The group continued recording sporadically over the spring, then spent most of July and August at work on the album. On August 8, the band arrived early at the studio and had themselves photographed as they walked across the street in the crosswalk out front, creating another iconic album cover. The album was named after the very street they were crossing: *Abbey Road.*

The album is a masterpiece of craftsmanship. In the days when albums were two-sided records, side one had a conventional collection-of-songs format, while side two was devoted to extended medleys. George Harrison blossomed as a songwriter on the album, writing not just one, but two bona fide classics: the tender love song "Something" and the equally gentle "Here Comes the Sun." John's presence wasn't as strong on the album, though his contributions are standouts: the funky "Come Together" (which opens the album), "Because," which features some of the best harmonizing the Beatles ever did, and the impassioned love song "I Want You (She's So Heavy)," which dissolves into a whirl of white noise. Ringo continued the aquatic adventuring he'd started on "Yellow Submarine" with another deep-sea story, "Octopus's Garden."

But it's Paul who dominates the album. On side one he provides some black-humored comic relief with "Maxwell's Silver Hammer," then puts on his best rock screamer voice for "Oh! Darling." He also oversaw the medleys on side two, singing most of the lead vocals, beginning the first medley with the melancholy "You Never Give Me Your Money," a reference to the Beatles' recent managerial and financial struggles. This segues into John's pretty, dreamy "Sun King," followed by a series of pen portraits: the unsavory "Mean Mr. Mustard," the racy "Polythene Pam" (both John songs, with typically pungent vocals), and the female drop-in Paul describes in "She Came In Through the Bathroom Window."

The first medley is followed by a second, with all the songs helmed by Paul. "Golden Slumbers" is based on the lullaby "Cradle Song," by 17th-century writer Thomas Dekker, here sounding a more forlorn note, especially when followed by "Carry That Weight," which leads unexpectedly into the only drum solo Ringo ever recorded while in the Beatles. Paul, George, and John then chime in with their distinctive guitar solos before the number climaxes with "The End," the final couplet about the love you take being equal to the love you make serving as something of an epitaph for the Fab Four. After a momentary pause, there's another surprise, with Paul's cheeky ditty "Her Majesty," which cuts off before the final note.

It's a remarkably accomplished work by musicians operating at their peak, making it all the harder to believe that these same musicians would never all work together again. Yet such was the case for the Beatles. *Abbey Road* was released on September 26, 1969, in the UK, October 1 in the US, topping the charts in both countries.

EMI Recording Studios had always been a popular place for Beatles fans to hang out, hoping for a chance to glimpse one of their idols. Now, with the album cover showing the Beatles crossing the road in front of that very studio, fans began referring to the studio as "Abbey Road," and the studios were eventually renamed, to Abbey Road Studios.

18 Paul Is Dead (Isn't He?)

The oddest rumor that circulated during the Beatle years was the speculation in the fall of 1969 that Paul was dead. He'd been killed in a car accident in November 1966 and been replaced by a looka-like/sound-alike imposter. And the Beatles were now revealing the news to their fans by placing clues in their song lyrics and album covers.

How do such things get started? The first known appearance of the rumor came in a September 17, 1969, story titled "Is Beatle Paul McCartney Dead?" that ran in *The Drake-Times Delphic*, the student newspaper of Des Moines, Iowa, college Drake University; the article's author, Tim Harper, had heard the rumor from a friend who had himself heard it at a party. The rumor spread to college campuses throughout the country, becoming increasingly embellished along the way. University of Michigan student Fred LaBour concocted an elaborate conspiracy theory around the rumor in a story that ran in the university's student paper, *The Daily*, on October 14, 1969. The story, "McCartney Dead; New Evidence Brought to Light," pointed out various supposed "clues" to Paul's demise that are now invariably mentioned when the rumor is discussed: the patch on the suit Paul wears on the *Sgt. Pepper* cover that says "O.P.D.," said to mean "Officially Pronounced Dead" (the patch actually reads "O.P.P." for Ontario Provincial Police); a picture in the *Magical Mystery Tour* album booklet showing Paul wearing a black carnation while the others wear red (the group was shooting the "Your Mother Should Know" number, and they'd simply run out of red carnations); and on the *Abbey Road* album cover, the Beatles aren't simply walking across the street, they're in a funeral procession, with George as the gravedigger, Paul as the dead man, Ringo as the undertaker, and John as the minister (Paul's also walking out of step with the other three Beatles). LaBour proudly called his article "The best bullshit I ever wrote, and it only took me an hour and a half."

Other clues concerned messages the Beatles placed in their songs, such as the line in "A Day In the Life" about the man who "blew his mind out in a car," which referred to the car accident. In the muttering heard at the end of "Strawberry Fields Forever," John supposedly says, "I buried Paul" (he claimed he was actually saying "Cranberry sauce"). If you play the ending of the song "I'm So Tired" backward (a feat which was possible on some turntables) you could hear John saying, "Paul is dead, man, miss him, miss him." And if you play the phrase "Number nine, number nine" that floats through the sound collage of "Revolution 9" backward, you'll hear "Turn me on, dead man."

The story, and clues, soon spread to the national media; there were actually stories about Paul's supposed death on the evening news broadcasts of all three major networks in the US. There was even a televised trial, of sorts, *Paul McCartney: The Complete Story Told for the First and Last Time*, that aired on November 30, 1969, with noted attorney F. Lee Bailey questioning LaBour; Peter Asher, the brother of Paul's former girlfriend Jane Asher and an A&R executive at the Beatles' company, Apple; and Allen Klein, one of the band's business managers, among others.

Paul was, of course, alive and well. But in late October 1969 he and his wife Linda went to his farm in Scotland, and so seemed to disappear from the public eye. He was eventually tracked down at his farm by journalists, much to his annoyance, but conceded to give some interviews to try to dispel the rumors; for their story, *Life* magazine pictured Paul on the cover, next to a headline assuring readings "Paul Is Still With Us."

An unexpected side effect of the rumor was that the just-released *Abbey Road* became a strong seller. As John said in an interview with Detroit radio station WKNR when he was asked about the Paul-is-dead story, "It's just insanity. But it's a great plug for *Abbey Road*." Capitol Records eventually got in on the fun, running an ad featuring a head shot of Paul surrounded by Beatles albums, reading: "Paul McCartney's Sounds Are Alive..."

Eventually, the rumor played itself out. John later got in a dig at his former partner in the song "How Do You Sleep?" with the line about "those freaks" being right about the rumor. But Paul had the last laugh. In 1993, he released a live album with the unequivocal title *Paul Is Live*, showing him crossing Abbey Road looking very much alive.

Further reading: *Turn Me On, Dead Man* (Andru J. Reeve)

19 The Lennon/McCartney Songwriting Team

One of the main reasons why the Beatles are such an enduring band is that they wrote their own songs. While singers, or singing groups, need not write their own material, for a band to have any credibility they must perform original songs. And while all four Beatles received songwriting credits on the Beatles' albums, the primary songwriters were John and Paul, who were jointly credited with writing most of the group's material.

Paul was already a budding songwriter when he met John; his first song, written in the wake of his mother's death, was "I Lost My Little Girl"—perhaps a subconsciously revealing title, though the song was about a romance, and not the death of a parent. John hadn't previously considered writing songs himself; now, spurred on by Paul, he decided he'd try his hand at it as well. Interestingly, his first song, "Hello Little Girl," was also inspired by his mother, specifically his memory of her singing Cole Porter's "It's De-Lovely"; "It's all very Freudian," he later admitted.

The two wrote a number of songs together during the Beatles' pre-fame years, though their claims of writing as many as 50, or even 100 songs, are exaggerated. Some of these songs were later recorded by the Beatles, including "Ask Me Why," "One After 909," and "I'll Follow the Sun," while others were never taken any further, like "Thinking of Linking" and "Winston's Walk." Paul later said they thought about bringing George in as another songwriter, but decided it would be simpler to keep the songwriting team to two people. Thus the Lennon/McCartney songwriting partnership was formalized.

Unlike songwriting teams where one person wrote the lyrics and the other the music (like composer Richard Rodgers and lyricist

Oscar Hammerstein, the team that wrote such classic musicals as *South Pacific* and *The Sound of Music*), both John and Paul wrote music and lyrics. In the early years of Beatlemania, they frequently worked "eyeball to eyeball…. playing into each other's noses," as John put it, in part because they were not only writing songs for the Beatles, but also for the other acts Brian Epstein managed. "The demand on us was *tremendous*," Lennon told *Playboy* without exaggeration. "So the [songwriting] cooperation was functional as well as musical." "Collaborating with another writer makes it twice as easy," McCartney agreed in his biography, *Many Years From Now*. "The ricochet is a great thing."

Early Lennon/McCartney songs were fairly simple. "In the early days lyrics didn't really count as long as we had some vague theme; she loves you, he loves her, and they love each other," Lennon explained. "It was the hook and the line and the sound we were going for." As the songs became more complex, each songwriter would be more likely to start a number on his own, then bring it to his partner to help refine it. In one well-known story, John recalled when Paul brought the song "Michelle" to a songwriting session, played him the first verse, then asked, "Where do I go from here?" John had recently been listening to Nina Simone's "I Put a Spell On You," with its refrain, "I love *you*, I love *you*," which, with a change in emphasis, became "I *love* you, I *love* you…" in "Michelle." "My contribution to Paul's songs was always to add a little bluesy edge to them," he explained to *Playboy*. "Otherwise, y'know, 'Michelle' is a straight ballad, right? [Paul] provided a lightness, an optimism, while I would always go for the sadness, the discords, the bluesy notes."

It was an astute examination of their differences. The songs that Paul predominantly wrote were generally more positive; even his songs that expressed sadness and disappointment never became as biting or as cynical as John's. Paul also noted the differences

Lennon and McCartney at the piano together.

in their musical styles: "If you analyze our songs, John's are often on one note, whereas mine are often much more melodic. I enjoy going places with melodies. I like what John did too, but his are more rhythmic."

In differentiating "John" songs from "Paul" songs, a general rule of thumb is that the dominant writer is the one singing the lead vocal. But you shouldn't pigeonhole either writer. John could write lovely melodies and Paul could write hard-hitting lyrics; Paul could rock out and John could sing a sweet ballad. Their strengths complemented each other perfectly, resulting in a catalogue of classic songs unrivaled by any other songwriting team in rock.

Lennon/McCartney vs. McCartney/Lennon

The song credits on Paul's live albums *Back in the US* (2002) and *Back in the World* (2003) drew attention because of his crediting Beatles songs as written by "McCartney/Lennon," instead of the usual "Lennon/McCartney."

It wasn't the first time this happened; Paul had done the same thing on his 1976 album *Wings Over America*, but no one commented on it at the time. Paul contended he wanted the name order to reflect who the dominant songwriter was for different songs, and he'd also asked Yoko if he could be credited as sole songwriter of "Yesterday" (a song John admittedly made no contribution to).

When John and Paul began writing songs together, they always added the heading "Another Lennon/McCartney original" to each new number, suggesting this name order was an agreed-upon standard. "Love Me Do" was credited to Lennon/McCartney, but initial pressings of "Please Please Me," "From Me to You," and the *Please Please Me* album were credited to McCartney/Lennon, before being switched back. In a 2002 press release, Paul claimed that John and Brian Epstein had told him at the time it would be Lennon/McCartney for now, and then switched at a later date. Which begs the question as to why Paul didn't ask for a credit change sooner.

But name order in songwriting credits means little to the general public, and many fans regarded the "Lennon/McCartney" credit as sacrosanct. So after a flurry of media stories, Paul let the matter drop.

America Meets The Beatles

Meet The Beatles was the album that broke the Beatles in America. It wasn't the first Beatles album to be released in the US (Vee-Jay's *Introducing The Beatles* beat it by 10 days), but Capitol had more powerful promotion and distribution, which helped the company retain the edge in the marketplace.

Once Capitol had decided to release the single "I Want to Hold Your Hand," they planned to follow up with an album drawn from the most recent Beatles album in the UK, *With The Beatles*. Capitol used the same cover, but put together their own song selection. "I Want to Hold Your Hand" gets the lead position, followed by the US and UK B-sides of the single, "I Saw Her Standing There" and "This Boy," respectively. The rest of the track listing was rounded out by all the Lennon/McCartney songs from *With The Beatles*, George Harrison's debut song "Don't Bother Me," and the sole cover "Till There Was You."

Aside from the songs cut (the *With The Beatles* tracks that were left off *Meet The Beatles* were all rock 'n' roll covers), the running order on *Meet The Beatles* largely follows that of *With The Beatles*, underscoring how strong that album's running order was. The only misstep is in closing the album with "Not a Second Time," a song whose fade-out ending leaves the album hanging; *With The Beatles* closed more powerfully with the Motown stomper "Money."

Not that that hurt *Meet The Beatles'* sales. The album was released on January 20, 1964, and by February 15 it was at the top of the *Billboard* charts, where it stayed for a total of 11 weeks, until it was replaced by *The Beatles' Second Album*, which stayed at No. 1 for five weeks. The soundtrack for *A Hard Day's*

Night, released the same year, was No. 1 for 14 weeks, meaning that Beatles albums were at the top of the charts for 30 weeks in 1964—over half the year.

21 The Long and Winding Road to the Beatles' US Invasion

While the Beatles found success in the UK fairly soon after signing with a major label, it took over a year for the band to break in America, during which time their records were also released on two different labels before Capitol finally claimed them.

EMI offered the Beatles' first single, "Love Me Do," to its US subsidiary, Capitol Records. But Capitol's producer Dave Dexter, who screened EMI records for possible US release, turned it down. He did the same when the Beatles' next single, "Please Please Me" was offered to Capitol. As "Please Please Me" had been a major hit in the UK, EMI then had their American agent, Transglobal Music Co., try to place the record with another label. Chicago-based label Vee-Jay agreed to release it, and on February 7, 1963, the first Beatles record was released in the US. Author Bruce Spizer says that Dick Biondi, a DJ with Chicago station WLS, may have been the first person to play a Beatles record in the states, as early as February 8 (without having playlists of every radio station operating in America at the time, it would be impossible to determine exactly who it was that gave the Beatles their first stateside radio play).

The single wasn't promoted very well; initial releases misspelled the group's name as "The Beattles," and ads plugged them as "R&B, C&W and Pop!," a clear sign that Vee-Jay wasn't sure what kind of group they were dealing with. Unsurprisingly, "Please

Please Me" didn't chart, but Vee-Jay tried again, releasing the Beatles' "From Me to You" single on May 6. This time, the single hit the charts, but plateaued at a less than impressive peak of No. 116, though it did better regionally, hitting the Top 40 on Los Angeles–based station KRLA, thanks to DJ Dick Biondi, who'd moved to LA after leaving WLS. (A young Richard Carpenter heard the song on KRLA, and promptly went out and ordered the single from his local record shop; the Carpenters' first major label single would be a cover of "Ticket to Ride.") Vee-Jay then planned to release a Beatles album, but the label's financial problems led to

A Record-Setting Achievement

April 4, 1964, was a remarkable day in Beatle history. They didn't just have the No. 1 single in the *Billboard* charts. They didn't have the top two singles. They didn't even have the top three singles. The Beatles stood at numbers one, two, three, four, *and* five in the charts. That's half of the Top 10.

The reason for this was that so many other American labels were releasing Beatle records that year. The No. 1 single that week was the Beatles' latest, "Can't Buy Me Love," on Capitol. The No. 2 single, "Twist and Shout," was on Tollie, a subsidiary of Vee-Jay, and rush released to take advantage of the Beatles' newfound popularity; it peaked at No. 2. At No. 3 was "She Loves You," initially released by Swan in 1963 with little success, and reissued in the hopes that it would now perform better, which it did, having topped the charts the previous week. Capitol's "I Want to Hold Your Hand" was at No. 4, on its way down from the top spot. "Please Please Me" was at No. 5, and had been previously released in 1963 on Vee-Jay. It was now on its way down from its peak at No. 3.

It was a stunning achievement that is unlikely to ever be repeated. And those weren't the only singles the Beatles had on the charts that week; there were seven more songs in the Top 100. On the album charts that same week, Capitol's *Meet The Beatles* was at No. 1 and Vee-Jay's *Introducing The Beatles* at No. 2, while MGM's compilation *The Beatles with Tony Sheridan and Their Guests* was at No. 77.

Transglobal ending their relationship with the company. So when the next Beatles single to be offered to Capitol, "She Loves You" was again turned down, Transglobal made a one-off deal with Swan Records, based in Philadelphia. Swan released "She Loves You" around September 16, but despite good reviews in *Billboard* and *Cash Box*, as well as getting airplay on Dick Clark's *American Bandstand* program, it failed to chart.

When Capitol initially turned down "I Want to Hold Your Hand" for US release, Brian Epstein decided he'd had enough. He called up Capitol's president, Alan Livingston, and asked that he please listen to the group's records himself. Livingston did, and finally agreed that Capitol would release Beatles records in the US. By this time, word about the Beatles was beginning to spread; Livingston had taken note of the coverage the group received in the UK, and in mid-November 1963, both *Time* and *Newsweek* ran stories on the band. Short pieces on the group also aired on NBC's *Huntley-Brinkley Report* on November 18, and the *CBS Morning News with Mike Wallace* on November 22 (before the airwaves were taken over with news of President Kennedy's assassination the same day). The Beatles' records were also being released by Capitol in Canada. And Livingston knew the Beatles were going to get plenty of national exposure when they appeared on three *The Ed Sullivan Show* programs in February 1964. Vee-Jay planned to piggyback on this growing interest by finally releasing an album of tracks they believed they still had the rights to, *Introducing The Beatles*, on January 10, 1964.

After working so hard to get the Beatles' records released by a major label in America, everything now began to happen at once. Finally, 16 months after "Love Me Do" had been turned down by Capitol, the Beatles had the No. 1 records in *Billboard's* singles and albums charts.

Further reading: *The Beatles Are Coming!* (Bruce Spizer)

Why Are There So Many US Records?

With both "I Want to Hold Your Hand" and *Meet The Beatles* setting sales records, 1964 in particular saw innumerable Beatles records flooding the US market—20 singles and 15 albums (in contrast to the four singles and three albums that were released in the UK). The US records were released on a variety of different labels, including not only Capitol, Vee-Jay, and Swan, but also United Artists (the *Hard Day's Night* soundtrack), and MGM and Atco (both of whom released records of the Beatles backing guitarist Tony Sheridan, recorded in 1961 and 1962 in Germany).

The core Beatles catalogue also differed between the UK and the US. In the UK, there were 12 main Beatles albums on Parlophone: *Please Please Me, With The Beatles, A Hard Day's Night, Beatles For Sale, Help!, Rubber Soul, Revolver, Sgt. Pepper's Lonely Hearts Club Band, The Beatles, Yellow Submarine, Abbey Road,* and *Let It Be.* In the US, there were 18 main Beatles albums on Capitol: *Meet The Beatles, The Beatles' Second Album, A Hard Day's Night, Something New, Beatles '65, The Early Beatles, Beatles VI, Help!, Rubber Soul, "Yesterday"...And Today, Revolver, Sgt. Pepper's Lonely Hearts Club Band, Magical Mystery Tour, The Beatles, Yellow Submarine, Abbey Road, Hey Jude* (aka *The Beatles Again*), and *Let It Be.*

Why the difference, when the albums featured most of the same songs? For one thing, Beatles albums in the US had fewer songs on them, in part because of the way royalties were calculated; just 12, in contrast to the 14 songs on the UK albums. And while US singles always appeared on US albums, such was not the case in the UK, where there were 31 songs that only appeared on singles or EPs (a seven-inch record with four songs) and not on the main

The Documentary Album

The Beatles' Story was one of the oddest Beatles records ever released during the '60s. It had no involvement from the Beatles, though two of the Beach Boys' songwriters, Roger Christian and Gary Usher, worked on the project, as producers, writers, and in Christian's case, one of the album's narrators.

The album's cover described the two-LP set as "A narrative and musical biography of Beatlemania." Over the four sides, the Beatles' story is related via song excerpts, sound bites from press conferences, instrumental versions of Beatles songs by the Hollyridge Strings, and hokey narration. Prose like: "Lady luck would be Beatle number five. And with the brilliant guiding hand of young Brian Epstein as their manager, the Beatles would soon lift off the Liverpool launch pad with enough force to put the entire music world into orbit!" makes the writing in the fan book *The True Story of The Beatles* seem like the height of sophistication in comparison.

Each Beatle is described in turn ("George is an interesting combination of beat and blasé, but takes his music seriously"; "James Paul McCartney; the baby-faced Beatle, an extremely handsome fellow"), and the record was also the first to feature a live Beatles song, an excerpt of "Twist and Shout" from the 1964 Hollywood Bowl show. *The Beatles' Story* was released on November 23, 1964, and made it to No. 7, but sold the least of any Capitol Beatles album in the '60s. It has yet to be released on CD.

albums. The US *Hard Day's Night* and *Help!* albums also included instrumental tracks drawn from the film scores that didn't appear on their UK counterparts.

The Beatles weren't happy about having their albums broken up, since they put a good deal of time in preparing the running order of their UK albums. The early US releases also sounded different, Capitol's Dave Dexter adding echo to various tracks. And while the cover of *Meet The Beatles* used the same artwork as the UK album *With The Beatles*, most of the US albums had different cover art. US and UK albums finally began matching up starting with the cover of *Rubber Soul*, but it wasn't until the release of *Sgt. Pepper* that the Beatles had sufficient creative control to insist the US and UK albums feature exactly the same tracks.

When the Beatles albums were first released on CD in 1987, it was decided that the UK albums would become the standard catalogue—with one exception. In the UK, the soundtrack for the *Magical Mystery Tour* album had been released in a two-EP set, complete with a booklet telling the film's story. In the US, the EP format was no longer in use, so the songs were put on an album, rounded out by the other singles the Beatles had released that year: "Penny Lane"/"Strawberry Fields," "All You Need Is Love"/"Baby You're a Rich Man," and "Hello Goodbye"/"I Am the Walrus." There were also two "new" albums created, *Past Masters Volume I* and *Past Masters Volume II*, which contained all the songs that had not appeared on a UK album. When the Beatles catalogue was reissued on CD in 2009, the two volumes were combined in one set simply called *Past Masters*.

Unlike fans in other countries, where different variations of Beatles albums also appeared, American fans remained particularly (some might say peculiarly) nostalgic for the Beatles' American albums. Eight of them were eventually released on CD in the box sets *The Capitol Albums Vol. 1* and *Vol. 2* released in 2004 and 2006, respectively. *Vol. 1* featured *Meet The Beatles, The Beatles' Second Album, Something New,* and *Beatles '65,* while *Vol. 2* contained *The Early Beatles, Beatles VI, Help!,* and *Rubber Soul,* with all tracks presented in mono and stereo mixes. *Vol. 1* reached No. 35 in the US charts, while *Vol. 2* peaked just outside the Top 40 at No. 46.

23 The Shea Stadium Concert

The high-water mark of the early Beatlemania years was probably the Beatles' first concert at Shea Stadium on August 15, 1965.

It wasn't the first time a rock act had played a baseball park; Elvis Presley played shows at such venues during the '50s. But the Beatles' show drew the largest audience for a rock show at the time—55,600, at least according to Mark Lewisohn's *The Complete Beatles Chronicle* (the Beatles also earned a record figure: $160,000 out of a $304,000 gross). All this made the Beatles' appearance not just a concert, but a bona fide event.

The Beatles got to the legendary gig in stages, first flying by helicopter from Manhattan to Queens, the borough where Shea Stadium was located, then traveling to the stadium itself locked securely inside a Wells Fargo armored van. Opening acts included Brenda Holloway and the King Curtis Band, Cannibal and the Headhunters, Sounds Incorporated, and the Young Rascals. The show was emceed by former WINS DJ Murray Kaufman, aka "Murray the K."

Finally, to the relief of the fans who'd been screaming themselves hoarse during the previous sets, Ed Sullivan appeared to introduce the main attraction: "Ladies and gentlemen; honored by their country, decorated by their queen, and loved here in America—here are the Beatles!" The Beatles, wearing beige Nehru-styled jackets and black pants, then ran across the field, hailed by deafening screams, to the stage setup at second base. Once on stage, they launched into "Twist and Shout," followed by "She's a Woman," "I Feel Fine," "Dizzy Miss Lizzy," "Ticket to Ride," "Everybody's Trying to Be My Baby," "Can't Buy Me

Love," "Baby's In Black," "Act Naturally," "A Hard Day's Night," "Help!," and concluding with "I'm Down."

A camera crew was in attendance and filmed the show for posterity. Because the sound recording was poor, the Beatles re-recorded most of the songs at a session on January 5, 1966; the film also uses a live recording of "Twist and Shout" from the August 30, 1965, show at the Hollywood Bowl, and the original studio recording of "Act Naturally," with crowd noises dubbed in to make it sound like a live performance. But what you see in the film is what happened that night, and the thrill of the event is clear. Frenzied teens scream in the stands; police officers hold their hands over their ears when the shrieking becomes unbearable, or race around

The Beatles perform at New York's Shea Stadium before thousands of screaming fans in 1966, a year after their first appearance there. (AP Images)

the field tackling fans desperate enough to try anything to get closer to their idols; the increasingly sweaty Beatles looking around at the crowd in amazement. The aptly titled *The Beatles at Shea Stadium* was first broadcast in the UK on March 1, 1966; a US screening followed on January 10, 1967. The 48-minute film doesn't feature the complete concert, as it adds in off-stage material and clips of the other acts on the bill; the complete Beatles set has yet to be officially released.

The Beatles returned to Shea Stadium the following year on August 23, 1966, but the show failed to sell out (the promoter, Sid Bernstein, later claimed the show would have sold out if he hadn't mislaid a box of 11,000 tickets). Paul later appeared as a special guest at Billy Joel's July 18, 2008, concert at Shea Stadium, the last show at the venue before it was torn down. Paul then appeared at the new stadium built on the site, now called Citi Field, for a run of three shows in 2009.

24 More Popular Than Jesus

The biggest controversy the Beatles experienced during their career came when John made the following comment to a journalist: "Christianity will go. It will vanish and shrink. I needn't argue about that; I'm right and I will be proved right. We're more popular than Jesus now; I don't know which will go first—rock 'n' roll or Christianity."

This quote by John first appeared in a profile entitled "How Does a Beatle Live? John Lennon Lives Like This," that ran in London's *Evening Standard* on March 4, 1966. It wasn't meant to be a controversial statement; John was simply talking to a journalist,

Maureen Cleave, he knew and liked (the two were rumored to have had an affair, but Cleave has always denied this). John's views on religion weren't even the focus of the article; it's just one moment in the day Cleave spends with her subject, in a portrait showing John to be at something of a loose end: pointing out gadgets he owns that don't work, admitting he's lazy ("Sex is the only physical thing I can be bothered with any more") and talking dismissively about his lavish suburban home ("I'm just stopping at it, like a bus stop.... I'll get my *real* house when I know what I want"). When the article ran in England, it was considered as just another profile of a Beatle.

The article was syndicated in publications around the world, including the *New York Times*, and there was no reaction. But when the US teen magazine *DATEbook* picked up the story for its August 1966 issue (which hit the stands on July 29), it provoked a fierce backlash in America's Bible Belt, with John's views condemned as blasphemy. Radio stations across the South and as far north as New York (though not including New York City) banned the Beatles' music, and some communities even held public burnings of Beatle merchandise. The British, Cleave observed in a later interview, knew that John's comments were "ironically meant. But the Americans have little sense of irony." But the backlash wasn't limited to the US. Radio stations in Holland, Spain, and South Africa also banned Beatles records from the airwaves, and even the Pope issued a statement in the Vatican's newspaper, *L'Osservatore Romano*: "Some things may not be dealt with profanely even in the world of beatniks."

John later insisted that people were misinterpreting his statement; he was not saying the Beatles were greater than Christianity, only more popular—after all, there were no religious records selling in the millions, nor were churches drawing the kind of standing-room-only crowds that came to Beatle concerts. And his subsequent comment in the original article—"Jesus was all right but his disciples were thick and ordinary. It's them twisting it for me"—even mirrored the views of religious scholars who spend their entire lives analyzing different interpretations and translations of the gospels, as well as debating what the apostles really said and did.

Images of the Beatles burn during one of many protests in the American South over Lennon's comments; this "Beatlemania Bonfire" was held near Fort Oglethorpe, Georgia, on August 12, 1966. (AP Images)

But the general public wasn't interested in such nuance. And with the Beatles scheduled to start another American tour on August 12 in Chicago, there was an urgent need for some damage control. Brian Epstein flew to New York City and held a press conference on August 6 to try to defuse the situation, and considered canceling the tour. But it was decided that the tour should go ahead, with a pre-tour press conference held on August 11 to address the issue. By then, John had become so worried about how his fellow Beatles might be taken to task for comments he alone had made that he broke down and cried before the conference. But he was back in control when he went before the press, trying in vain to explain his remarks, before finally giving up and saying, "I apologize if that will make you happy. I still don't know quite what I've done. I've tried to tell you what I did do, but if you want me to apologize, if that will make you happy, then okay, I'm sorry."

The press was suitably mollified, though an air of tension hung over the rest of the tour. Members of the Ku Klux Klan turned up to protest shows in Washington, D.C., and Memphis; in the latter city, an anonymous death threat was also phoned in, and when a firecracker was thrown on the stage during the evening show, it did nothing to ease anyone's nerves. But there were no further incidents on the tour, which would be the Beatles' last. The controversy soon subsided, and the radio bans were eventually lifted (except in South Africa, where John's records are still banned). To the end, John insisted he'd been misunderstood. In one of his last interviews, with *Playboy* magazine, he said, "People got the idea I was anti-Christ or antireligion. I'm not at all. I'm a most religious fellow. I'm certainly not an atheist."

25 Visit London

There are innumerable reasons to visit London, one of the world's most fascinating cities; as English author Samuel Johnson put it, "When one is tired of London, one is tired of life." Being able to visit myriad Beatle sites is just an added bonus.

The Beatles spent much of their professional life in England's capital city. And though much has changed—EMI House, where the covers of *Please Please Me* and the *1962–1966* and *1967-1970* compilation were taken, has been torn down —a number of key sites are still standing. Most important is Abbey Road Studios, a site even casual fans may want to visit; the outside wall is scrawled with graffiti, and fans are forever holding up traffic by trying to replicate the cover of *Abbey Road* in the crosswalk nearby.

The Beatles were so integrated into London's life, there's a Beatles connection with a range of sites a tourist might visit anyway. There's a permanent Beatles exhibit at the British Museum, featuring original handwritten lyrics (including the lyrics to "Yesterday"). See a show at the London Palladium or Prince of Wales Theatre and you'll be at one of many venues where the Beatles performed. An early Beatles photo session was held at the London Zoo, and Paul frequently took his dog Martha for a walk in the park where the zoo is located, Regent's Park. Marylebone Station was the site where the early scenes of *A Hard Day's Night* were shot. Euston Station, is the same station the Beatles also used when they traveled to North Wales to attend a seminar by the Maharishi Mahesh Yogi; you also catch trains to Liverpool from this station.

There are a number of resources to help you track down Beatles sites in London. The most comprehensive guide is *The Beatles' London*, by Piet Schreuders, Mark Lewisohn, and Adam

Smith. The 2008 edition has over 200 pages of sites, meaning you could conceivably plan a trip to London doing nothing but visiting Beatles landmarks; it's also packed with enough info and photos to make it a good read even if you don't have a London visit on your schedule. If you'd like to be part of a tour group, there are walking tours of Beatle sites given by London Walks (www.walks.com). The tours are hosted by Richard Porter, who has also written his own tour book (*Guide to The Beatles' London*), and runs the Beatles Coffee Shop at St. John's Wood tube (subway) station, the closest stop to Abbey Road Studios. International Tours and Events, who offer tours of Liverpool during International Beatle Week, also add on London trips as part of their tours (www.toursandevents.com).

Rubber Soul: The Beatles Grow Up

Rubber Soul signaled the Beatles' transformation from Mop Tops to serious artists. It marked the moment when the days of Beatlemania became something they looked back on, not something they were caught in the middle of. It was also when the band began thinking about their albums in terms of being a complete piece of work, not merely a collection of singles.

There was also a new lyrical sophistication afoot, particularly in John's songs, which are some of his best work. The yearning "Girl" is a song of profound ambivalence, the singer consumed with desire for a woman who alternately enthralls and intimidates him; "Norwegian Wood" is a cynical tale of modern romance with a sinister ending, as the rejected suitor takes his revenge by literally burning down the house; "Nowhere Man" is a portrait of a man mired in his safe little world of isolation—"a bit like you and me,"

John adds, gently chiding his audience and himself as much as the song's subject. Conversely, John also crafted the poignant "In My Life," a clear-eyed view of nostalgia that emphasizes the present is what is most important (though Paul contends that he provided the bulk of the melody for the song).

Paul's standout song on the album is the lovely ballad "Michelle," an immediate standard destined to be nearly as popular as "Yesterday." His other songs are in the same conventional mode, with "You Won't See Me" and "I'm Looking Through You" describing troubled relationships. But there's a sly twist in the album's opening track, "Drive My Car," with a rising starlet enlisting a would-be suitor as her chauffeur before he learns she hasn't even got a car. Love is also the subject of "The Word," but it's love in its broadest, spiritual sense; the first Beatles song to address the concept of universal love and peace. George Harrison also reveals his growing complexity as a songwriter with the unabashedly spiteful "Think For Yourself" and the backhanded compliment of "If I Needed Someone" (which says, in essence, when I get bored with my current relationship I'll give you a call).

Though the Beatles had made use of instruments outside the basic guitar/bass/drums lineup since "Love Me Do," on *Rubber Soul* they began making increasing use of different sounds. Most noticeable is the sitar line on "Norwegian Wood," played by George, who'd become intrigued by the instrument after watching a musician play it on the set of the film *Help!* The piano part that George Martin played on "In My Life" was given a baroque flavor when the recording was sped up, a harbinger of things to come on future Beatles records. It also marked the first time songs went through complete revisions; the original arrangements of "Norwegian Wood" and "I'm Looking Through You" (both later released on *Anthology 2*), are substantially different from their final versions. And the vocal harmonizing on "Nowhere Man," "The Word," and "If I Needed Someone" is superlative.

The strength of the good stuff is such that it easily overrides the album's lesser material. The weakest track is "What Goes On," the token Ringo song, a light country/western number that gave Ringo his first (shared) songwriting credit. "Wait" was resurrected from the *Help!* sessions, while "Run For Your Life" was a song John said he always "hated" as he considered it a piece of hack work (though its theme of jealousy was one he'd often return to, most famously in "Jealous Guy"). The album was released on December 3, 1965, in the UK, December 6 in the US, and topped the charts in both countries. For the first time, the US album had the same front and back cover as the UK album, though Capitol still rejigged the song selection. The elongated look on the Beatles' faces was the result of a happy accident; when photographer Robert Freeman was projecting slides of possible cover photos onto an album-sized piece of cardboard, the board slipped, stretching out the group's faces. The band were excited by the look, and asked to have the cover printed in the same fashion, creating another distinctive cover for the group.

The Beatles Break Up...

To the general public, it seemed that the Beatles broke up in April 1970, when the newspapers announced that Paul was leaving the group. But the breakup had actually been underway for some time.

It was the band's most amiable member, Ringo, who left first, walking out of a recording session on August 22, 1968. As the Beatles' music became increasingly elaborate, Ringo ended up spending much of his time sitting around during sessions (he passed the time during the *Sgt. Pepper* sessions by learning to play chess). Finally fed up with feeling he was no longer an important part of the band, he left while the group was working on the song "Back in the USSR." That there was no announcement of his departure suggests the other Beatles knew Ringo was only experiencing some momentary frustration, and indeed he soon returned to the group on September 4, just in time for the filming of the promotional clips for "Hey Jude" and "Revolution." At the band's next studio session the following day, Ringo walked in to find his drum kit had been covered with flowers.

George Harrison was the next to leave, on January 10, 1969, during filming sessions for what would become the movie *Let It Be*. George's departure was more serious; he felt tired of being shunted into the background by John and Paul, and hadn't been keen on making a film in the first place. He agreed to return if they moved the filming to the Beatles' Apple Studio and abandoned the idea of doing a proper live show. Sessions continued with the full band on January 21.

Eight months later, it was John's turn. On September 13, he'd performed at the Rock 'n' Roll Revival concert in Toronto, and been so enthused by the experience he decided to leave the Beatles. He announced his decision during a business meeting with the other Beatles on September 20. Paul had been suggesting projects for the group to do, which John continually shot down, finally saying he was leaving the group, bluntly stating, "I've had enough. I want a divorce." But as the band had just released *Abbey Road*, and had signed a new contract with Capitol, John was persuaded to say nothing publicly. As a result, Paul seemed to think John's decision carried little weight, saying, "Oh, that means nothing's really happened if you're not going to say anything." Perhaps he assumed it was simply a momentary walkout on John's part, as Ringo's and George's had been.

But it was not to be. John never attended another Beatles recording session (of which there were only four more, adding overdubs to the *Let It Be* album). He never did talk publicly about his decision to leave, but it was clear to any astute observer that the Beatles were now spending their time working on their own outside projects. Indeed, Paul himself acknowledged the group's split in an interview in *Life* magazine's November 7, 1969, issue, frankly admitting, "The Beatle thing is over. It has been exploded, partly by what we have done and partly by other people."

But Paul's remark was strangely overlooked at the time. No one took full notice of the group's split until he wrote a Q&A interview with himself that was issued with review copies of his first solo album, *McCartney*, released in April 1970, which featured such questions and answers as: *Are you planning a new album or single with the Beatles?* "No." *Is your break with the Beatles temporary or permanent, due to personal differences or musical ones?* "Personal differences, business differences, but most of all because I have a better time with my family. Temporary or permanent? I don't know." *Do you foresee a time when Lennon-McCartney becomes an active songwriting partnership again?* "No."

Paul's answers weren't absolute and did leave the door open to the possibility of the Beatles working together again. But the media preferred to think otherwise, and on April 10, 1970, headlines like the *Daily Mirror*'s "Paul Is Quitting The Beatles" began running on the front page of newspapers around the world. Though the other Beatles had left in the group in the past, none of them announced it publicly, which allowed the group to continue. Now that Paul had made a public statement, the matter was out in the open. There was no turning back.

28 ...But When Are They Getting Back Together?

No one seemed to want to accept that the Beatles had broken up. Despite the apparent split in April 1970, rumors of a Beatles reunion regularly appeared in the media over the next decade.

In fact, rumors of a reunion began circulating within months of Paul's April 1970 announcement he was leaving the group. When George Harrison jokingly told a journalist, "I guess we'll have to get another bass player" in the wake of the many Paul-has-left-the-Beatles stories, a rumor immediately swept through the British media that the Beatles were looking for a replacement bassist.

But relations between the members were touchy for some time, especially when Paul filed suit against the other Beatles, and their company, Apple Corp., at the end of 1970, a move he believed was the only way to break up the partnership. Paul was definitely the odd man out for a few years; while John, George, and Ringo all played on each other's records, no one played with Paul.

The first serious chance for a reunion came in 1971, with George's charity concerts for Bangladesh, two shows held August 1 at Madison Square Garden. Ringo readily agreed to participate, but John declined when he was told Yoko wouldn't be able to perform with him. Paul also declined, fearing that the man looking after John's, George's, and Ringo's business interests at the time, Allen Klein, might then take the credit for a Beatles reunion.

A partial reunion did take place in 1973, when all the Beatles appeared on the album *Ringo*, though they didn't all appear on the same track (the only track featuring three Beatles was "I'm the Greatest," written by John; George also appeared on the song). And as the decade progressed, various promoters began offering increasingly larger sums of money to the Beatles if they'd only reunite. Sid

Bernstein, who'd promoted the Shea Stadium concerts, had been trying to lure the Beatles back since 1969 and continued to up the ante, hoping for a reunion show. Promoter Bill Sargent offered the Beatles $10 million for a concert that he envisioned would also feature the Rolling Stones and Bob Dylan; when that didn't pan out, he offered $50 million, then $100 million. David Geffen (whose Geffen Records label would later release John's comeback album, *Double Fantasy*) offered $30 million for a new Beatles album. In 1979, United Nations secretary general Kurt Waldheim asked the Beatles to do a charity concert for Vietnamese refugees. When Paul's band Wings performed later that year at a London charity concert for the people of war-torn Kampuchea, rumors flew that the other Beatles would also show up. They didn't, but the December 29, 1979, show was still notable for being the final live performance by Wings.

A partial reunion had happened earlier that year, at the May 19 wedding reception for Eric Clapton and Pattie Boyd (who'd married on March 27). A jam session broke out at the reception, during which George, Paul, and Ringo had all taken up instruments, prompting a small flurry of "Beatles reunion" stories. And there was one reunion offer that nearly did get a response. On April 24, 1976, Lorne Michaels, producer of the late-night comedy show *Saturday Night Live*, lampooned the outlandish offers people had been making by offering the Beatles $3,000 for a reunion show. "All you have to do is sing three Beatle tunes," Lorne said with a straight face. "'She loves you, yeah, yeah, yeah'—that's a thousand dollars right there." Little did Lorne know that John was watching the show at his New York home along with Paul. In one of his last interviews, John revealed that the two nearly went down to the studio for a joke, but decided they were too tired.

There was another project that might have brought the Beatles together during the '70s. Longtime Beatles aide Neil Aspinall had been working on a documentary film about the group, provisionally entitled *The Long and Winding Road.* In 1980, John gave a deposition for a suit the Beatles' company, Apple Corp., had brought against the producers of the *Beatlemania* show (a tribute show featuring Beatles impersonators), stating that the Beatles planned to film a reunion concert as the climax for a documentary, though at the time no definite plans for such a show had been made.

Even John's murder on December 8, 1980, didn't put an end to the reunion rumors, which became increasingly far-fetched, such as suggesting John's son Julian could stand in for his father as part of a "Beatles reunion." As Ringo wryly put it, "It doesn't matter how many times we deny the reunion stories, it'll still go on. Even if there's only one of us left, they'll say he's getting it together with himself."

The Beatles Anthology: In Their Own Words

The 1990s *Anthology* project was threefold, enabling the Beatles to tell their story in their own words in a range of media: music, print, and film.

The *Anthology* had its roots in a documentary that Beatles aide Neil Aspinall had been working on since 1970, when the film was originally planned for release. Though that didn't happen, Aspinall didn't give up on the project, and over the years he continued to comb film archives around the world for footage, assembling a documentary provisionally entitled *The Long and Winding Road*, after the song of the same name on the album *Let It Be.* It then remained in limbo for some time, despite occasional efforts to get it released.

Finally, in 1992, the project was revived. The deciding factor had been George's financial woes. In 1978, he'd started the film company HandMade Films, with attorney Denis O'Brien, who also became George's business manager. George then discovered O'Brien had been ripping him off to the tune of several million dollars. George filed and won a lawsuit against his former manager, but O'Brien had no money to pay the debt, which left George in serious financial straits; among other things, he was in danger of losing his beloved home, Friar Park. So he agreed to give the green light to the documentary, though he did request a name change, not wanting the film to go out with the title of a Paul song. Instead, the project took on the more neutral title of *The Beatles Anthology*.

Paul, George, and Ringo all did new interviews for the film; Neil Aspinall, George Martin, and Apple publicist and close friend Derek Taylor were also interviewed, while John's contributions were taken from archive footage. What had begun as a 90-minute film now expanded to over 10 hours; an edited version of the film was prepared for television broadcast, held over three evenings in the US, six in the UK (though the overall running times were the same), beginning on November 19, 1995.

No archival releases were originally considered to accompany the documentary; as late as 1993, George Martin said in an interview there was only "junk" in the vaults. But once it was realized that a tie-in release could make a considerable amount of money, three double-CD sets were assembled, drawing on rehearsal tapes, alternate versions of songs, and unreleased material. Inevitably, the idea of adding new music to the releases came up, and the new songs "Free as a Bird" and "Real Love" were added to *Anthology 1* and *2*, respectively.

Anthology 1 was released on November 20, 1995, in the UK, November 21 in the US; it topped the US charts, with record sales of 855,000 in its first week, but only reached No. 2 in the UK. *Anthology 2* followed on March 18, 1996, in the UK, March 19 in the US, and topped the charts in both countries; *Anthology 3*, released October 28, 1996, in the UK, October 29 in the US,

The Biggest-Selling Album Of The 21st Century.

It's such an obvious idea: an album featuring every Beatles song that topped the UK and US charts. Yet the *1* album wasn't released until 2000.

The Beatles hadn't released a "Best Of" set since 1982's *20 Greatest Hits* (infamous for including an edited version of "Hey Jude" on the US edition). Perhaps that accounts for *1*'s phenomenal sales. It was hoped that *1* would do well, but its eventual success exceeded all expectations. It topped the charts in 35 different countries. Though released near the end of 2000, on November 13 in the UK, November 14 in the US, by the following month it had become the best-selling album of the year. Sales continued well into the next year, making it the fastest selling album in history. It remains the biggest-selling album of the decade—and, so far, of the 21st century.

As a melding of US and UK No. 1s, there were some surprises among the 27 selections, if you weren't familiar with how songs did in each country. "Love Me Do" only topped the US charts; "From Me to You" only topped the UK charts. "Eight Days a Week" and "Yesterday" weren't even released as singles in the UK. As a double-sided single, both "We Can Work It Out" and "Day Tripper" topped the UK charts, while only "We Can Work It Out" topped the US charts. It was actually a good idea to compile the album from both countries' hits, as it resulted in a record that better represented the breadth of the Beatles' work.

The success of *1* also showed that the Beatles' music remains as wildly popular as it was during the height of Beatlemania.

again topped the US chart, but peaked at No. 4 in the UK. Some of the songs had circulated on bootlegs, but there were also songs on the albums that had not appeared on any bootleg, such as a previously unknown song by George, "You Know What to Do." Unfortunately, the decision was also made to compile composite tracks, from two or more takes, thus creating a few new "rarities."

1996 also saw the release of the longer *Anthology* cut on video; when it was re-released in 2003 on DVD, there was a disc with an additional 81 minutes of material, primarily group interviews with the three Beatles, which were especially poignant to see, as George had died in 2001. Sales of the CDs and videos had been huge, spurring the *London Observer* to write: "In 1996 the Beatles have achieved what every group since them has failed to do: become bigger than the Beatles."

And there was still more to come. In October 2000 came the release of *The Beatles Anthology*—the book. The lavishly designed book ran to 367 pages, and featured far more interview material than even the full-length cut of the film. There were dozens of previously unseen photographs, many from the Beatles' private collections, and reproductions of letters, postcards, itineraries, handwritten song lyrics, and other ephemera.

Certainly, the Beatles' version of their story was selective and subjective, with less pleasant events played down. But it was still great to hear the Beatles share their memories, and their music.

30 The Reunion Singles

The *Anthology* project didn't just bring the Beatles together to tell their story. It resulted in two new Beatles songs as well: "Free as a Bird" and "Real Love."

As the *Anthology* project got underway, there was a suggestion that the Beatles might record some incidental music for the film. Eventually, those discussions led to the idea of recording new songs. Paul says it was his idea to approach Yoko and see if she had any demos of John she could share; Yoko says it was George who approached her. Whoever asked her, Yoko was initially hesitant about the idea: "John always said there could be no reunion of the Beatles because, if they got together again, the world would be so disappointed to see four rusty old men." But in the end she decided not to stand in the other Beatles' way. And when Paul came to New York to induct John into the Rock and Roll Hall of Fame at the organization's annual dinner on January 19, 1994, Yoko gave him cassette tapes of songs John had recorded at home in 1977.

There were still some details to be worked out. George said he would only participate if Jeff Lynne (who'd played with George in his post-Beatles group the Traveling Wilburys) was chosen as producer; George Martin, the Beatles' original producer, wasn't asked. The others agreed, and sessions began on February 11, 1994, at Paul's country home in East Sussex. The three Beatles—whom the media would soon nickname "the Threetles"—chose "Free as a Bird" to work on, largely because the lyrics were unfinished and so they could add something to it, making the song more of a collaborative number. There were some awkward moments at the beginning—Paul initially didn't like the slide guitar part that George wanted to play on the track—but the group managed to put their differences aside. As Ringo put it, "Once we get the bullshit behind us, we all end up doing what we do best, which is making music."

A later session on June 22 at Paul's home to work on the song "Now and Then" didn't go nearly as well. But during subsequent sessions on February 6 and 7, 1995 (also at Paul's home), they completed work on "Real Love" (another version of this demo had played during the credits of the 1988 documentary *Imagine: John Lennon*). But further sessions that year on March 20 and 21 and May 15 and 16 were again problematic and no other songs were finished. George complained, "It's just like being back in the Beatles," and the three never reconvened to make music together again.

Thus there were only two new songs to promote, with "Free as a Bird" placed on *Anthology 1* and "Real Love" placed on *Anthology*

2. There was still much anticipation about hearing the first new Beatles songs to be released in 25 years (the last new single being "The Long and Winding Road," released in the US only in May 1970). A terrific video, directed by Joe Pytka, was put together for "Free as a Bird," which debuted on ABC on November 19, 1995, playing at the end of the broadcast of the first *Anthology* episode. The song itself was slow, even somewhat ponderous (due in part to the poor quality of the cassette with John's vocal and piano part), but it nonetheless worked well with the imaginative video, with the "Bird" of the title being the camera itself, gliding through a Liverpool landscape that cleverly worked in all kinds of references to Beatles songs that were fun to spot, like a young woman with a tray of poppies ("Penny Lane"), and a newspaper taxi ("Lucy in the Sky with Diamonds"), as well as Beatle landmarks (the Cavern, the Strawberry Field gates). The single was officially released December 4, 1995, in the UK, reaching No. 2, and December 12 in the US, reaching No. 6. The song won a Grammy for Best Pop Performance by a Duo or Group with Vocal, and the video also won a Grammy for Best Music Video, Short Form.

The "Real Love" video, directed by Kevin Godley, begins with a shot of John's white piano rising from Liverpool's River Mersey, soaring into the sky and eventually joined by the Beatles' other instruments, intercut with shots of the "Threetles" recording the song in Paul's home studio and other archive footage. The single was released March 4, 1996, in the UK, reaching No. 4, and March 5 in the US, reaching No. 10. There was some controversy in the UK when Radio 1 declined to add the song to their playlist, saying it was of no interest to their youthful demographic.

Was the recording of new songs worth it? That depends. Some felt the songs were little more than gimmicks to hype the *Anthology.* Other fans enjoyed hearing the "Threetles Plus John" making new music together.

31 The Death Of Brian Epstein

You could certainly say that the moment when the Beatles quit touring and thus stopped sharing that communal on-the-road life-together feeling was when the group's breakup really began. But as the release of *Sgt. Pepper* showed, there was just as much demand for their music as ever—possibly even more so, since their live appearances had been curtailed. The real turning point came later on during the summer of 1967, when their manager, Brian Epstein, died.

Once the Beatles decided to stop touring, Brian worried that his role as a manager would be increasingly superfluous. He was also concerned that when his contract with the group came up for renewal in October 1967, the Beatles would not re-sign with him. And with less to occupy his time, his personal life became increasingly turbulent, with a growing dependence on pharmaceutical drugs and alcohol, and unhappy relationships. He became sufficiently depressed that he attempted suicide, both in late 1966 and early 1967.

He pulled himself together when his father died in July 1967, inviting his mother to move in with him for a time. She returned to Liverpool on Thursday, August 24, and Brian headed down to his country home in Sussex the next day, Friday, August 25, to spend the Bank Holiday weekend with his friends, Peter Brown and Geoffrey Ellis. Brian had hoped more interesting male companionship could be found to share the weekend, but when no one was available, he drove back to London that same Friday night. He called his friends in Sussex in the late afternoon on Saturday and said he would return to the country by train that night and would call again before he left.

The Beatles kick back and relax in a Paris hotel in 1964. From left to right, John Lennon, George Harrison, Brian Epstein, Ringo Starr, and Paul McCartney.

But the call never came, and on Sunday, August 27, Brian's housekeepers, a Spanish couple, became increasingly anxious. They contacted one of Brian's secretaries, who came over to his house, soon followed by a doctor that Peter Brown had contacted. The door to Brian's room was broken down, and he was found dead in his bed. He was 32 years old.

The official cause of death was an accidental overdose of Carbatrol, a sleeping aid. Over the years, rumors of something more sinister happening have become rife; that Brian's death was suicide (ruled out due to testing showing the drug had not been taken all at once), or a murder, either because of the money lost through Brian's poor handling of the Beatles' merchandising deals, or a violent sex game gone wrong. But no real proof for any other cause of death has ever been found.

Brian was buried at Long Lane cemetery in Liverpool. On October 17, the Beatles attended a memorial service for Brian held at the New London Synagogue in London. By then it had been announced that Brian's brother Clive would become the new chairman of the NEMS management organization, though he would not be the Beatles' personal manager ("No one could possibly replace Brian," Paul said). The Beatles would remain with NEMS and a press release assured the public, "Things will go on as before." And though Paul was seemingly optimistic, getting the group on board to further develop the *Magical Mystery Tour* project, others in the group were more worried. In later reflecting on Brian's death in a *Rolling Stone* interview, John admitted: "I knew we were in trouble then. I didn't really have any misconceptions about our ability to do anything other than play music and I was scared. I thought, 'We've fuckin' had it.'"

32 An Apple a Day

Apple Corp., Ltd. was the Beatles' company, founded in 1967 as The Beatles Ltd., and renamed Apple Corp., Ltd. in 1968. The Beatles explained that the company's purpose was to spread their wealth, using their money to encourage other artists "to see if we can't get artistic freedom within a business structure," as Paul explained. But that was merely a side concern. The real reason Apple was set up was because by forming the company the Beatles would be able to have their earnings subject to corporation tax and not income tax; corporation tax rates were substantially less than income tax rates.

And there was no shortage of other ventures the Beatles wanted to get involved with. Apple Records was an obvious division, soon joined by Apple Publishing, Apple Films, Apple Publicity, Apple Management, and some less expected areas like Apple Retailing, Apple Tailoring, and Apple Electronics.

The Beatles also solicited talent via an ad which pictured longtime Beatles aide Alistair Taylor dressed up as a street musician, under the heading: "This man has talent…"—the ad going on to ask other people to send in tapes of their own musical creations. "If you come and see me and say, 'I've had such and such a dream,' I will say, 'Here's so much money. Go away and do it,'" Paul grandly announced. As a result, Apple's offices were deluged with proposals for various projects, most envelopes never being opened, let alone read. It was an early indication of how quickly Apple's abilities to achieve even their short-term goals would soon spin out of control.

Apple's offices were initially located at 94 Baker Street in London. As more people were hired, an additional branch was set up at 95 Wigmore Street. On July 15, 1968, most of Apple's departments moved to 3 Savile Row, which became the company's official HQ. Each Beatle had his own office, and a studio was installed in the basement, used by the Beatles and other artists. Apple Records was proudly launched in mid-August, with a special package of the label's first releases, labeled "Our First Four," containing the singles "Hey Jude" (by the Beatles), "Those Were the Days" (by Mary Hopkin), "Sour Milk Sea" (by Jackie Lomax), and "Thingumybob" (by the Black Dyke Mills Band), the first two becoming worldwide smashes.

Yet by January 1969, John was telling a journalist the company was being badly run: "It doesn't need to make vast

The Saga of Northern Songs

Northern Songs, Ltd., was the company that held the publishing rights to most of John and Paul's Beatles songs. It was set up by publisher Dick James in 1963, with John and Paul holding 20 percent each, Brian Epstein 10, and James and his partner Emmanuel Silver 50. Northern became a public company in 1965, and when shares went on sale, James remained the majority holder with 37.5 percent of the shares, with John and Paul owning 15 percent each (George and Ringo each owned 1.6 percent).

After Brian's death, John and Paul hoped to renegotiate their arrangement with James. Instead, James sold his shares to entertainment conglomerate ATV. A struggle for control of the company ensued. The Beatles lost, and John and Paul eventually sold their shares to ATV in October 1969 (Ringo held on to his, and George had previously sold his shares).

Paul claimed he approached Yoko in 1981 about their jointly buying the ATV catalogue; she disputed this story, and in any case the deal fell through. Associated Communications Corporation, ATV's holding company, was next purchased by Robert Holmes à Court in 1982. In 1984 he put ATV up for sale, and with Paul and Yoko still unable to come to terms, sold it to Michael Jackson in 1985. Jackson merged the catalogue with Sony to create Sony/ATV Music Publishing; on his death in 2009, his share passed to his estate.

More on this complicated story can be found in *Northern Songs* (Brian Southall and Rupert Perry) and *Beatles For Sale* (John Blaney).

profits, but if it carries on like this, all of us will be broke in the next six months." While a decided exaggeration, it was true that people were taking advantage. Some employees ran up huge food and liquor bills. Equipment from stereos to televisions to typewriters was regularly stolen; even the secretaries' wage packets were pilfered. "All our buddies that worked for us for 50 years were just living and drinking and eating like fucking Rome," John complained.

Nor were all of Apple's ventures proving profitable. The original Apple location on Baker Street had also housed the Apple shop, which carried clothes designed by a group of Dutch artists who called themselves The Fool. The shop opened with a flourish on December 7, 1967, but closed just over seven months later, on July 31, 1968, with the entire stock given away free to the public. None of the film projects suggested for Apple Films—such as a version of *Lord of the Rings*, starring the Beatles—came to fruition. The same was true of many projects Apple wanted to do. And the Beatles and Mary Hopkin were Apple Records' only truly successful artists.

Paul brought in his future in-laws, Lee Eastman and his son John, both attorneys, to help put Apple in order; the others brought in record executive Allen Klein. There was a restructuring at the company, with many people let go, but it proved to be too late. Eastman and Klein could not work together, which drove a fatal wedge between the Beatles. After the recording of *Abbey Road*, the Beatles largely stopped working together, though their breakup wouldn't be formally announced until April 1970.

But that wasn't the end of Apple. No new records were released after 1976, but Neil Aspinall, Apple's managing director, stayed on at the company, undertaking the long process of getting the Beatles' affairs in order (a few films also came out under the Apple name, such as George's *The Concert for Bangladesh*). In the '90s, records by other Apple artists were reissued on CD, and today the Apple logo can still be found on all Beatles releases.

Further reading: *The Longest Cocktail Party* (Richard DiLello), *Apple to the Core* (Peter McCabe, Robert D. Schonfeld), *Those Were The Days* (Stefan Granados), *The Beatles on Apple Records* (Bruce Spizer)

Beatles Times Two: The "White Album"

The Beatles, released in the fall of 1968, was the only double album released while the group was still together. With a total of 30 tracks, it's unsurprisingly the most diverse record the band ever released.

Sessions for the album were held from May to October 1968. There was an abundance of songs to draw from, and producer George Martin felt they should only work on a single album's worth of the best tracks. But the Beatles thought otherwise. The sessions were also fraught. John had his new girlfriend, Yoko Ono, constantly by his side, so Paul frequently brought his new love interest, Francie Schwartz, to the sessions. In August, Ringo left for a brief period; longtime engineer Geoff Emerick also walked out and never returned. And Martin absented himself by going on holiday during the sessions.

But despite all the distractions, the Beatles made an exceptional album. Songs like Paul's "Helter Skelter" and John's "Yer Blues" showed that the band hadn't lost their rock 'n' roll edge. And they were still having fun, as could be heard in the Beach Boys-esque harmonies of "Back in the USSR," the calypso hijinks of "Ob-La-Di, Ob-La Da," and the rollicking rave-up "Birthday." George contributed four songs (the most he had on any Beatles album), including the ambiguous "Long, Long, Long" (it's a love song that could be referring to either a romantic partner or God), and two more sarcastic numbers, "Savoy Truffle," inspired by his friend Eric Clapton's fondness for chocolates, and "Piggies," a jaunty attack on authority figures. But "While My Guitar Gently Weeps" was his masterpiece, an epic number with Eric Clapton tapped to provide the glorious guitar solo. Ringo also got a look in with the twisted country & western number "Don't Pass Me By"—his first sole songwriting credit.

Paul and John remained the dominant songwriters, and never before had their songwriting styles seemed so divergent. Paul looked to the outside world for inspiration, creating characters like the honky tonkin' "Rocky Raccoon," the Hollywood starlet of "Honey Pie" (both exhibiting some of the whimsy that would later surface in his solo work), and "Mother Nature's Son," something of a sequel to "Fool on the Hill." "I Will" was a short, sweet love song, while "Blackbird," another acoustic number that Paul has said was a nod to the civil rights struggle in America, has a quiet elegance. And he proved to be something of a one-man band; he recorded linking tracks like "Wild Honey Pie" and "Why Don't We Do It In the Road" all on his own, and he was frequently the only Beatle to appear on a number of his other tracks. "Martha My Dear," a delightful ode to his sheepdog, was seemingly the only song where he touched on anything personal.

Conversely, John plumbed his psyche for most of his songs, none of which were as upbeat or breezy as Paul's. "Happiness Is a Warm Gun," for example, starts out as an anguished love song, and finishes up as a parody of doo-wop, the song's title taken from a headline in an American gun magazine that John called "a fantastic, insane thing to say." Then there's the delicate "Julia," who's also called "Ocean Child" in the song; Julia was his mother's name, while Yoko's name translates to *Ocean Child*, a juxtaposition of mother and lover that's tailor-made for a Freudian psychiatrist.

The meaning of "I'm So Tired" is self-evident, but not all of John's songs were so grim. "The Continuing Story of Bungalow Bill" is his wry commentary about a big-game hunter he met in India, a trip that also inspired the scornful "Sexy Sadie" and the gentle "Dear Prudence" (about Prudence Farrow, actress Mia Farrow's sister). "Revolution 1" has a wonderfully slow groove, while the apocalyptic sound collage "Revolution 9" was the album's most polarizing track. John hit just about all the bases, from the giddy "Everybody's Got Something to Hide Except Me and My Monkey," to laying false trails for overly analytical Beatles fans in "Glass Onion," to the nursery rhyme setting of "Cry Baby Cry," to the album's closing number, the lush lullaby "Good Night," sung with heartfelt sincerity by Ringo.

The album was packaged in a plain white cover—hence the name it's more commonly known by, "the White Album"—and also included four 8 x 10 portraits of the band members and a large poster. *The Beatles* was released on November 22, 1968, in the UK, November 25 in the US, and topped the charts in both countries; people were positively enthralled by the wealth of material on the album. The UK release date was five years to the day of the release of the Beatles' second album, *With The Beatles*. The songs on *The Beatles* certainly showed how much the group had grown in those five years. But the highly individualized nature of the songs also showed how much the group was growing apart.

34 Love and Marriage— and Divorce

John was the first Beatle to get married. He met Cynthia Powell while both were attending the Liverpool College of Art. When Cynthia became pregnant, the two married on August 23, 1962, at the same registry office where John's parents had been married on December 3, 1938. There was no time for a honeymoon; after a celebratory lunch at a café across the road, the Beatles were scheduled to play a show that night in Chester. In 1963, Cynthia and their son, Julian (born on April 8, 1963), joined John in London, moving into a flat in Kensington; the following year the family moved to a luxury home in the London suburb of Weybridge, the so-called "stockbroker belt." The couple divorced on November 8, 1968. Cynthia published two memoirs about her relationship with John, *A Twist of Lennon* and *John*. At time of writing, she lives with her fourth husband, Noel Charles, in Spain.

Ringo met Maureen Cox in Liverpool, when the Beatles were still playing the Cavern and Maureen was training to be a hairdresser. They drifted apart as the Beatles' career took off, but became more serious when Maureen came down to London to be at Ringo's side when he had his tonsils removed in December 1964. She soon became pregnant, and the couple married on February 11, 1965, spending their honeymoon in the coastal town of Hove. That same year they moved to Weybridge, just down the road from John and Cynthia. Their first son, Zak, was born on September 13, 1965; a second son, Jason, was born August 19, 1967, and a daughter, Lee, was born on November 11, 1970. Infidelities on both sides (including a brief affair Maureen had with George) led to the couple's divorce on July 17, 1975. Maureen later married Isaac Tigrett, co-founder of the Hard Rock Café; she died of leukemia on December 30, 1994.

George met model Pattie Boyd on the set of *A Hard Day's Night*; Pattie was cast as one of the schoolgirls the Beatles encounter on their train journey to London. In 1965, Pattie moved into George's home in the London suburb of Esher; the two married on January 21, 1966, and spent their honeymoon in Barbados. As George became increasingly interested in Eastern religion, he became distanced from his wife, leading her to have an affair with guitarist Eric Clapton, who'd written the song "Layla" for her. George and Pattie eventually broke up in 1974, and divorced in 1977. Pattie married Eric Clapton in 1979; the two divorced in 1988. Pattie later published a memoir, *Wonderful Tonight: George Harrison, Eric Clapton, and Me*.

On April 18, 1963, the Beatles appeared at London's Royal Albert Hall, as part of a package show entitled "Swinging Sound '63." Afterward Paul met actress Jane Asher, who'd attended the show, and the two quickly became an item. Paul later moved into the Asher family home in central London before buying his own home on Cavendish Avenue, a few blocks away from Abbey Road Studios. There already was a connection between the Beatles and the Asher family, as Jane's mother, Margaret, had taught George Martin the oboe when he was at the Guildhall School of Music and Drama. Paul later gave a song he had written, "Woman," to the group Jane's brother was in, Peter & Gordon, who released it on a single that reached No. 14 in the US, No. 28 in the the UK (the song was credited to "Bernard Webb," as Paul wanted to see if a song he wrote would sell without having the Lennon/McCartney songwriting credit attached to it). Paul and Jane became engaged at the end of 1967, but the engagement was called off in July 1968, after Jane had arrived at Paul's home unexpectedly and found him in bed with another woman, said to be Francie Schwartz. Jane has never subsequently given any interviews about her relationship with Paul (Francie gave her side of the story in her 1972 memoir *Body Count*). Jane continued her acting career and married illustrator Gerald Scarfe (who provided stage sets and animation for the stage and film versions of Pink Floyd's *The Wall*) in 1981.

Yoko and John: East Meets West

The Beatles' wives and girlfriends had generally stayed in the background. That changed when John met the artist Yoko Ono, who became very much a part of his life; her presence also proved to be very controversial.

What Happened To: John?

The breakup of the Beatles hardly slowed down John's involvement in myriad projects. After a short stint of "primal scream" therapy in the US with therapist Arthur Janov, he released what many feel was his finest album, the stark *John Lennon/Plastic Ono Band*, at the end of 1970. The next year saw him release his utopian anthem "Imagine," also the title track of the album of the same name. 1971 was also the year John and Yoko moved to New York City; John would never see England again.

John's next albums, *Some Time in New York City* (1972), *Mind Games* (1973), and *Walls and Bridges* (1974), received mixed reviews. He played a few charity concerts, but never went on a major tour. He played on Yoko's records, and also made guest appearances on records by Ringo, David Bowie, and Elton John. In 1973, he and Yoko separated, and he became embroiled in a battle with US immigration to be able to live in America. In 1975, he reconciled with Yoko, and the couple had a son, Sean Taro Ono Lennon, on October 9 (John's own birthday). John also released the album *Rock 'n' Roll* in 1975, his last record for five years.

In 1976, he finally won his battle with immigration and received his Green Card. He traveled abroad, but mostly stayed close to home at his apartment in the Dakota building in New York City, looking after Sean and recording the occasional demo. In 1980, John and Yoko returned to the studio and recorded the album *Double Fantasy*, released on November 17 in the US and the UK. John had plans to make another record, and spoke about touring, but it was not to be. On December 8, 1980, he was murdered outside his home by Mark David Chapman, a mentally ill man.

Since his death, Yoko has kept John's legacy alive with numerous record releases. There have also been authorized films, and books featuring John's drawings, his letters, and photographs.

Yoko Ono was born on February 18, 1933, in Japan. In 1953, she moved to the US, where her father worked as a bank executive, and attended Sarah Lawrence College. She had studied classical piano as a child, and now discovered the work of avant-garde composers like John Cage. In 1956, she married composer Toshi

Ichiyanagi and moved to New York City, where she began to host performance events called "happenings" at her loft. She later joined a loose-knit group of artists called Fluxus and published a book of "instructional poems" called *Grapefruit*. The poems were both amusing and cryptic, such as "Map Piece," whose sole instruction was "Draw a map to get lost."

In 1966, Yoko came to London with her second husband, Tony Cox, and their child, Kyoko. John met her at a preview of her latest exhibition, *Unfinished Paintings and Objects* at London's Indica Gallery in early November (John had a fondness for the number nine and said the meeting happened on November 9, but other historians have noted that since the two met at the exhibit's preview it was more likely to have been a day or two earlier). John enjoyed the whimsical absurdity of Yoko's work—such as an apple on display that sold for £200—and the two began running into each other at different events. Author Peter Doggett says Yoko attended the "Fool on the Hill" recording sessions in September 1967; John also put up funding for her exhibition "Yoko Plus Me," which opened on October 11, 1967, at London's Lisson Gallery. The friendship became a romance in May 1968 when John invited Yoko over while his wife Cynthia was out of town. The following month he told Cynthia he wanted a divorce, and on June 15 John and Yoko staged their first "event," planting "acorns for peace" at Coventry Cathedral. For the next five years they never left each other's side.

This provoked much consternation among the Beatles, especially when Yoko was brought to recording sessions; during the *Abbey Road* sessions, a bed was even set up in the studio for her, as she was recovering from a car accident. The other Beatles weren't especially pleased with their outside activities either; the couple's first album, *Unfinished Music No. 1: Two Virgins* (recordings they'd made during their first night together at John's home), had a cover shot of them completely naked. But they were afraid to confront

John directly, feeling that if they did so John would react by further distancing himself from the group.

But that was happening anyway. Yoko energized John creatively, and over time he found he preferred working with her instead of the other Beatles. The Beatles hadn't performed live since 1966; now John and Yoko were making all kinds of live appearances, appearing as guests at the taping of *The Rolling Stones Rock 'n' Roll Circus* television special in December 1968, added to the bill of Toronto's Rock 'n' Roll Revival Festival in September 1969,

John and Yoko at their "bed-in for peace" at the Hilton Hotel in Amsterdam on March 25, 1969.

headlining a "Concert for Peace" in London in December 1969. The couple also made films, released records, and put on exhibitions. Even their marriage on March 20, 1969, became an event. Knowing that the media would be eager to cover it, they staged a "bed-in" at their hotel in Amsterdam, inviting anyone who wanted to interview them to come in. At a subsequent bed-in at the Queen Elizabeth Hotel in Montreal, they taped the single "Give Peace a Chance."

The couple faced much hostility from the press and general public; Yoko's wailing vocals, which predated '70s punk by several years, also came in for harsh criticism. But John was completely devoted to Yoko, even having his name legally changed from "John Winston Lennon" to "John Ono Lennon." And despite the tensions with John's new partner, "The Ballad of John and Yoko" was released as a Beatles single (on May 30 in the UK, June 4 in the US), though only John and Paul played on the recording.

Further reading: *Yoko Ono: Arias and Objects* (Barbara Haskell, John G. Hanhardt), *Yes: Yoko Ono* (Alexandra Munroe, Jon Hendricks)

36 Linda McCartney: The Lady Behind the Lens

Paul was the last Beatle to get married. When he finally did tie the knot with Linda Eastman, it proved to be a wise choice, for the marriage would last nearly 30 years, until her death in 1998.

Linda Louise Eastman was born on September 24, 1941. Her father, Lee Eastman, was a prominent entertainment attorney, and Linda grew up used to having well-known show business personalities dropping by the house. Songwriter Jack Lawrence even wrote a song for her, "Linda," later recorded by Buddy Clark (Jan & Dean also recorded it). In an interesting twist, considering that he was to go on to manage the Beatles, and Paul's business affairs, Lee, the son of Russian Jewish immigrants, was originally named Leopold Epstein.

Linda, like Yoko, attended Sarah Lawrence College, though the two were not there at the same time. She then transferred to the University of Arizona, where she married Mel See, with whom she had a daughter, Heather. She also took up photography. Her marriage soon broke up, and Linda moved back to New York in 1965 (she was in the audience at the Beatles' Shea Stadium concert that year). In 1966, while working as an assistant at *Town & Country* magazine, she snagged an invitation to a press reception for the Rolling Stones held on a yacht; as an attractive young woman, she was the only photographer allowed on the boat, and her career in photography began. Over the next few years, she took pictures of major acts like the Who, the Doors, Jimi Hendrix, Janis Joplin, Bob Dylan, and Aretha Franklin.

In May 1967, she went to England to photograph bands for a book, *Rock and Other Four Letter Words*. She met Paul one night at London's Bag O'Nails club; he asked her to come along to the speakeasy with his friends, then invited everyone over to his house, though "memories are hazy as to whether Linda stayed that night," Howard Sounes wrote in his biography of Paul, *Fab*. She later encountered Paul at the press launch for *Sgt. Pepper* that Brian Epstein held at his home. The two met up again in May 1968, when John and Paul were in New York promoting Apple. Now things quickly started becoming more serious. When Paul was in Los Angeles the next month, again promoting Apple, he invited Linda to come join him at his hotel. By July, his relationship with his fiancé Jane Asher had ended. He then asked Linda to move in with him in September.

Linda now became Paul's constant companion, whom he also brought to Beatles recording sessions, though he didn't go as far as setting up a bed in the studio for her. When Linda became pregnant, the two married on March 12, 1969; their daughter Mary was born on August 28 (they would have another daughter, Stella, on September 13, 1971, and a son, James, on September 12, 1977). Paul also brought in Linda's father, Lee, and her brother John, also an attorney, to help with the Beatles' business affairs; after the Beatles' split, Lee and John continued working for Paul.

Linda had no ambitions to be a performer herself; she was happy simply providing support for Paul. She continued taking pictures, shooting a number of excellent photos of the Beatles during this period. But Paul wanted to have her working with him, and on his first solo album, *McCartney*, she contributed backing vocals on a number of songs, as well as shooting photos for the album's cover. And when Paul started his band, Wings, Linda gamely agreed to play keyboards. At the time she unfairly faced criticism from people who accused her of "muscling in" on Paul's group, not realizing it was Paul who wanted her beside him. In 1977, Linda released a single under a pseudonym, Suzi and the Red Stripes, and the animated short *Oriental Nightfish* also featured her song of the same name. Her solo album *Wild Prairie* was released after her death. Linda died of breast cancer on April 17, 1998.

Linda's interest in animals led to the entire McCartney family becoming vegetarian, and she and Paul became active campaigners for animal welfare. Linda wrote vegetarian cookbooks and created a line of frozen vegetarian meals. She also published numerous books of her photographs.

Further reading: *Linda McCartney's Sixties: Portrait of an Era* (Linda McCartney)

37 Hamburg Days

Liverpool was certainly the city where the Beatles got their start. But it's no exaggeration to say that as a band they came of age in Hamburg, Germany.

Consider this. From 1957 to August 1960, the band had performed around 60 shows. Meaning that in their first two weeks in Hamburg they played more hours on stage than they had in the previous three years and eight months combined. Their first Hamburg stint in 1960 in particular made them a vastly better band, transforming them from scruffy amateurs to seasoned professionals.

The Beatles were sent to Hamburg through a series of unusual circumstances. Allan Williams, a small-time entrepreneur, ran a coffee bar in Liverpool called the Jacaranda, among his many other endeavors. The Jacaranda also featured live music, a West Indian group called the Royal Caribbean Steel Band. One day in the spring of 1960, Williams arrived at the Jacaranda to find that the band had left, having been offered a better gig in Hamburg, Germany. Hamburg was a port city, and its notorious Reeperbahn district was home to numerous clubs, sex shows, and open prostitution.

The steel band members invited Williams to check out the scene for himself. While there, Williams met club owner Bruno Koschmider and regaled him with stories of how British groups were much better at playing rock 'n' roll than the German musicians Koschmider had engaged. As a result, Koschmider began going to London in search of new talent, and on one such trip he and Williams crossed paths again, at London's famous 2i's Coffee Bar, where Williams was trying to find work for another Liverpool act, Derry Wilkie and the Seniors. Koschmider promptly booked the group, who began their Hamburg residency on July 31.

Koschmider soon needed another group for a club he planned to open, and Williams offered the job to the Beatles, whose lineup then consisted of John, Paul, George, and Stuart Sutcliffe. They quickly tapped Pete Best, whom they knew from playing his mother's club, the Casbah, to play drums, and left for Hamburg on August 16.

From August 17 to October 3 the Beatles played the Indra Club; when the Indra was closed due to noise complaints, they were moved to the Kaiserkeller, where they played from October 4 to November 30. It was a backbreaking schedule; they were expected to play four and a half hours a night during the week, six hours on Saturdays and Sundays. "We loved it," Tony Sheridan, another British musician playing in Hamburg at the time, told me. "It sounds like a lot of work, and it *was* a lot of work, especially because we didn't really look after ourselves. We didn't eat properly and we didn't sleep enough; we were doing too much beer and all sorts of funny things, doing speed now and again. But that was all part of that scene, and out of that a lot of things happened. Mainly it was the music. The music was the central thing, always."

Prior to arriving in Hamburg, the Beatles rarely played shows that went on longer than an hour. Now they were forced to expand their repertoire, to help fill up the longer hours. They didn't just play their rock 'n' roll favorites; they mixed in show tunes and standards; everything from "Over the Rainbow" to George Gershwin's "Summertime." They also learned how to extend numbers—making Ray Charles' "What'd I Say" last half an hour, for example. The amphetamine diet pills that were readily available helped fuel their antics, and club attendees would regularly send up crates of beer along with their song requests.

The Beatles' first Hamburg stint ended ignominiously. First, George was sent home when it was discovered he was too young to

Visit Hamburg

Sadly, the Beatlemania museum in Hamburg, which had opened in 2009, closed its doors at the end of June 2012. But some Beatle sites remain in the city.

At time of writing, both the Indra and the Kaiserkeller, where the Beatles first performed, are still open. The building which held the Bambi Kino—the movie house where the Beatles slept in the back rooms—has been slated for demolition. The Top Ten has gone through numerous changes, and at time of writing wasn't offering live music, but is still open. The Star-Club burned down in 1983, and new buildings now occupy the space. But you can still drop in at the Gretel & Alfons café, which the Beatles frequented, for a drink and a snack. And you can still book a room at the Hotel Germania, where the Beatles stayed in November 1962.

Other sites of interest: the police station where Paul and Pete Best were detained before being deported; Paul Hundertmark, the shop on the Reeperbahn where the Beatles bought their cowboy boots; and you can still have your picture taken in the doorway in Jägerpassage where Jürgen Vollmer took the picture of John that ended up on the cover of his *Rock 'n' Roll* album. The corner of Reeperbahn and Grosse Freiheit has been designated Beatles-Platz 1, featuring a Beatles sculpture.

Walking tours of Beatles-related Hamburg sites are offered by the German-based company Beatles-Tour Hamburg (www.beatles-tour.com). International Tours and Events, the US company that organizes Beatles tours to the UK, also sometimes adds a Hamburg leg to the itinerary (www.toursandevents.com). *Beatles Guide Hamburg* is a great pocket-sized guidebook by Ulf Krüger, that's unfortunately now out of print.

legally play Hamburg's clubs; then, when the Beatles announced they were moving to another club, Koschmider retaliated by reporting Paul and Pete to the authorities, saying they'd tried to burn down the building where they slept at night, in an old cinema that Koschmider also owned (Paul said they'd pinned a condom to the wall and set it alight while they packed; other accounts say they burned the building's molding tapestry). The two were duly arrested and deported. As

Stuart was put up at the home of his fiancé, Astrid Kirchherr, John was forced to make his own way back home.

But the Beatles were anxious to return to Hamburg. Once the legal complications were sorted out, they returned to the city on four more occasions, playing the Top Ten Club from March 27 to July 2, 1961, and the Star-Club three times in 1962: April 13 to May 31, November 1 to 14, and December 18 to 31. A lot happened during their three years in Hamburg: they lost a bass player, lost and gained a drummer, and made their first professional recordings. They returned to Hamburg in triumph in 1966 for a final two shows in the city that had fashioned them into a world-beating group, playing the Ernst Merck Halle on June 21, 1966. As John told the Beatles' first publicist, Tony Barrow, "I aged 10 years every time I went back to Hamburg, but it was a wonderful way to grow old!"

Further reading: *The Beatles In Hamburg* (Spencer Leigh)

38 The Very First Record to Feature The Beatles

The Beatles made their first professional recordings in Germany. During their second stint in Hamburg in 1961, Bert Kaempfert visited the Top Ten Club one night, where the Beatles were in residence. Kaempfert was a composer and a producer then working for Polydor Records. He'd come to the Top Ten on the recommendation of an associate, Alfred Schact. After watching the Beatles playing with Tony Sheridan, he told them he'd like to record them. "He was basically looking to make a quick buck," Tony Sheridan told me. "I think his main thing was to capture this atmosphere that he saw happening in front of his eyes."

Arrangements were made for sessions to be held on June 22 and June 23, 1961, at Friedrich-Ebert-Halle, a concert hall in Harburg (a suburb of Hamburg), next to a children's school (some sources say there was a session on June 24 as well). A curious selection of songs were recorded: rock 'n' roll versions of "My Bonnie Lies Over the Ocean" and "When the Saints Go Marching In" entitled "My Bonnie" and "The Saints," respectively; "Take Out Some Insurance On Me, Baby," previously recorded by Jimmy Reed; "Nobody's Child," first recorded by Hank Snow; and "Why," an original co-written by Sheridan. "The choice of songs was basically a product of a discussion—perhaps a heated discussion sometimes!—with us about what to do and what not to do," Sheridan explains. "The typical example is, 'My Bonnie,' 'cause nobody really wanted to do that for the first record. But we did it, and we did it as best we could, and it turned out quite well."

The Beatles served as a backing group on the songs with two memorable exceptions: the standard "Ain't She Sweet," which features a nice raw and raucous vocal by John, and the instrumental "Cry For a Shadow," a parody of the British group the Shadows, co-written by John and George. But it was "My Bonnie"/"The Saints" that were the first songs to be released on Polydor in Germany the following October, credited to Tony Sheridan and the Beat Brothers, as the name "Beatles" sounded too much like *peedles,* German slang for penis. Some versions of "My Bonnie" also featured a slow intro in German; others had an English intro.

This was the first record to feature the Beatles, albeit as a backing group. And it was a request for this record that led to Brian seeking the group out. Once Brian began stocking the single in NEMS, there was eventually sufficient interest to release the single in Britain, again on Polydor, which happened in January 1962. That April, it was released in America on Decca—ironically enough, as the label's UK branch had just turned down the Beatles after their audition on New Year's Day.

When Brian Epstein wrote to Kaempfert after he became the Beatles' manager, Kaempfert was happy to let his contract with the group expire in June 1962, but asked that they record one more session. Brian agreed, and on May 24, 1962, the Beatles and keyboardist Roy Young recorded backing tracks for "Sweet Georgia Brown" and "Swanee River" at Hamburg's Studio Rahlstedt; Sheridan recorded his vocals later.

"My Bonnie" was successful in Germany, and in Liverpool, where news of its recording made the front page of *Mersey Beat*. But it wasn't until the Beatles became successful that the other songs from the sessions were released (except for "Swanee River," which was lost). "Ain't She Sweet" reached No. 19 in the US, "My Bonnie" No. 26, and "Why" No. 88, all in 1964. Sheridan also recorded a new vocal for "Sweet Georgia Brown" with new lyrics referencing the Beatles' success. The songs were also put on many albums that were usually filled out with other tracks that featured Sheridan but not the Beatles, which made it confusing for fans; even later editions that featured all eight songs were padded with extra tracks. The TimeLife/Universal 2011 release *First Recordings: 50th Anniversary Edition* is a good way to get all the recordings that feature the Beatles.

Further reading: *The Beatles: From Cavern to Star-Club* (Hans Olof Gottfridsson)

39 Stuart Sutcliffe: Artistic Influence

Stuart Sutcliffe was John's best friend. More of an artist than a musician, his aesthetic sensibilities and outlook gave the Beatles a more artistic quality than their peers had—especially when he attracted the attention of a woman who would do much to shape the Beatles' visual appeal.

Stuart Fergusson Victor Sutcliffe was born on June 23, 1940, in Edinburgh, Scotland, and moved with his family to Liverpool in 1942. Determined to pursue a career as a painter, Stuart was accepted at the Liverpool College of Art at the age of 16, so promising was his talent. When John entered the college a year later, he was introduced to Stuart by a mutual friend, Bill Harry (who would later found the Liverpool music paper *Mersey Beat*). John, who was indifferent to his studies, was intrigued by Stuart's intense devotion to his art, and the two became close friends.

Stuart shared John's interest in rock 'n' roll and attended the Quarrymen's shows. More practically, as a member of the Students' Union committee, he arranged for the college to purchase an amplifier that the band could use when they played college dances; the gear soon found its way into the band's permanent collection of equipment.

In 1959, one of Stuart's paintings was chosen for the prestigious biennial John Moores Exhibition, held at Liverpool's Walker Art Gallery. When the exhibition closed on January 17, 1960, his painting had been purchased by John Moores himself, for the impressive sum of £65. Stuart was encouraged to use his cash prize to buy a bass guitar, so he could fully join the band. There are differing opinions as to how well he could actually play, but as John's friend, his place in the group was assured.

While playing in Hamburg in 1960, the Beatles came to the attention of a group of art students, who were enthralled with their music. One of them, Astrid Kirchherr, became Stuart's girlfriend. "He was so tiny, but perfect, every feature," she told Beatles biographer Philip Norman. "So pale, but very, very beautiful. He was like a character out of Edgar Allen Poe."

Stuart already had a distinctive style of dress, having a penchant for wearing skintight jeans and sunglasses—even after dark—to

Astrid Kirchherr and Stuart Sutcliffe in Hamburg in April 1961 in a photo taken by Juergen Vollmer.

heighten his allure, and Astrid further refined his look. It was she who first brushed Stuart's greased-back hair forward, in the style that would later be known as the "Beatle cut," the Mop Top. She designed a leather suit for Stuart, which the rest of the Beatles soon copied. She also dressed Stuart in a collarless jacket the others laughed at initially; in a few years, such jackets would be an integral part of the Beatles' stage outfits.

Two months after meeting, Astrid and Stuart became engaged, and his interest in the Beatles began to wane. There was also growing tension within the group; Paul in particular was jealous of John's closeness to Stuart, and he was frequently the target of relentless teasing. During the band's second season in Hamburg in 1961, Stuart decided to leave the Beatles, and returned to his art studies, enrolling in the Hamburg College of Art. Paul became the band's bassist by default, after John and George both staunchly refused to consider taking up the instrument.

Stuart was now fully wrapped up in his studies, his relationship with Astrid, and his new life in Germany. Unfortunately, time was running out for him. He'd begun to suffer from severe headaches that sometimes led to seizures. But the doctors could find nothing wrong. On April 10, 1962, his condition deteriorated and he was sent to the hospital with Astrid; he died in the ambulance in her arms. He was 21 years old.

The official cause of death was a brain hemorrhage. Astrid was also told that Stuart's brain was actually expanding, a rare medical condition that could not have been cured. There is speculation that Stuart could have suffered brain damage because of a head injury, perhaps sustained in a fight in Liverpool or Hamburg, but no one knows for certain.

Three tracks of Stuart jamming with the Beatles appear on *Anthology 1*. Numerous books of his artwork have been published, as well as a few biographies, and his story was the subject of the film

The Exis

Three of the German students who dubbed themselves the Exis—for "existentialist"—became especially close to the Beatles.

Klaus Voorman first discovered the Beatles, when he wandered in to the Kaiserkeller one night in the fall of 1960. Brian Epstein later managed his band, Paddy, Klaus & Gibson. He was also in Manfred Mann, and played bass on records by John and Ringo, and at George's Bangladesh charity concerts. And he designed the covers for the *Revolver*, *Ringo*, and *Anthology* albums.

Astrid Kirchherr took some of the best photographs of the Beatles—moody, atmospheric black and white shots, with their faces often dramatically half in shadow. After the Beatles' success, her photos were widely published without her permission; she has since copyrighted her work. She also served as an advisor on the 1994 film *Backbeat*, about her relationship with Stuart.

Jürgen Vollmer photographed the Beatles several times in Hamburg; John would later choose one of his photos for the cover of his 1975 *Rock 'n' Roll* album. But his most important contribution to the Beatles may have been when John and Paul, visiting Vollmer in Paris in 1961, had him restyle their hair by brushing it forward; a style favored by German students that would soon become known as the "Beatle cut."

Backbeat. The Beatles also paid tribute to him by including him in the collage on the front cover of *Sgt. Pepper*.

Further reading: *Backbeat: Stuart Sutcliffe: The Lost Beatle* (Alan Clayson, Pauline Sutcliffe); *The Beatles' Shadow: Stuart Sutcliffe and His Lonely Hearts Club* (Pauline Sutcliffe with Douglas Thompson)

40 The Best of Cellars

The Beatles played Liverpool's Cavern Club more than any other venue during their career—around 300 times.

The Cavern is located at 10 Mathew Street, in Liverpool's city center. Previously a warehouse, it was purchased by Alan Sytner in 1956. Sytner was a jazz fan, and he named his new establishment the Cavern, after a club he'd visited in Paris called Le Caveau. The Cavern opened on January 16, 1957, with the Merseysippi Jazz Band, the Wall City Jazzmen, the Ralph Watmough Jazz Band, and the Coney Island Skiffle Band on the bill. The Quarrymen played the Cavern later that same year, though the exact date is unknown. The band is listed in an ad for a show on August 7, 1957, but the Quarrymen's Rod Davis told me that was simply the first time the band had been mentioned in an ad, and that they'd played the club on previous occasions.

In any case, the Quarrymen played too much rock 'n' roll to suit the club's clientele; the band wasn't terribly welcome in a jazz club. But by the time new owner Ray McFall took over in 1959, jazz was fading in popularity. Rock bands were increasingly being booked for the club's lunchtime sessions, and by the fall of 1960, rock 'n' roll was taking over the evening sessions as well. When the Beatles returned from their first trip to Hamburg, Pete Best's mother Mona urged McFall to book them. Bob Wooler, the club's DJ (who would open his sets with the phrase "Hello, all you Cavern dwellers, welcome to the best of cellars"), also recommended them to McFall, and so on February 21, 1961, the Beatles played their first show at the Cavern since 1958.

For the next two years, the Beatles played the Cavern every week, at lunchtime and evening shows, excepting the times they were in Hamburg. Eighteen stone steps led down into the club, which was divided into three tunnels, each 10 feet wide. The middle tunnel was where the small stage was set up; there was little light and no ventilation, so when the club was full—as it often was when the Beatles played—the heat from all those tightly packed bodies led to condensation dripping from the walls. But to Beatles fans, it was their own personal clubhouse; there were

Bob Wooler: The Cavern's DJ

Bob Wooler was one of the Beatles' biggest supporters in Liverpool, booking a landmark show for them in 1960 and working hard to promote them in 1961, before Brian Epstein became the group's manager.

Wooler was born Frederick James Wooler in Liverpool on January 19, 1926. He worked as a clerk for British Rail, but had an interest in music as well. During the skiffle era he briefly managed the Kingstrums, which got him involved in Liverpool's music scene. He had aspirations to be a songwriter, but more often ended up being an emcee and DJ at local shows, especially at the Cavern.

Though he'd met the Beatles a few times, it wasn't until their return from Hamburg in 1960 that Bob became more involved with the group. He booked their December 27, 1960, gig at Litherland Town Hall, and afterward recommended them to other Liverpool promoters. He loaned them records from his collection and gave them tips on their stage presentation. And he regularly plugged the group in his column for *Mersey Beat*, "The Roving I." "I was virtually managing the Beatles in '61," Bob told me in an interview.

But he was happy to have Brian take over as manager at the end of 1961. Brian even offered him a job when NEMS Enterprises relocated to London, but Bob turned it down. Brian also arranged to have Bob's lyric for a song called "I Know" set to music by George Martin and recorded by Billy J. Kramer and the Dakotas as the B-side of "I'll Keep You Satisfied" (though Wooler was unfortunately misspelled as "Wooller").

At the end of the '60s, Bob quit working as a DJ and worked for a theatrical agency. He later teamed with Allan Williams to produce Liverpool's first Beatles conventions, and was a regular guest at subsequent conventions. He never wrote an autobiography, but cooperated with Spencer Leigh on the book *The Best of Fellas: The Story of Bob Wooler*. Bob died on February 8, 2002.

even membership cards. But no alcohol; the Cavern only sold soft drinks.

The first sound footage of the Beatles was shot at the Cavern by Granada TV on August 22, 1962, just after Ringo had joined the band. The band was filmed playing Richard Barrett's "Some Other Guy." This exciting performance not only captures the Beatles on the verge of their stardom, but also gives a good idea of what conditions were like in the Cavern.

By 1963, the Beatles were in Liverpool far less frequently, and their popularity was now such that the Cavern was too small a venue for them to play. When they played their final show at the club on August 3, 1963, it was their first date at the club since the previous April. They wouldn't have even played that show, but Brian Epstein hadn't been able to get the Beatles out of a booking for a show the previous night at Liverpool's Grafton rooms, and decided that if the Beatles had to be in Liverpool they might as well get some other work in the area. It was not announced as the band's last show, and it drew the by-now expected overflow crowd. The Mersey Beats, the Escorts, the Road Runners, the Sapphires, and Johnny Ringo & the Colts were also on the bill.

The club was closed in 1973 to make way for a ventilation shaft for the city's underground railway. But the shaft was never built, and the bulldozed area became a parking lot. In 1984, a new "Cavern Walks" office and shopping complex was built on the site, and the Cavern was re-created, using bricks from the original club. The new Cavern is substantially bigger; it's not precisely where the first Cavern stood, but about half of the original club is incorporated into the new space (the current fire exit door is where the original entrance was). Paul played a memorable homecoming show at the club on December 14, 1999, later released on the DVD *Paul McCartney Live at the Cavern Club.*

Further reading: *The Cavern: The Most Famous Club in the World* (Spencer Leigh)

41 Pete Best: The Other Beatles Drummer

Pete Best was the Beatles' drummer during a key two-year period, when they rose through the ranks to become one of Liverpool's top bands. Unfortunately, it would not pay off for Pete, who was fired from the group a month before they recorded their first single.

Randolph Peter Best was born on November 24, 1941, in Madras, India, where his father, Johnny Best, an officer in the English army, was stationed (some accounts say Johnny was actually Pete's stepfather, his real father being a marine engineer who was killed during World War II). The family returned to Johnny's home of Liverpool in 1945.

Pete enjoyed rock 'n' roll, but had no thought of being a musician himself until 1959, when Ken Brown left the Quarrymen after a short stint of playing with them at the Casbah, a club in the basement of Pete's house. Ken asked Pete to start a new band with him, and so Pete became the drummer of the Blackjacks, who regularly played at the Casbah, one time drawing a crowd of over 1,300 people.

But by the summer of 1960, the Blackjacks were on the verge of splitting up, leaving Pete at loose ends. The Beatles came to see the Blackjacks at the Casbah on August 6, and on learning about Pete's situation, later contacted him, saying they'd been offered a residency in Hamburg but needed a drummer. The Hamburg engagement was due to start on August 17, and after a perfunctory audition on August 12, Pete joined the Beatles.

He remained in the drummer's seat for the next two years, participating in the recording sessions with Tony Sheridan in Germany, playing at an audition for Decca Records on January 1, 1962, and still with the band when they made their radio debut on March 7,

The Beatles perform at the Cavern Club in 1962. The leather-clad Lennon and McCartney play on the left, while soon-to-be-replaced drummer Pete Best is visible in the back.

1962. His position in the group seemed secure. But on August 15, 1962, he played what would be his last show with the Beatles at the Cavern. The next day, he went to NEMS to meet with Brian Epstein, and was stunned to be told that he was being fired from the group. Amazingly, he was also asked if he'd mind staying with the band until the weekend, and he initially agreed. But in the end, he not surprisingly failed to turn up for any of the dates.

What happened? Pete had no idea that such a breakup was imminent. There have been suggestions that the other Beatles

The Casbah Coffee Club

Liverpool's Casbah Coffee Club is where the Beatles had their first residency. The Casbah was in the basement of the Best family home. Pete Best had been using the basement as a den where he hung out with his friends when his mother Mona came up with the idea to make it into a club. The Les Stewart Quartet was booked to play, but broke up before the club's opening night. George, who'd been a member of the Quartet, suggested to fellow member Ken Brown that they join up with his friends John and Paul; the new group, playing under the name the Quarrymen, got the honor of opening the Casbah on August 29, 1959. The band played every Saturday night at the club until mid-October, when a dispute led to Brown leaving the group.

After Pete Best joined the Beatles, the group next played the Casbah on December 17, 1960, and regularly appeared at the venue until Pete was fired from the band. The Beatles' last show at the Casbah was June 24, 1962, and the Casbah itself would close by the end of the month.

As Beatles tourism began to take off in Liverpool, a restored Casbah was opened to visitors during Beatle Week and on other occasions. The club is now open year round, though advance booking is required, and there's a recording studio on the premises as well. Info: www.petebest.com/casbah-coffee-club.aspx.

were jealous of Pete's popularity, and indeed Paul's father had berated Pete when he was mobbed by fans after a June 11, 1962, radio appearance, thus delaying the Beatles own departure. There were certainly signs that the other Beatles were gradually distancing themselves from him; they didn't immediately tell Pete that Decca had turned them down, nor did they tell him about George Martin's plans for their upcoming recording sessions in September.

In retrospect it's clear that the other Beatles had been unhappy with Pete for some time, but hadn't found the right occasion to get rid of him. Now they had one, for after their first session with George Martin on June 6, Martin had told Epstein he hadn't liked Pete's drumming; they could keep Pete on for live dates, but in the studio, Martin would prefer to use a studio drummer. That was all the Beatles needed to hear, and they insisted to Brian that Pete be fired. Brian would have been happy to go along with George Martin's suggestion, but he'd always told the Beatles he would not interfere with their music, so he agreed that Pete had to go.

Pete continued playing in other bands for the next few years, but with little success, and by 1968 he'd left show business. But 20 years later, he returned, first playing at Liverpool's annual Beatles convention, then putting together a group, the Pete Best Band, who have since toured around the world. Pete also received a financial windfall when 10 songs he'd recorded with the Beatles were included on *Anthology 1*.

Further reading: *Beatle! The Pete Best Story* (Pete Best, Patrick Doncaster), *The Best Years of The Beatles* (Pete Best, Bill Harry); *The Beatles: The True Beginnings* (Pete Best, Roag Best, Rory Best), *Drummed Out! The Sacking of Pete Best* (Spencer Leigh)

42 The Songs Inspired By Liverpool

The "Penny Lane"/"Strawberry Fields" single, released in February 1967, clearly showed that the Beatles were moving in a new direction musically.

When the Beatles entered the studio on November 24, 1966, for the first time since the previous June, they weren't planning to work on a single, but on tracks for an upcoming album, and by the end of the year they'd worked on three songs, "Strawberry Fields," "When I'm Sixty-Four," and "Penny Lane." Under pressure from their record company, "Strawberry Fields" and "Penny Lane" were handed over for a new single, as both Parlophone and Capitol were anxious to have a new record to promote. The Beatles had released no new tracks since August, nor had they made any live or TV appearances. There was a fear that the Beatles' popularity might be on the wane.

In fact, the group had spent the intervening months involved in other projects: George went to India, Paul traveled around Europe and Africa, Ringo stayed home with his wife and son, and John appeared in the film *How I Won the War* (directed by Richard Lester, who'd also directed *A Hard Day's Night* and *Help!*). It was during location shooting for the film in Spain that John began writing "Strawberry Fields." The name came from a Salvation Army home near John's house in Liverpool, though it was named Strawberry *Field*—singular. The languid song looks back at childhood, but it's a rather unsettling picture, beginning with the opening invitation to take the listener to a place where "nothing is real." The song conveys a decided sense of isolation, but it's wrapped in enough lyrical ambiguity to keep it from becoming too disturbing. The Beatles recorded two versions, one with a more subdued instrumental backing, the other a lavish production featuring cellos and trumpets. John told George Martin that he liked the first part of the original version, and the second part of the more orchestral version. Though the two versions were in different keys, Martin found that by speeding up the first version and slowing down the second version he could get them into the same key, and then join the two versions together.

Paul's "Penny Lane" was a brighter, more upbeat song. It too was a place in Liverpool, and the song refers not just to the street itself, but also the entire neighborhood. John's first home was not far from Penny Lane, and the Quarrymen once played a show at the St. Barnabas Church Hall, which is on Penny Lane; Paul also sang in the St. Barnabas choir as a child.

Paul's lyric drew pen portraits of Penny Lane's characters—a barber, a banker, a fireman—ordinary folk that he then "arted up a bit," as he explained, to give the song a veneer of surrealism (as in the banker who never wears a coat, even when it's raining). The song also featured orchestral instruments: brass, flutes, and woodwinds. Hearing Bach's Brandenburg Concerto No. 2 on television gave Paul the idea to add a piccolo trumpet part.

The Beatles shot promotional film clips for each song, though whereas previous clips had always shown the Beatles miming to their songs, these clips had no "performance" element to them. For "Penny Lane," shots of the real Penny Lane were intercut with shots of the Beatles walking around a city (not actually Liverpool, but London's Stratford neighborhood), and riding horses in the country while wearing red riding jackets. In one shot, they ignore the bandstand where their instruments have been set up as they ride by it on their horses; later, while sitting outdoors at a table drinking champagne from tea cups, a group of footmen hand them their instruments, which they look at as if not knowing what to do with them. It's a sequence that seems to suggest that they've put their performing days behind them.

"Strawberry Fields" was even stranger. The Beatles, dressed in psychedelic finery, are shown cavorting in a field, with some trick photography used, as when Paul is shown apparently leaping up onto a platform in a tree. At the end, under cover of night, they pour paint on a destroyed piano, then walk off, with Paul's sheepdog Martha trailing behind them.

The single was released February 13, 1967, in the US, February 17 in the UK. The single stalled at No. 2 in the UK—the first single to not top the charts there since 1963. But "Penny Lane" easily went to No. 1 in the US, with "Strawberry Fields" peaking at No. 8. The single was packaged in a picture sleeve—a first for the UK, though not for the US—featuring the "new look" Beatles, with all of them sporting moustaches. It was the first of many surprises that 1967 would see.

43 The Most Popular Beatles Cover Song

It was 10:00 PM on the evening of February 11, 1963, and the Beatles were taking a much-needed break during recording of their debut album, *Please Please Me*, at Abbey Road Studios. They needed one more song for the record, so everyone went to the studio canteen to discuss the matter over coffee. The debate went on for a bit until someone—no one remembers who—hit on the perfect number to close the album: "Twist and Shout."

"Twist and Shout," by Phil Medley and Bert Russell, was originally titled "Shake It Up, Baby," and was first released on a single by the Top Notes in 1961. But it was the Isley Brothers who had the first hit version of the song in 1962 when it was retitled "Twist and Shout," reaching No. 17 on the pop charts and No. 2 on the R&B charts. The Beatles quickly added the song to their act.

John was suffering from a cold, and had been sucking on throat lozenges all day—in between smoking cigarettes. Now he stripped to the waist to ready himself for one of the landmark performances of his career. It's a masterful piece of work, everything the best rock 'n' roll should be: full of passion, excitement, and raw, naked energy. And that's not only due to John's raucous vocal. Paul and George provide the Beatles' trademark "Woos!" in the background, and when all three voices come together in building a chord that steadily rises in intensity and volume, it's the kind of moment where you feel your heart is about to burst. John actually recorded two takes of the song; the first take was the final choice, as during the second take his voice gave out completely.

There could be no other song to close the *Please Please Me* album, which was released in March 1963. In the wake of the Beatles' success in America, "Twist and Shout" was first released as a single in the US on Tollie Records (a subsidiary of Vee-Jay) in February 1964. It reached No. 2 in *Billboard's* chart (and No. 1 in *Cash Box* and *Record World*)—the strongest chart performance of any song recorded, but not written by, any member of the Beatles. It became as much a signature song of the early Beatles era as "She Loves You" and "I Want to Hold Your Hand."

Ironically, John himself wasn't pleased with his vocal on the song. "I was always bitterly ashamed of it because I could sing it better than that," he said. "You can hear that I'm just a frantic guy doing his best." It's safe to say that most people find his "best" to be more than good enough.

44 Where They Recorded (Most of) Their Songs

Though the Beatles recorded in a number of studios during their career, Abbey Road Studios is where they recorded the majority of their records, and it's the studio that is most associated with them.

As previously mentioned, during the 1960s the facility was known as EMI Recording Studios, not Abbey Road Studios—a name which refers to the building's location, at 3 Abbey Road in London's St. John's Wood neighborhood (where Paul also has a house). The building was initially a private home built in the 1830s, later converted into apartments. The Gramophone Company— later renamed EMI—purchased the building in 1929 and, after substantial remodeling, opened it as a studio in November 1931, with Sir Edward Elgar conducting London Symphony Orchestra at the studio's opening ceremony. Prior to the Beatles' arrival, a variety of acts like Sir Edward Elgar, Vera Lynn, Glenn Miller, the Goons, and Cliff Richard all recorded at the studio.

And the Award Goes to...

The Beatles have won a number of the music industry's highest award, the Grammy. The first came in 1964, when they won the honors for Best New Artist and "A Hard Day's Night" won Best Performance by a Vocal Group. In 1966, Paul won Best Contemporary Pop Vocal Performance, Male, for "Eleanor Rigby"; the Beatles won Song of the Year for "Michelle," and Klaus Voorman's design for *Revolver* won Best Album Cover/Package. *Sgt. Pepper* won four awards, for Best Engineered (Non-Classical) Recording, Best Album Cover, Best Contemporary Album, and Album of the Year. In 1969, *Abbey Road* won Best Engineered (Non-Classical) Recording, and in 1970 *Let It Be* won Best Original Score Written for a Motion Picture or TV Special. *Let It Be* also won the band's only Oscar, for Best Original Song Score.

Post-1970 Beatles Grammy wins include Best Pop Performance by a Duo or Group with Vocal for "Free as a Bird" in 1996; the song's video also won Best Music Video, Short Form. The same year *The Beatles Anthology* won the Grammy for Best Music Video, Long Form. *The Beatles Love* album won Best Surround Sound Album and Best Compilation Soundtrack Album for Motion Picture, Television or Other Visual Media in 2007, while the documentary about the show, *The Beatles Love: All Together Now*, won Best Long Form Music Video in 2009. The 2009 reissue of the band's catalogue on CD, *The Beatles (The Original Studio Recordings)*, won the Grammy for Best Historical Album in 2011.

The Beatles were inducted into the Grammy's Hall of Fame in 1975. Paul received the organization's Lifetime Achievement Award in 1990; John received it in 1991. The band also has many songs and albums in the Grammy Hall of Fame, including: "I Want to Hold Your Hand," *Meet The Beatles*, *A Hard Day's Night*, "Help!," "Yesterday," *Rubber Soul*, "Eleanor Rigby," *Revolver*, "Strawberry Fields Forever," *Sgt. Pepper*, *The Beatles*, "Hey Jude," *Abbey Road*, and *Let It Be*.

The Beatles were inducted into the Rock and Roll Hall of Fame in 1988. John was the next to be inducted as a solo artist in 1994, with Paul inducted in 1999 (producer George Martin was inducted the same year as a non-performer), and George in 2004.

The Beatles' first session at Abbey Road was on June 6, 1962, when drummer Pete Best was still in the band. The last time all four Beatles were at Abbey Road was August 20, 1969, mixing and editing the song "I Want You (She's So Heavy)" and working on the running order for the *Abbey Road* album. The last Beatles session at Abbey Road where new material was recorded (as opposed to non-recording work, like a mixing session) was on April 1, 1970, when Ringo recorded additional drum parts for "Across the Universe," "The Long and Winding Road," and "I Me Mine."

The studio was renamed Abbey Road Studios in 1970, after the release of the *Abbey Road* album. All four Beatles continued to record at Abbey Road in their post-Beatle careers; Paul liked Abbey Road's Studio Two so much he re-created it in the basement of his MPL (McCartney Productions Ltd.) Communications building at 1 Soho Square, giving it the jokey name "Replica Studios."

There are no regular tours offered of Abbey Road, though special events are held at the studio on occasion. Tour groups like International Tours and Events also sometimes include an inside visit to Abbey Road in their tour packages. The studio also has a web cam (www.abbeyroad.com/crossing) focused on the famous crosswalk where you can watch tourists trying to emulate the Beatles' walk across the street.

Further reading: *Abbey Road* (Brian Southall, Peter Vince, Allan Rouse); *Abbey Road: The Best Studio in the World* (Alistair Lawrence)

Fabs On Film No. 2: Magical Mystery Tour

The *Magical Mystery Tour* film was the first major project the Beatles embarked on after Brian Epstein's death. It turned out to be a major turning point for the group—the moment when the first cracks in their invincibility began to show.

Paul got the idea for the film when returning home from a visit to the US to see his girlfriend, Jane Asher, in April 1967. A "mystery tour" in England was a bus trip people signed up for not knowing what the destination was going to be; it usually ended up being a trip to the seaside. Paul's idea was about doing a psychedelic version of the tour, a concept perhaps also inspired by the growing hippie scene in San Francisco, which he'd visited during his US trip.

The Beatles recorded the title track in April and May of 1967, but didn't return to the project until late August. At a meeting at Paul's house on September 1, just five days after Brian's death, they decided now was the time to push on with the film. Paul had drawn a pie chart divided into different sections, each representing a different segment of the film. He then assigned each section to one of the Beatles, saying they had to create something for that sequence of the film. Because the Beatles had learned how to create elaborate musical productions in the studio, they—or at least Paul—felt that turning their hands to other art forms would be similarly easy. A week of location shooting, a week of shooting at a studio, another week to edit, and they'd be done.

But the proposed schedule proved to be wildly optimistic, and the project's disorganization was evident from the first day, September 11, when the bus scheduled to pick up the actors and crew arrived two hours late. There was no formal script; the Beatles simply invited their friends and a few character actors to accompany them, and all the scenes were improvised (Victor Spinetti, who'd appeared in *A Hard Day's Night* and *Help!*, was asked to reprise his role as a drill sergeant in the stage play *Oh! What a Lovely War* in one scene). Filming was further hampered by the fans and press that followed the bus; the bus itself got stuck on a bridge at one point. Location shooting ended September 15.

The Beatles hadn't realized how far in advance studios needed to be booked, so they ended up filming from September 19 to 24 at the West Malling Air Station, a US base during World War II, using both the air field and the large hanger. Editing began on September 25, and lasted for the next 11 weeks. Additional sequences were shot in Nice, France, the London strip club Raymond Revuebar (where the art rockers the Bonzo Dog Doo-Dah Band backed stripper Jan Carson while performing the only non-Beatles song in the film, "Death Cab for Cutie"), and Ringo's home.

The loosely knit story had Ringo and his aunt Jessie (Jessie Robins) signing on for the tour, which is overseen by "four or five magicians." Unsurprisingly, the musical sequences turned out to be the best part of the film. Paul's lyrical "Fool on the Hill" showed him in various picturesque rural settings in France; the eerie "Blue Jay Way" had George posing as a street pavement artist, shrouded in mist and subdued lighting; the finale, "Your Mother Should Know," was a tongue-in-cheek tribute to vintage film musicals, the Beatles attired in white tuxes, descending a staircase that leads into a ballroom full of dancers. The highlight was the nightmarish "I Am the Walrus," an imaginatively edited sequence, which had the Beatles in colorful psychedelic outfits one second, and wearing creepy animal masks the next, with policemen and a row of "egg men," bound together in the same white bag, providing additional surrealistic touches to one of John's most fanciful compositions.

The hour-long film was first broadcast in the UK on the day after Christmas (a holiday called Boxing Day) and received terrible reviews. "Take your pick from the words, 'Rubbish, piffle, chaotic, flop, tasteless, nonsense, emptiness and appalling!'" one critic wrote. "I watched it. There was precious little magic and the only mystery was how the BBC came to buy it." Paul quickly did some interviews in the interest of damage control, telling one journalist: "It was our first attempt. If we goofed, then we goofed. It was a challenge and it didn't come off. We'll know better next time." A major miscalculation was having the film debut on BBC 1, which only transmitted in black and white, thus losing the impact of the vibrant colors on display (it later aired on BBC 2, in color). The poor reviews meant no US networks were interested in picking it up for broadcast, so the film was relegated to the midnight movie circuit, or screenings at college campuses.

The soundtrack proved more successful. In the UK, the film's six songs were packaged in a double EP set, released on December 8, 1967, and reaching No. 2 in the charts. In the US, an album was created of the film songs and other singles the Beatles had released in 1967. Released on November 27, 1967, the album topped the charts. The film is now available on DVD and stands as an interesting, if flawed, opulent "home movie."

46 The First US Concert

The Beatles' first live performance in the US was on *The Ed Sullivan Show*. But their first full concert was performed in the nation's capital, Washington, D.C., on February 11, 1964.

Brian Epstein had booked the show less than a month before, when the Beatles were performing in Paris. During their stay, he met with a representative of the General Artists Corporation talent agency, and the February 11 date was chosen as a sort of "out of town opening" date for the Beatles' performances at Carnegie Hall the following night. The Beatles were meant to fly from New York City to D.C., but it was snowing so heavily on the morning of February 11 that they refused to fly. Arrangements were hastily made to travel by train instead (Brian had no qualms about traveling via plane himself, and he flew to D.C. in the afternoon). During the short journey, the Beatles were able to relax and joke with the press, who were pleased to find the band members so animated.

On arriving in D.C., the group first checked in at the Shoreham Hotel, and were then taken to the venue where they would perform that night, the Washington Coliseum. They attended a press conference and gave a few other interviews before taking the stage at 8:30 PM, following opening acts by the Caravelles, Tommy Roe, and the Chiffons.

The stage was set up in the middle of the arena, with Ringo's drums on a revolving platform that had to be operated manually. When Ringo had too much difficulty in turning the platform, road manager Mal Evans and publicist Brian Somerville came on stage to turn it every few songs; this enabled the Beatles to face everyone in the arena at some point during the show.

The show was the first Beatles concert to be professionally recorded in its entirety (it was being recorded for later screening via a closed-circuit broadcast held in US theaters the next month on March 14 and 15). As such, it's an invaluable record of the Beatles' live act at the time, at a point when they were full of elation at having finally conquered America. Despite the pervasive screaming, which begins the moment the Beatles enter the arena and continues throughout the entire show, the performance is infectious, with the Beatles clearly enjoying themselves, especially on the upbeat numbers. Even the faltering microphones can't impede the good vocal harmonizing on numbers like "This Boy," and every time they shake their heads the crowd erupts in fresh screaming. It was one of the most exciting performances in the Beatles' career. The setlist for the complete performance is: "Roll Over Beethoven," "From Me to You," "I Saw Her Standing There," "This Boy," "All My Loving," "I Wanna Be Your Man," "Please Please Me," "Till There Was You," "She Loves You," "I Want to Hold Your Hand," "Twist and Shout," and an especially explosive "Long Tall Sally."

Afterward, the group paid a visit to the British Embassy, where they were treated with no little condescension by some attendees, who mocked their appearance and behavior; one young woman even snipped off a chunk of Ringo's hair. The Beatles later received an apology from the British ambassador and his wife, but they decided privately to never attend such functions again. The next day, before returning to New York, the Beatles posed for some shots on the Mall, with the Capitol Building appearing dramatically in the background.

Footage of the Washington, D.C., show has been seen in numerous films, and it's also been readily available on the collector's circuit (though the footage cuts off before "Long Tall Sally"). But a complete, official version of the show has yet to be released.

47 The Last US Concert

The Beatles' 1966 tour of America was relatively brief—between August 12 and August 29 they performed just 19 shows—but it was one of the more trying experiences of their performing career. It began with an opening press conference where John was made to apologize for his "the Beatles are more popular than Jesus" remark. The Ku Klux Klan turned up to picket at two shows; a famous clairvoyant predicted the Beatles' plane would crash; the show in Cleveland was halted for half an hour when over 2,000 fans swarmed over the field; the Shea Stadium show failed to sell out; rioting fans trapped the Beatles in their limo for two hours after a show in Los Angeles.

The band had also become increasingly fed up with the presentation of their shows. The crowds seemed more interested

Trouble In the Philippines

The "Beatles bigger than Jesus" kerfuffle wasn't the only controversy the Beatles faced during the summer of 1966. They were also in actual physical danger during their stay in the Philippines.

It had been a stressful trip from the beginning. When the Beatles arrived on July 3, 1966, military guards boarded the plane and took the group to a boat in Manila Harbor. The Beatles were alarmed at being separated from their entourage, and at Brian Epstein's insistence they were eventually taken to the Manila Hotel. (Imelda Marcos, the wife of the country's president, Ferdinand Marcos, told author Howard Sounes the Beatles were placed aboard a ship for their "protection.")

The First Lady had also invited the Beatles to lunch at the presidential palace on July 4. Brian turned down the invitation, as the Beatles disliked attending official functions. But the word was apparently not passed on to Mrs. Marcos, who still expected the Beatles to arrive for lunch. The Beatles played two shows on July 4, and were unaware of anything being amiss. But the next morning, when they switched on their televisions, they watched in growing horror at an endless stream of stories about how they'd snubbed the First Family by failing to turn up at the palace, accompanied by footage of disappointed children and other invited guests. Newspapers were also full of the story, and when room service sent up spoiled food, they realized the precariousness of their situation.

Everyone quickly left for the airport, where they were further stymied by getting no help from luggage porters, and forced to deal with escalators that had mysteriously ceased to function. As they made their way to the departure gate, they were kicked and punched. Road manager Mal Evans and publicist Tony Barrow were then called off the plane and questioned about the tour's paperwork. Brian was forced to surrender their tour earnings. They were finally allowed to leave. Mrs. Marcos later referred to the incident as a "sad misunderstanding." But the unpleasant experience definitely played in a role in the Beatles' decision to stop touring.

A fan is pulled off the stage during a Beatles performance in Boston in August 1966. (AP Images)

in partaking in the spectacle of a Beatles concert—what George referred to as "the mania"—than in listening to the music, shrieking non-stop from the moment the Beatles took the stage. The Beatles had become bored with grinding out the same half-hour set that no one was apparently listening to. "There was no satisfaction in [touring]," George told Hunter Davies. "Nobody could hear. It was just a bloody big row. We got worse as musicians, playing the same old junk every day."

And so, before the Beatles stepped out on stage at San Francisco's Candlestick Park on August 29, they'd privately agreed it would be their last show. Paul even asked their publicist, Tony

Barrow, to record the show on his cassette tape recorder (the tape ran out during the last song). The 11-song set featured: "Rock and Roll Music," "She's a Woman," "If I Needed Someone," "Day Tripper," "Baby's in Black," "I Feel Fine," "Yesterday," "I Wanna Be Your Man," "Nowhere Man," "Paperback Writer," and "Long Tall Sally"—a setlist notable in that it includes not a single song from the band's latest album, *Revolver*. Afterward, a camera was placed on an amplifier and the timer set up to take a picture of the band, as a souvenir.

Sadly, Brian Epstein was not on hand to see the last show of the group he'd helped launch to stardom. While staying in Los Angeles, his briefcase—which had contained a substantial sum of money as well as drugs and personal correspondence—had been stolen by one of his errant boyfriends. The theft left Brian sick with worry, and too distraught to attend the concert. So he wasn't with the band when they jetted out of San Francisco after the show and headed back to LA, to hear George pronounce as he sat in his seat, "Well, that's it. I'm not a Beatle any more."

48 Fabs On Film No. 3: *Let It Be*

It should have been a Beatle fan's dream: a film that got up close and personal with the group, as they worked in the studio. Instead, the *Let It Be* documentary depicted a band for whom it was clear the pleasure of making music together had all but disappeared.

The roots of *Let It Be* were twofold. The group had hoped the *Yellow Submarine* animated film released in 1968 would satisfy the three-picture deal they had with United Artists, but this was determined not to be the case. At the same time Paul had been urging the Beatles that they needed to get back to live performing. The other Beatles conceded, and it was announced that the group would be playing the Roundhouse (a London venue) in December 1968. That fell through, as did other concert plans, though a January 18, 1969, date was eventually tentatively scheduled. Rehearsals for the show would also be filmed for an accompanying documentary, called *Get Back*.

And so the Beatles arrived at Twickenham Films Studios, in suburban London, on January 2, 1969, for what would be the most contentious rehearsals of their career. The final film edited out the most fraught moments, but enough remains to convey the underlying disinterest John, George, and Ringo have in the project. For one thing, the Beatles all look miserable; unkempt and unshaven, they appear to be suffering from a permanent hangover. The Twickenham soundstage was huge and sterile, and the group was forced to work during the day, instead of the all-night schedule they were used to. The lack of enthusiasm is palpable. As John put it, "I just didn't give a shit, you know. Nobody did."

On January 10, George walked out. He was not only frustrated with Paul's overbearing direction, but also John's apparent abdication from the proceedings, happy to let Yoko speak for him. He didn't like the Twickenham setup, nor did he want to do a show. At a meeting on January 15, he agreed to come back if the public show was cancelled and they continued working elsewhere. The Beatles agreed, and the group relocated to their Apple HQ where a studio was supposed to have been built in the basement by Alex Mardas, aka "Magic Alex," the head of Apple Electronics. Alex proved to have little idea how to put a recording studio together, and the sessions were further delayed as a mobile recording unit was brought in.

But when the sessions finally recommenced, everyone's attitude had decidedly improved. George had also suggested they bring in a keyboard player as a guest musician, and Billy Preston, whom the

Beatles had met when Preston was in Hamburg playing with Little Richard's band, was invited to the sessions. Eventually, the Beatles even agreed to perform live, climbing up to Apple's roof on January 30 and playing a set that lasted around 40 minutes. The sessions ended the next day.

There were now hours and hours of tapes and film to be gone through. The Beatles had wanted to record without any overdubbing, and so had recorded countless takes of each song. They also recorded endless hours of jamming, running through the kind of rock 'n' roll classics they'd played in Hamburg. Glyn Johns, a recording engineer who served as producer on the project when George Martin was absent, assembled a few versions of an album then called *Get Back*, but none of them were deemed satisfactory.

In the meantime, the Beatles began recording *Abbey Road*, which was released in September 1969. It was also decided to use the documentary footage to create a feature film, and thus fulfill the United Artists contract that way. The film was finally scheduled for release in May 1970, and given that the "Get Back" single would be a year old by then, the film was retitled *Let It Be*, after the single of the same name was released in March 1970. The film also needed an accompanying soundtrack, and as no one had been happy with Glyn Johns' versions, Phil Spector was hired to be the album's producer. While some numbers on the album remained fairly unadorned, Spector did add lush orchestrations to "Across the Universe," and "The Long and Winding Road." John was pleased, saying of Spector, "He was given the shittiest load of badly recorded shit with a lousy feeling to it ever, and he made something out of it. He did a great job." But Paul was not happy with the end result, and it would take another 24 years before the songs were released how he wanted them.

Let It Be had its world premiere in New York City on May 13, 1970. The album was released in the UK on May 8, the first edition packaged in a box with a book of pictures from the sessions. The

US release followed on May 18, without the book, and the album topped the charts in both countries. Despite receiving some mixed reviews, there is much to enjoy on the album. "The Long and Winding Road" and "Let It Be" are two of Paul's classics. George's "I Me Mine" is a stinging critique of self-absorption. "I've Got a Feeling" is one of the best rockers the Beatles ever did. And "Two of Us" captures the spirit of the early days, when the group was just starting out, with no idea what lay ahead of them.

Further reading: *Drugs, Divorce, and a Slipping Image* (Doug Sulpy, Ray Schweighardt), *Let It Be/Abbey Road* (Peter Doggett)

49 The Very Last Beatles Show

The Beatles' last official concert was on August 29, 1966, at San Francisco's Candlestick Park. But their very last live performance together was a unique one-off event that happened two years and five months later, on January 30, 1969.

During the filming of *Let It Be* in January 1969, it was decided on January 26 that the Beatles would do a brief live show from the roof of their Apple Corp. HQ on Savile Row. Equipment was set up in the morning, and at lunchtime the Beatles climbed up the stairs to the roof, greeted by a cold, overcast day. The performance began with a quick run-through of the chorus of "Get Back," followed by two complete versions of the song. Next came a strong version of "Don't Let Me Down," with John forgetting the lyrics at one point and singing gibberish, followed by equally good performances of "I've Got a Feeling" and "One After 909." After "Dig a Pony," the Beatles returned to both "I've Got a Feeling" and

"Don't Let Me Down," though these performances aren't as good as the earlier versions.

The impromptu show naturally attracted the attention of passersby and people in nearby buildings. Some lucky folks were able to climb up on their own rooftops to get a better view of what was happening. Others in the area were less amused and contacted the police, who duly arrived at 3 Savile Row and politely knocked on the door. Film cameras captured all the action as the police ascended to the roof, talked with Beatle aide Mal Evans, and ultimately agreed to let the Beatles perform one more song, which turned out to be another version of "Get Back," with Paul ad-libbing at the song's end about the arrival of the police: "You've been playing on the roofs again! And that's no good. Because you know your mommy doesn't like that. She gets angry. She gonna have you arrested!" The Beatles were in fact disappointed that they weren't arrested, as they thought it would've been a good climax for the film. Instead, it was left for John to have the final word with his joking comment: "I'd like to say thank you on behalf of the group and ourselves, and I hope we passed the audition!"

The second take of "Get Back," the first versions of "Don't Let Me Down" and "I've Got a Feeling," "One After 909," "Dig a Pony," and the final version of "Get Back" all appeared in the *Let It Be* film ("I've Got a Feeling," "One After 909," and "Dig a Pony" also appeared on the *Let It Be* album, with John's "audition" comment spliced onto the end of a studio performance of "Get Back"). As the *Let It Be* film has more than its share of dreary moments, the rooftop performance, which appears as the film's end, provides a welcome respite, as it's clear the Beatles are enjoying themselves. Which makes it a shame they couldn't have worked out a way to do more live performances together in their later years.

50 All About Those "Yeah Yeah Yeahs"

The "Love Me Do" single introduced the Beatles to the world. "Please Please Me" was their first big success. "From Me to You" proved the group were not just one-hit wonders.

And then came "She Loves You."

You can't overstate the excitement this single generated. Its exuberant sound captured the very spirit of Beatlemania. And the fans must have sensed what was coming, as even before the single was released in the UK (on August 23, 1963), it had racked up advance orders of half a million copies.

The song was written while the band was on tour, as they were during so much of 1963. On June 26, they found themselves in Newcastle-upon-Tyne, and despite their hectic schedule, John and Paul were determined to put every spare moment to good use. "We must have had a few hours before the show so we said, 'Oh, great! Let's have a ciggy and write a song!'" Paul recalled. The two roughed out the song that day, and decided to take on a new approach with the lyrics. Instead of a straightforward you-and-I narrative, a third party was introduced, with the singer carrying the message of assurance—she loves you—between the two. The song was finished the next day at Paul's home in Liverpool. On hearing the number for the first time, Paul's father suggested that they sing "yes, yes, yes," instead of "yeah, yeah, yeah," telling his son, "There's enough of these Americanisms around." But the songwriters knew that "yes, yes, yes" didn't have the right ring to it. "Yeah, yeah, yeah" remained.

"She Loves You" was recorded four days later, on July 1. After Ringo's barreling introduction on the drums, the song goes straight into the chorus (a move George Martin suggested), bursting with energy from start to finish. The Beatles pull out all the stops; in addition to punctuating each line of the chorus with "yeah, yeah, yeahs," they throw in a few "woos!" for good measure (which were invariably followed by screams from their fans when they performed the song live). The song ends with John, Paul, and George each singing the notes that make up a G sixth chord. George Martin, who recognized it as something commonly used during the Glenn Miller era, thought it a corny touch. But the Beatles insisted on keeping it, enthusing over the "great sound," and it does provide a distinctive ending to the record.

"She Loves You" quickly reached No. 1 in the UK; in fact, the Beatles set a record when it topped the singles charts in *Record Retailer* on September 12, for the group were also at the top of the album charts (with *Please Please Me*) and the EP charts (with *Twist and Shout*) the same week. "Yet another record achievement from EMI artists!" a contemporaneous ad boasted. In the US, the single was released on September 16, 1963, on Swan Records. Like the release of previous Beatles records in the states, it failed to chart. But as "I Want to Hold Your Hand" began to take off in early 1964, Swan reissued the single, and by March it topped the charts.

The single became the Beatles' first million seller, selling over 1 million copies in the UK by November 1963. It remains the Beatles' biggest-selling single, and held the record for best-selling British single of all time, until 1977, when it was outsold by Paul's single "Mull of Kintyre."

51 Fabs On Film No. 4: *Help!*

The success of the film *A Hard Day's Night* guaranteed there would be a second Beatles movie. It also meant there would be more money to spend on the film as well, so *Help!* became the first Beatles movie to be in color.

The plot revolves around the efforts of an Eastern religious sect to get back a sacrificial ring that has ended up on Ringo's finger (a mad scientist and his daft assistant also join the pursuit). The Beatles again played "themselves," though Ringo was given a bigger role due to the acclaim his performance had received in *A Hard Day's Night*. The group was placed in a pop art fantasy world, a hyperreality of bright colors and gadgetry. This is established at the film's beginning, when the Beatles are seen entering different doors in a row of terrace houses, only for the camera to reveal that the separate entrances lead into one large flat, with a sunken pit for a bed, an organ that rises from a trap door in the floor, and a wall lined with vending machines.

The film was also a send-up of the fast-paced antics of the James Bond action films; the film's incidental music (not written by the Beatles) even parodies the signature guitar sound of the James Bond theme music. As John astutely noted, *Help!* was a forerunner of the satiric, comic book caperings that were the hallmark of later TV shows like *Batman*.

A Hard Day's Night director Richard Lester was again at the helm. The increased budget enabled the hiring of name actors like Leo McKern (later the star of the TV series *Rumpole of the Bailey*), Eleanor Bron (later to star in the comic classic *Bedazzled*), and Patrick Cargill (who later appeared in *The Magic Christian*, which also starred Ringo). Victor Spinetti, who played a frustrated TV director in *A Hard Day's Night*, returned to play the mad scientist. They were also able to film at more exotic locations, including the Bahamas (chosen because the Beatles planned to set up a tax shelter there, though the effort failed) and the Austrian Alps. Closer to home, scenes were shot at Cliveden House (formerly the residence of Lord Astor) and Stonehenge.

The film's original title was *Eight Arms to Hold You*, inspired by the multi-armed statue of the religious sect's god, and that title appeared on early US copies of the "Ticket to Ride" single. But when it proved to be too difficult to come up with a song to match that title, the film was renamed *Help!* at Lester's suggestion. The song's lyrics were primarily written by John, who later said that he felt he was subconsciously crying out for help in the song, as a reaction to the overwhelming demands of the Beatle phenomenon. But at the time, "Help!" just seemed like an upbeat pop song. Of the film's other songs, the languorous "Ticket to Ride" is the stand-out, and was used in the movie's best visual sequence, showing the Beatles frolicking in the snow in the Alps (not as frantic as the "Can't Buy Me Love" sequence in *A Hard Day's Night*, but in the same spirit of fun). John's "You've Got to Hide Your Love Away" clearly showed the influence of Bob Dylan, and also expressed the dominant theme of the film's songs, which are either about disappointment in love (Paul's "The Night Before," George's "I Need You") or moving on without regret (Paul's "Another Girl," John's "You're Gonna Lose That Girl").

In America, the film's soundtrack only featured the songs that appeared in the movie, along with the film's incidental music; the UK version of the soundtrack, like *A Hard Day's Night*, featured a second side of Beatle music and no incidental music. The most notable of the non-film songs was Paul's "Yesterday," the delicate ballad followed somewhat improbably by a raw cover of "Dizzy Miss Lizzy," howled out by John. Conversely, John regularly cited "It's Only Love" as one of his least favorite songs ("The lyrics were abysmal"). As on the preceding album *Beatles For Sale*, the quality control slipped a bit (as on the somewhat draggy "Tell Me What You See"), but there are still enough classic songs (like Paul's folky "I've Just Seen a Face," a live favorite during the Wings era) to make it an enjoyable album.

Help! had its world premiere in London on July 29, 1965. Critical reaction to the film was not as strong as for *A Hard Day's Night*, but it was a huge success with fans and has aged well as a pop art satire and is great fun to watch. The soundtrack was released on August 6, 1965, in the UK, August 13 in the US, and topped the charts in both countries.

52 Animated Fabs

From 1965 to 1969, kids in America could get a weekly dose of Beatlemania on TV by watching *The Beatles*—the cartoon series.

The series was the idea of Al Brodax, an executive at King Features Syndicate, who approached Brian Epstein during the Beatles' first visit to America in February 1964 about doing an animated series about the Beatles. Epstein agreed, and Brodax quickly went to work, lining up sponsors and writers. Because it was felt that American children would have trouble understanding British accents, American voiceover specialist Paul Frees was hired to provide the voices of John and George (among his many credits, Frees was also the voice of Boris Badenov in the *Rocky and Bullwinkle* cartoons, and the Pillsbury Doughboy in the food company's commercials). But British character actor Lance Percival was also hired to provide the voices of Paul and Ringo.

Each half-hour show featured two five-and-a-half-minute cartoons and two sing-along spots. The plots generally involved the Beatles ending up in some kind of sticky situation, usually while trying to escape from their fans; vampires, monsters, and witches make frequent appearances. The stories were each based around a Beatles song, and the sing-along sequences featured additional songs, meaning kids got a lot of exposure to the Beatles' music on the program. A range of toys was also produced to exploit new-found interest in the group among the pre-teen demographic. The toys are all now quite collectable; a complete set of inflatable dolls based on the cartoon characters will set you back at least $500.

The show debuted on September 25, 1965, on ABC, and was an instant success, the first 26 episodes generating high ratings. But soon after, the ratings began to slump, as those 26 episodes were rerun not just once, but twice before any new episodes aired. The second season, in 1966, featured seven new episodes, with episodes from season one mixed in during rerun periods. The third season, in 1967, featured only six new episodes. After they aired, all 39 episodes were simply rerun, the last air date being September 7, 1969.

The Beatles themselves had nothing to do with the series, and were said to have not liked it very much, at least initially, one of the reasons why the series was not shown in England. They later modified their views—somewhat, as in George's backhanded compliment, "They were so bad or silly that they were good, if you know what I mean."

The success of *The Beatles* led to cartoon series about other rock groups, both real (*The Jackson Five*) and fictional (*The Archies*). The show was seen in syndication through the 1980s (MTV rebroadcast edited versions of the show in 1986 and 1987). Apple purchased all rights to the series in the '90s, and though they've licensed the cartoon images for various official products (such as T-shirts), the shows themselves have yet to be officially re-released.

Further reading: *Beatletoons: The Real Story Behind the Cartoon Beatles* (Mitchell Axelrod)

53 Fabs On Film No. 5: Yellow Submarine

Yellow Submarine had the least direct Beatles involvement of any of their films. Though receiving mixed reviews at the time of its release in 1968, it went on to become a worldwide smash and today is often the route through which youngsters are introduced to the Beatles.

The Beatles had signed a three-picture deal with United Artists, and after *A Hard Day's Night* and *Help!* they still owed the company one more film. They'd been searching for a suitable project, but hadn't found anything to their liking. Al Brodax, who produced *The Beatles* cartoon feature, had been pushing to do a feature-length film, and Brian Epstein finally agreed, thinking the movie would satisfy the UA deal (that ultimately turned out not to be the case, which led to the release of the *Let It Be* documentary).

The story (written in part by future *Love Story* novelist Erich Segal) had the evil Blue Meanies sucking all the light, music, and joy out of a fairytale place called Pepperland. The Lord Mayor dispatches the sailor Old Fred to get help, and Fred travels by yellow submarine to Liverpool, where he meets the Beatles, who agree to return with him to Pepperland. Their journey takes them through a variety of strange and sometimes threatening places—the Sea of Time, the Sea of Monsters, the Sea of Holes—but they eventually arrive safely in Pepperland and unsurprisingly overturn the reign of the Blue Meanies.

Director George Dunning wanted to avoid any hint of Disney-esque cuteness. It was the height of the psychedelic era, and *Yellow Submarine* fairly bursts with color, and features a weird and wonderful cast of characters. The villains are especially inventive: the Snapping Turtle Turks, whose stomachs open up to reveal rows of shiny teeth; the towering Apple Bonkers, who drop lethal apples on the unsuspecting; the menacing Flying Glove that smashes things into oblivion. There are plenty of visual jokes, a surfeit of punning dialogue, and a dazzling array of animation styles.

The Beatles wanted as little to do with the film as possible. The soundtrack drew on previously recorded tracks (mostly drawn from 1967), and the band only recorded four new songs: "Only a Northern Song" and "It's All Too Much" (both by George), "Hey Bulldog" (initially cut from US prints of the film), and the closing ditty "All Together Now." Their attitude to the songs is perfectly expressed by John's description of "Hey Bulldog": "It's a good sounding record that means nothing." But the Beatles did agree to make a cameo appearance at the film's end, ushering in a sing-along to "All Together Now."

The film had its world premiere on July 17, 1968, in London. But the soundtrack wouldn't be released for another six months, on January 13, 1969, in the US, January 17 in the UK. Originally, the plan was to release the four new songs on an EP. But since that format was no longer used in the US, an album was created by adding "Yellow Submarine" and "All You Need Is Love" to side one, and filling side two with the incidental music George Martin had written for the film. Despite the paucity of new material on the album, it still reached No. 2 US, No. 3 UK.

When the film was released on DVD in 1999, it was accompanied by what was called the *Yellow Submarine Songtrack*, which featured fifteen songs from the movie, and none of the incidental music. The songs were not only remastered, but also remixed, building anticipation for the overhaul of the Beatles' catalogue on CD, though that wouldn't happen for another decade.

The Beatles eventually came to like the film—especially when it became a commercial success—though some ambivalence remained, as in Paul's comment: "I don't mind it much now as I did back then.... For me, *Yellow Submarine* is a bit like *Magical*

Mystery Tour—a bit disappointing at the time but now it looks a lot better." Ringo says that to this day children still ask him why he pushed a button in the submarine, an action that promptly ejected him into the Sea of Monsters. "Kids from all over the whole bloody world kept shouting 'Why did you press the button?' at me as if it was real," he marveled. "They actually thought it was me."

54 The Decca Audition

As 1962 began, the Beatles must have felt they were about to enter the big time. The previous December 6, the Beatles had agreed to let Brian Epstein become their manager. The main thing Brian had promised the band was that he would land them a record contract. And just seven days later, on December 13, Mike Smith, an A&R man from Decca Records, came to Liverpool to watch the Beatles in action at the Cavern at Brian's invitation. Liking what he saw, Smith decided to see how the band would fare in the studio, and arranged a session at Decca's London studios on January 1, 1962. Less than a month after obtaining management, the Beatles were going to audition for the one of the biggest record companies in England.

The band, with road manager Neil Aspinall at the wheel, drove down to London on December 31 (Brian traveled more comfortably by train). There were no major highways in Britain at the time, and the journey took ten hours; a snowstorm even caused Neil to get lost at one point. New Year's Day was not yet a national holiday, but Mike Smith still arrived late for the 11:00 AM session, due to the celebrations of the previous night, making the Beatles even more nervous.

Smith's first move was to say that the group couldn't use the battered amps they'd hauled all the way down from Liverpool; Decca's in-studio equipment was in far better shape. Over the next few hours, a total of 15 songs were recorded. This wasn't a formal recording session; Smith simply wanted to get an idea of what the band sounded like in studio, so the songs were laid down quickly, with no overdubs.

The songs were drawn from numbers that were already in the Beatles' repertoire, reflecting their many influences—the rock 'n' roll, rockabilly, and R&B of Chuck Berry ("Memphis Tennessee"), Carl Perkins ("Sure to Fall"), Buddy Holly ("Crying, Waiting, Hoping"), the Coasters ("Three Cool Cats," "Searchin',"), and Motown ("Money"). Unexpected song choices like the 1920s hit "The Sheik of Araby" and the Latin standard "Bésame Mucho" weren't as unusual as they seemed. British singer Joe Brown had recorded a version of the former song in 1961, as had Fats Domino, who was a great favorite of the Beatles, while the Coasters had released their version of "Bésame Mucho" in 1960; most likely the Beatles were influenced by these versions. Paul was always partial to standards and musicals, making "Till There Was You" from Meredith Wilson's *The Music Man* a natural choice for him. Much the same could be said of the decision to perform "September in the Rain" (with Paul again on lead) a standard that Dinah Washington had a Top 30 pop hit with in 1961. "Take Good Care of My Baby" had caught the Beatles' eye not because of who sang it—Bobby Vee—but who wrote it, Gerry Goffin and Carole King, the Brill Building songwriting team that Lennon and McCartney aspired to emulate. "To Know Her Is to Love Her" was the sole hit of the Teddy Bears, the Los Angeles–based vocal group that included Phil Spector, who would go on to work with the Beatles (and with John and George as solo artists).

Of most interest are the three Lennon/McCartney originals the group performed: "Like Dreamers Do," "Love of the Loved," and "Hello Little Girl," with Paul taking lead on the first two songs and John singing lead on the third (with a harmony vocal from Paul). The songs are bright lively pop tunes, but lack the dynamic punch of the Beatles' later work—especially evidenced by the fact that the Beatles never recorded formal versions of these songs themselves, but ended up passing them off for other artists to record. It's also worth pointing out that George Harrison had lead vocal on four tracks ("Three Cool Cats," "The Sheik of Araby," "Crying, Waiting, Hoping," and "Take Good Care of My Baby"), emphasizing that he sang leads more often during the group's early days.

Smith assured the band, and Epstein, that the audition had gone well, and everyone returned to Liverpool assuming a record contract was as good as signed. So it must have been a shock when word arrived in February that Decca had decided to turn the group down. Brian returned to London to meet with Decca's head of A&R, Dick Rowe, in an attempt to get him to change his mind. But Rowe stood firm, telling Epstein that groups with guitars "were on the way out." "You've got a good business, Mr. Epstein," Brian was told. "Why not stick to it?" Another factor was said to be that Mike Smith had auditioned Brian Poole and the Tremeloes on the same day as the Beatles, and had been told he'd only be able to sign one group, and as the Tremeloes lived closed to London, Smith opted to sign them.

Of course, had the Beatles' performance been stronger, that might have tipped the balance in their favor. Though the band is certainly competent and energetic, a number of the performances—such as "Money"—sound rushed, and the group doesn't come over as sounding entirely comfortable. The Beatles themselves didn't feel they were at their best. "We were terrified and nervous," John later admitted. Paul agreed: "We couldn't get the numbers right, and we couldn't get in tune." The entire session has been extensively bootlegged; five of the songs were eventually released officially on *Anthology 1* ("Searchin'," "Three Cool Cats," "The Sheik of Araby," "Like Dreamers Do," "Hello Little Girl").

Brian, and the Beatles, must have been crushed by Decca's decision. But the session would have an unexpected payoff. While in London having the audition tape transferred to disc, the songs caught the attention of the recording engineer, who referred Brian to Sid Colman of music publishers Ardmore & Beechwood. On learning Epstein was looking for a recording contract for his group, Colman referred him to George Martin, head of A&R at Parlophone Records, who would ultimately sign the Beatles. So, the Decca audition did eventually lead to a record deal for the Beatles—just not with Decca Records.

55 A Royal Honor

Harold Wilson, who became Britain's prime minister in 1964, had a full appreciation of the publicity value that could result from associating oneself with the Beatles. When he was still Leader of the Opposition, he attended an awards luncheon held by the Variety Club of Great Britain on March 19, 1964, and handed the Beatles their awards for Show Business Personalities of 1963, making sure he was photographed with them. After becoming prime minister, he decided to acknowledge the Beatles' contribution to Britain's economy by adding their names to the Queen's annual "Birthday Honours" list, and on June 12, 1965, it was announced that each of the Beatles would receive an MBE award—"Member of the Most Excellent Order of the British Empire." As soon as the news was announced, the Beatles did two interviews sharing their reactions to getting the award (George:

"Well, I sort of went 'Wow! That's great'"; Ringo: "Yes. I think we all felt pretty well the same").

The MBE is the lowest of Britain's honors; the highest is the Knight Grand Cross and Dame Grand Cross. But it was the first time any rock musician had been given such an honor at all, and it provoked a good deal of controversy; a number of MBE recipients returned their medals in protest, saying the honor had been degraded. But Beatles fans were thrilled by the news, and the *Daily Mirror* noted approvingly, "Now they are in the topmost chart of all." At the time, John said, "Lots of people who complained about us getting the MBE received theirs for heroism in the war. Ours were civil awards. We deserve ours for not killing people. If you get a medal for killing, you should certainly get a medal for singing and keeping Britain's economics in good nick!"

The investiture was held on October 26, 1965, at Buckingham Palace, and a sizeable crowd gathered outside to watch as the Beatles arrived. John would claim that the group smoked a marijuana joint in the palace toilets while waiting for the ceremony to start, but George later denied that was the case; the group had merely smoked cigarettes (Ringo said he couldn't remember; Paul had no comment). During the wait, the group was also asked for their autographs by other people waiting to pick up their awards. "They were all nice, you know," said Paul. "But one fellow said, 'I want it for my daughter, but I don't know what she sees in you!'"

The Queen spoke briefly to the Beatles when she gave them their medals. When she asked how long the group had been together, Paul and Ringo spontaneously broke into the chorus of an old music hall number: "We've been together now for 40 years, and it don't seem a day too much!" "She had this strange, quizzical look on her face," Ringo later recalled. "Like either she wanted to laugh or she was thinking, 'Off with their heads!'" Afterward, the Beatles held a press conference at the Savile Theatre (which Brian Epstein would later own).

Beatles fans try to break through a police line at Buckingham Palace on October 26, 1965, as the Beatles recive the Member of the British Empire (MBE) decoration from the Queen.

Both Paul and George wore their MBEs on the *Sgt. Pepper* album cover. But John remained uncomfortable about having accepted the award, feeling that it meant he had finally sold out to the establishment. He had originally given the award to his aunt Mimi, who proudly kept it on display at her home. But he eventually decided to return it, and, on November 25, 1969, sent it back to the palace with the following note: "Your Majesty, I am returning my MBE as a protest against Britain's involvement in the

Nigeria-Biafra thing, against our support of America in Vietnam and against 'Cold Turkey' [his latest solo single] slipping down the charts. With love, John Lennon." The crack about his new single was meant to inject an element of levity into the event, but not surprisingly also drew some criticism.

Paul had no such qualms about being honored, and on March 11, 1997, happily accepted a knighthood from his Queen, for his services to music. Speaking to reporters after the ceremony, he joked that while he was now entitled to being addressed as "Sir Paul McCartney," Ringo and George had teasingly been calling him "Your Holiness."

56 The First No. 1 Single

When the Beatles arrived at Abbey Road Studios on November 26, 1962, to record their second single, they were ready with the strongest track they'd written up to that time, "Please Please Me."

The song was John's, and originally a ballad sung in the style of Roy Orbison; John mentioned being inspired both by Orbison's "Only the Lonely" and a line from a Bing Crosby song that used the words "please" and "pleas" in a lyric: "I was always intrigued by the double use of the word 'please,'" he explained. Unlike the band's first single, "Love Me Do," "Please Please Me" was very sexually aggressive; John doesn't modestly request, but outright demands that his loved one keep him satisfied.

The band had first performed the song for George Martin at the second "Love Me Do" session on September 11, 1962. Martin's first suggestion was a key one: increase the tempo. "And suddenly there was that fast Beatles spirit," Paul later recalled. The group recorded an early version at that same session (available on *Anthology 1*), but the song wasn't quite there yet. The November 26 session would give the song its final polish.

"Please Please Me" gets off to an upbeat start with a burst of John's harmonica, which punctuates the song throughout. John tackles the lead, with Paul providing a high-pitched harmony vocal. Most exhilarating is the moment when everyone's voices coalesce on the chorus, climbing up to the high notes on the line "Please please me, whoa yeah," before dropping back down. George Martin was duly impressed with the band's work. "The whole session was a joy," he later said. "At the end, I pressed the intercom button and said, 'Gentlemen, you have just made your first number one.'"

And after its UK release on January 11, 1963, "Please Please Me" did reach No. 1 in three of England's national charts. The single was soon released in America, on February 7, 1963, on Vee-Jay, though it attracted little interest at the time. The single was reissued in the US in January 1964, and this time it fared far better, peaking at No. 3.

57 The Beatles and the Beeb

Though the Beatles appeared on just about every British television program that featured rock bands, they were heard many more times on British radio. Between March 1962 and June 1965 they appeared 52 times on BBC (British Broadcasting Corporation, affectionately called "the Beeb" in the UK) radio shows, appearing on 16 different programs, and recording a total of 275 songs.

Now, that 275 figure includes each time the Beatles performed a particular song; "Please Please Me," for example, was performed

12 times on various BBC shows. Once you take that into account, you find that the Beatles performed 88 different songs during the three years they made radio appearances; 32 songs were Lennon/McCartney originals, and the rest were cover versions. What's most fascinating is that 36 of the songs performed on the Beeb were never recorded by the Beatles for their singles or albums; the only versions that exist are the BBC versions.

One of Brian Epstein's first accomplishments when he became the Beatles' manager was to arrange for an audition with the BBC. The audition was held at the BBC's Broadcasting House in Manchester on February 12, 1962, and the group was promptly booked for a March 7 appearance on *Teenager's Turn*, which was recorded before a live audience and then broadcast the next day. The Beatles performed three songs on the program: "Dream Baby (How Long Must I Dream)," "Memphis Tennessee," and "Please Mr. Postman"; the latter song was the only one they would officially record. Their next BBC appearance was for the same program, recorded on June 11 and broadcast on June 15. The group again performed three songs: "Ask Me Why," "Besame Mucho," and "A Picture of You." "Ask Me Why" thus became the first Lennon/McCartney song to be broadcast on the radio. It was also drummer Pete Best's last radio appearance with the Beatles.

As the Beatles' career began taking off, their number of radio appearances increased, and by mid-1963, they were given their own radio program, *Pop Go the Beatles*, which was first broadcast on June 4. A second series of shows, broadcast in 1963 and 1964, was given the title *From Us to You*. The wide variety of songs performed reveals a lot about the Beatles' influences. On their records, they naturally preferred to record their own songs, but on the radio they could inject some more diversity. Many songs were favorites they played at their club gigs: songs by Chuck Berry ("Johnny B. Goode"), Little Richard ("Lucille"), Carl Perkins ("Lend Me Your Comb"), Ray Charles ("I Got a Woman"), Chan Romero

("The Hippy Hippy Shake"), the Everly Brothers ("So How Come [No One Loves Me]"), and Little Eva ("Keep Your Hands Off My Baby"). There were also more unusual choices, such as Ann-Margret's hit "I Just Don't Understand" and "The Honeymoon Song" from the 1959 movie *Honeymoon*. A highlight of the BBC performances is John's impassioned version of Arthur Alexander's "Soldier of Love," which they performed only once on the radio in 1963.

The last radio show the Beatles appeared on was the special *The Beatles Invite You to Take a Ticket to Ride*, which was broadcast on June 7, 1965; the Beatles' popularity was now such that they no longer needed exposure via radio programs. On the 20th anniversary of the Beatles' first radio appearance, the BBC put together a special program called *The Beatles at the Beeb*, which was broadcast in both the UK and US. The show not only included the songs, but also the between-songs chat, which usually involved the Beatles cracking jokes while the DJ tried to maintain some sense of order. Twelve years later, 56 songs were officially released on the album *Live at the BBC*, released on November 30, 1994, in the UK, where it topped the charts, and on December 6 in the US, where it reached No. 3.

Further reading: *The Beatles at the Beeb 1962-65* (Kevin Howlett)

The Night "Beatlemania" Was Invented

The Beatles' popularity had been growing consistently throughout 1963. But it wasn't until their appearance on *Val Parnell's Sunday Night at the London Palladium* on October 13, 1963, that the national media began to notice, and even gave the fan hysteria a name: Beatlemania.

The *Palladium* program was Britain's top-rated variety show, and was broadcast live from the Palladium theater in London's West End theater district. It was their most prestigious appearance up to that time, and a clear sign that the group had truly arrived. "There was nothing bigger in the world than making it to the Palladium," said Ringo, who also recalled how a friend of his mother's would encourage him as a young musician by saying, "See you on the Palladium, son. See your name in lights." Now it was about to come true.

The Beatles arrived earlier in the day for rehearsals, and as crowds gathered in the street outside, the group was forced to remain inside the theater all day. The screams of the fans outside were such that they could be heard inside the theater; a few even made it past the police barricades and got inside the auditorium during rehearsals, before they were caught and ushered out. Ringo later admitted he was so nervous he threw up before taking the stage.

The show's host, Bruce Forsyth, acknowledged that he knew who the evening's main draw was by having the Beatles make a brief appearance during the show's opening, then sending them offstage and telling the audience, "If you want to see them again, they'll be back in 42 minutes!" He continued to tease the audience when the Beatles returned, building up the suspense throughout his introduction, shouting to be heard over the rising screams: "Are you *ready*? Are you *steady*? Five, four, three, two, one, zero—*The Beatles!*" The group promptly burst into "From Me to You," and went on to play "I'll Get You," "She Loves You," and "Twist and Shout." Afterward, the house band played a jazzy version of "Twist and Shout" while the Beatles made their way up to the show's trademark revolving stage, where all the evening's guests gathered during the show's finale for a final wave to the audience. As Forsyth noted, "That night we could have gone round 50 times and those young fans would have kept screaming."

By the time the Beatles finished their set, 2,000 fans had gathered outside the Palladium. "Screaming girls launched themselves against the police, sending helmets flying and constables reeling," wrote the *Daily Herald*. "The pop group dived down the theatre steps into a car. The teenagers charged forward and the Beatles' car went off into Oxford Street chased by the crowd." The *Herald* was just one of the British dailies that wrote about the frenzy the Beatles had inspired and that national journalists had just begun to notice,

The Beatles rock the Palladium in front of thousands of screaming fans on October 13, 1963.

for scenes of similar frenzy had been common at Beatles shows around the country for some time. The *Daily Mirror* summed up the night's events in the single word "Beatlemania," and the phrase stuck.

Brian Epstein and his publicist Tony Barrow had spent months trying to drum up national media interest in the Beatles. Now, overnight, they went from soliciting coverage to fielding a deluge of offers, as Beatles stories dominated the daily newspapers for the rest of the year. An estimated 15 million people had watched the *Palladium* broadcast, and there was now a huge audience eager to know everything about the new stars. The *Palladium* appearance didn't just make the Beatles the top group in Britain; it made them a national phenomenon.

59 Rockin' the Royals

On the heels of their *Palladium* appearance came an even more prestigious show that vaulted the Beatles into the upper tiers of Britain's show business establishment. On November 4, 1963, they performed at the Royal Variety Show, a charity event held before members of Britain's royal family.

When the group were approached the previous August about the show, they considered turning it down, precisely because it was such an establishment gig, with its well-heeled, upper-class attendees hardly representative of their primary audience. But Brian Epstein convinced the Beatles that the publicity would be invaluable, and he was right. By remaining their cheeky, lovable selves in front of the aristocracy, the Beatles effortlessly charmed their way into the nation's hearts.

The show was held at the Prince of Wales Theatre on November 4, and would be subsequently broadcast on television on November 10. Queen Elizabeth, who was pregnant with her fourth child, did not attend; instead, the royals were represented

The Beatles rehearse before the Royal Variety Performance at the Prince of Wales Theatre.

by the queen's sister, Princess Margaret, Margaret's husband Lord Snowdon, and the Queen Mother. Three thousand fans waited outside to cheer the arrival of both the Beatles and the royals, as well as the other stars appearing that night.

The Beatles were seventh on the bill, out of a total of 19 acts, which also included Marlene Dietrich, Wilfrid Brambell (who would later co-star with the Beatles in *A Hard Day's Night*), and the pig puppets "Pinky and Perky." They hit an energetic note right from the start, playing "From Me to You" as the curtains swept open. They could hear themselves playing for a change, as the largely adult audience was not predisposed to screaming, making this an especially engaging performance to watch. Though the Beatles later admitted to being quite nervous, they covered it well, Paul offering a friendly "Good evening—how are ya? All right?" after the first song. The group next performed "She Loves You," their biggest hit at that time, then, in a nod to their more refined audience, "Till There Was You," Paul announcing it as a song that had also been recorded "by our favorite American group—Sophie Tucker," a rather unfortunate reference to Tucker's size, but which nonetheless provoked some laughter.

They saved the best for last. "For our last number, I'd like to ask your help," John announced, then paused for effect. "Will the people in the cheaper seats clap your hands? And the rest of you, if you'll just rattle your jewelry!" John had teased Brian about the remark before the show, joking that he would ask the audience to "rattle their fucking jewelry," which caused his ever-scrupulous manager to blanche. But it was simply a case of John having a little fun at his manager's expense; the John Lennon of 1963 would never have jeopardized his career by making such an outrageous comment.

And without the expletive, the "rattle your jewelry" line struck just the right note, enough of a tease to be funny without being disrespectful, and it generated good-natured applause and laughter. The band finished their set with "Twist and Shout," then bowed to the audience, and the royal box, before leaving the stage.

The reviews were unanimously positive. Even the Queen Mother gave them the royal seal of approval, saying: "They are so fresh and vital. I simply adore them." The *Daily Mirror's* review, simply entitled "Yeah! Yeah! Yeah!," fully captured the giddy, innocent spirits of the time: "You have to be a real sour square not to love the nutty, noisy, happy, handsome Beatles. If they don't sweep your blues away—brother, you're a lost cause. If they don't put a beat in your feet—sister, you're not living. How refreshing to see these rumbustious young Beatles take a middle-aged Royal Variety performance by the scruff of their necks and have them Beatling like teenagers…. They're young, new. They're high-spirited, cheerful. What a change from the self-pitying moaners, crooning their lovelorn tunes from the tortured shallows of lukewarm hearts. The Beatles are whacky. They wear their hair like a mop—but it's WASHED, it's super clean. So is their fresh young act. They don't have to rely on off-colour jokes about homos for their fun." It was the moment when the Beatles became an indelible part of British culture.

Please Please Me: The Debut Album

As the "Please Please Me" single began climbing the charts in early 1963, an album was required to take advantage of the Beatles' newfound success. The band was becoming increasingly busy, having begun their first national tour (opening for Helen Shapiro) on February 2. But there was no time to waste, and on their day off, on February 11, the Beatles were hustled into Abbey Road to record their debut album.

Both sides of the "Love Me Do" and "Please Please Me" singles would appear on the record, meaning the group only needed to record another 10 tracks, which they did, in one marathon 10-hour session. Producer George Martin had contemplated recording the band live at the Cavern, or perhaps live in the studio, before an invited audience, the underlying idea being to try to capture the intensity that the Beatles generated in concert. In the end, there was no recording at the Cavern, and no invited audience, but *Please Please Me* did feature the kind of setlist that was typical of what you might hear at the Cavern.

The album gets off to a fantastic start with one of the band's best-ever rockers, "I Saw Her Standing There," counted off by Paul with an enthusiastic "One, two, three, *four!*" It's a clear demonstration of how the Beatles were able to absorb the influences of rock 'n' roll, and then create something uniquely their own. And it's a song that remains in Paul's concert setlist to this day. Despite its lovelorn title, "Misery" is a brisk pop number with appealing harmonies. On "Anna," the first of the album's six cover songs (originally performed by Arthur Alexander), John stakes his claim as the Beatles' most expressive vocalist. George chimes in next with the upbeat "Chains" (originally released by girl group the Cookies), followed by Ringo's spirited take on "Boys" (also originally recorded by a girl group, in this case the Shirelles).

The songs from the singles followed next: "Ask Me Why," "Please Please Me," "Love Me Do," "P.S. I Love You." Then another Shirelles cover, with John on lead, crooning through "Baby It's You." Unusually, George was given another lead vocal on "Do You Want to Know a Secret," something that wouldn't happen again until the *Help!* album; it's not the strongest song, or the strongest vocal, but is somehow all the more endearing because of that.

Perhaps the oddest song choice on the record is the cover of Lenny Welch's "A Taste of Honey," though the dramatic ballad does give Paul a chance to indulge himself on lead vocal. "There's a Place" is perhaps the most interesting track, hinting as it does at introspection, a theme that John in particular would return to in his future work. And "Twist and Shout" brought the album to an exhilarating close, featuring one of John's best-ever vocal performances.

The album's title, *Please Please Me*, was an obvious reference to the Beatles' recent hit (and a subhead on the cover added the

"Best Of" Beatles

There have been numerous Beatles compilations released since the group's breakup. Many have been compiled around a theme: *Rock 'n' Roll* (1976), *Love Songs* (1977), *The Beatles Ballads* (1980), or *Reel Music* (1982), a collection of songs featured in the Beatles' movies. The UK *Rarities* (1978) just featured non-album tracks, while the US *Rarities* (1980) had entirely different songs.

The most successful compilations before the 1990s were the 1973 compilations *1962-1966* and *1967-1970* double-album sets. These collections were a combination of greatest hits and popular album tracks; they've come to be known as the "Red" and "Blue" albums, respectively, because the *1962-1966* set came in a red-bordered package and *1967-1970* came in a blue one. The covers featured the picture from the *Please Please Me* album, with the group looking down from the stairwell at EMI headquarters, and a later shot of the band re-creating the pose at the end of the '60s. Red and Blue went No. 3 and No. 1, respectively, in the US, No. 3 and No. 2 in the UK.

At time of writing, the most recent compilation is the digital-only *Tomorrow Never Knows* (2012), billed as a collection of the Beatles' "most influential rock songs," perhaps a wildly subjective description for songs like "It's All Too Much" and "Savoy Truffle."

line "with Love Me Do and 12 other songs"). More thought was put into the cover shot, which featured the Beatles grinning down from the staircase in EMI House in Manchester Square. To those unaware of the location, the shot appeared to show the group posing in the stairwell of an apartment building. "No one seen in the Top Twenty since Tommy Steele had made so overt a declaration of being working class," Philip Norman noted in his Beatles biography *Shout!*

Please Please Me was released on March 22, 1963 (in mono; the stereo album followed on April 26). By May 9, it was at the top of the UK charts, where it stayed for an astonishing 30 weeks, until it was replaced by the group's second album, *With The Beatles*. The album still sounds fresh today, a sturdy collection of songs in the Beatles' repertoire at the time they became stars, with a few tantalizing hints of what lay ahead.

61 Turn Me On

When Paul admitted to the media in 1967 that he'd taken LSD, it was headline news around the world. What no one knew at the time was that the loveable Mop Tops had been using drugs for years.

The first drugs the Beatles indulged in were cigarettes and alcohol—perfectly legal for adults, though the Beatles admitted they began drinking and smoking well before they were of legal age. They began using harder drugs in Hamburg, when they took speed, in the form of Preludin, a diet pill, to help maintain the stamina to play all night, enhancing the effect by drinking alcohol. It's been said that John had previously experimented with Benzedrine strips, which British writer Royston Ellis showed him how to extract from a Vicks Inhaler. "I've always needed a drug to survive," John later told *Rolling Stone*. "I always had more of everything because I'm more crazy probably."

While the Beatles were said to have been introduced to marijuana by Bob Dylan, they'd actually smoked it before. In the *Anthology* book, George said the Beatles had first smoked it in Liverpool, "and we all learnt to do the Twist that night." But they didn't become regular smokers of the drug until meeting Bob, on August 28, 1964, when he came to their hotel after a show. A "crazy party," resulted, in Paul's words, after Bob broke out the weed. "It was fabulous," Ringo remembered. "I laughed and I laughed and I laughed." Paul thought he'd found the meaning of life while on the drug, and wrote it down on a piece of paper. When he read what he'd written the next day, he was surprised to find the single sentence: "There are seven levels."

The Beatles enjoyed pot's relaxing effects, though in general they didn't take drugs while recording, finding that it hindered their performance. They didn't feel the same about their film work though, and were routinely "smoking marijuana for breakfast" in John's recollection while they were filming *Help!* in 1965.

That same year, John and George were introduced to LSD, which was legal at the time. It had been slipped into their after-dinner coffee at a party one night, but didn't take effect until they were out at a club later in the evening (accompanied by George's girlfriend Pattie and John's wife Cynthia, who'd also been "dosed"). "Suddenly I had the most incredible feeling come over me," George recalled. "It was something like a very concentrated version of the best feeling I'd ever had in my whole life." John's perception was somewhat different: "We were just insane. We were out of our heads." Ringo was the next to take it, and finally Paul. "I must have had a thousand trips," John later said. The other Beatles, especially George, like to emphasize the spiritual revelations they'd had on the drug.

Paul used cocaine around the time of *Sgt. Pepper*, though he soon stopped using it as he didn't like the "come down" after the drug wore off. John also used it, though he also called it a "dumb drug. Your whole concentration goes on getting the next fix." In 1968, John began using heroin, claiming it relieved the "pain" he experienced from criticism about his relationship with Yoko. He soon developed a fairly serious addiction to the drug; his song "Cold Turkey" describes the torment of withdrawal. He wouldn't be fully free of the drug's grip until 1972.

But ironically, it was marijuana John was busted for, though he always insisted that the drugs had been planted. He'd been informed that the police were going to raid his residence at the time (a London flat owned by Ringo), so he and Yoko had made sure to thoroughly clean the place. Nonetheless, when the police arrived on October 18, 1968, about half an ounce of the drug was found in various locations around the flat (including a binoculars case). John denied the pot was his, but pleaded guilty and paid a fine to settle the case quickly; he was also afraid that if Yoko was charged, she would be deported. This drug conviction would cause him great problems with US immigration in the 1970s.

George was the only other Beatle busted during the '60s. On March 12, 1969, the same police officer who'd busted John, the infamous Sgt. Norman Pilcher, arrived at George's house in Esher, finding a piece of hashish in a shoe; George later said it had been planted ("I'm a tidy man. I keep my socks in the sock drawer and stash in the stash box"). But he also pled guilty to the offense and paid a small fine.

For the most part, the Beatles' drug use was recreational, and they tended to play down any influence it may have had in their work. But there were drug references in some of their songs, such as the phrase "turn me on" in "She's a Woman," and "I'd love to turn you on" in "A Day In the Life." "Doctor Robert" was based on a real life doctor who gave amphetamine-laced "vitamin shots" to his celebrity clientele. Paul has described "Got to Get You Into My Life" as an "ode to pot."

In his last major interview, John said he'd mostly stopped using drugs, though he still smoked cigarettes. The other Beatles eventually quit smoking, and in the late '80s, Ringo went through rehab to become clean and sober. Paul remained an unrepentant pot smoker, busted at least five times for the drug over the years. But in 2012 he announced he was quitting pot for the sake of his youngest daughter, Beatrice, deciding that, at age 69, "I smoked my share."

62 With The Beatles: A Pure Pop Delight

The *Please Please Me* album drew on songs already in the band's repertoire. They prepared their second album in the wake of their first flush of success, when the band was full of excitement at their ever-growing fame. As a result, *With The Beatles* has a giddy enthusiasm throughout, evident from the opening notes of the joyous "It Won't Be Long," followed by John's smoldering "All I've Got to Do" (influenced by Smokey Robinson and the Miracles), and then the buoyant drive of Paul's "All My Loving"—a killer opening trio.

The high standard is pretty much maintained throughout, only slipping with "Little Child" and "Hold Me Tight," the former a slight piece of pop, the latter suffering from a surprisingly subpar vocal from Paul. But the album also has the delightfully energetic "I Wanna Be Your Man" (with Ringo on lead vocals), and features George's debut as a songwriter with "Don't Bother Me," one of his three vocal leads (the others are covers of the Cookies' "Devil in Her Heart" and a "Roll Over Beethoven" that rocks even harder than the Chuck Berry original). John in particular shines on his cover songs, making the Marvelettes' "Please Mr. Postman" a desperate cry from the heart, and equally emotive on the simmering "You Really Got a Hold On Me" (originally by Smokey Robinson and the Miracles). And following the restless, bittersweet "Not a Second Time," the album comes to a forceful close with a raging version of Barrett Strong's "Money," with another impressive lead vocal from John.

With The Beatles was released in the UK on November 22, 1963, and easily replaced *Please Please Me* at the top of the album charts. The cover was a striking black-and-white shot taken by Robert Freeman, featuring the Beatles' faces in half-shadow. It's been suggested that the look was inspired by Astrid Kirchherr's arty Hamburg photographs, a notion Freeman dismissed in an interview with me as "Absolutely rubbish! I never saw any photographs of the Beatles beforehand; I never want to see any pictures of anybody I have to photograph 'cause I don't want preconceived ideas." Instead, Freeman got the idea from a picture of three graphic designers he'd taken the previous year (which can be seen in his book *The Beatles: A Private View*). "It was a big leap for them to go from [the cover art of] *Please Please Me* to *With The Beatles*," he says. "And I think *With The Beatles* stamped an image for them that I sustained for over three years. I went for a neutral look. Not gloomy, not provocative, not pretentious, just straightforward. I couldn't have one of them smiling, or all of them smiling. I just went for a kind of relaxed, natural look." Freeman had wanted the shot to fill the entire record cover, with no band name or title, but that idea was considered too radical for Parlophone. The cover image has been much parodied (by the Residents and Genesis, to name just two acts), and Freeman went on to photograph covers for the next four UK Beatles albums.

The other notable thing about *With The Beatles* is how seriously it was taken by the critics, who tended to dismiss pop music as kid stuff. In a December 27, 1963, article in *The Times*, William Mann hailed John and Paul as "the outstanding composers of 1963," even as he praised compositional skills they didn't realize they had, as when he wrote: "One gets the impression that they think simultaneously of harmony and melody, so firmly are the major tonic sevenths and ninths built into their tunes, and the flat submediant key switches, so natural is the Aeolian cadence at the end of 'Not a Second Time' (the chord progression which ends Mahler's *Song of the Earth*)." (Asked about Aeolian cadences in one of his final interviews in 1980, John said, "To this day I don't have *any* idea what they are. They sound like exotic birds.") It was part of a progression that saw the Beatles moving from being mere pop stars to becoming artists. As Mann summed it up in the closing line of his story, "They have brought a distinctive and exhilarating flavor into a genre of music that was in danger of ceasing to be music at all."

Further reading: *The Beatles: A Private View* (Robert Freeman)

63 Fabs On Film No. 6: What's Happening

What's Happening! The Beatles in the USA was the first documentary film about the Beatles, and expertly captured the vibrant energy surrounding the group's first visit to America.

The film was made by the legendary documentary team of Albert and David Maysles. Two hours before the Beatles were due to arrive at John F. Kennedy International Airport on February 7, 1964, the brothers received a call from Britain's Granada television network asking if they'd be interested in filming the Beatles for an upcoming television program. The two hustled over to the airport and remained by the group's side throughout their trip, in New York, Washington, D.C., and Miami.

The resulting film is a wonderfully evocative portrait of what the Beatles were like out of the spotlight, even as they shamelessly perform for the camera—but only because they're having such a good time. They're clearly thrilled as they ride around Manhattan in a limo, listening to news about themselves being broadcast over the transistor radios they're carrying. They clown around for the newsmen on the train taking them to and from Washington, George donning a porter's coat and pretending to serve drinks, Ringo loading himself down with cameras and staggering down the aisles. They wave from their hotel balcony in Miami at the shrieking fans below who are writing the name of their favorite Beatle in the sand. The sequence where they're hanging out at the Peppermint Lounge in the company of WINS DJ Murray Kaufman (whose constant catchphrase "We're what's happening, baby!" gave the film its title), looks exactly like the scene when the Beatles visit a nightclub in *A Hard Day's Night*.

There's no better record of the initial blast of Beatlemania that America experienced in February 1964. The Beatles are upbeat and energized by what they're experiencing; everything's new, fresh, and fun, and they're clearly having the time of their lives. The Maysles technique was to stay in the background filming, so there are no voiceovers or any Q&A sessions delivered to the camera. It was pure *cinéma vérité*, with the Maysles not attempting to set up any encounters, but simply filming events as they unfolded.

The first cut of what was then called *Yeah! Yeah! Yeah! The Beatles in New York*, was 36 minutes, and aired on Granada TV on February 12, while the Beatles were still in America; demand was such that it was rescreened the following night. A longer, 45-minute cut aired in America on CBS on November 13, 1964, with the film retitled *What's Happening! The Beatles in the USA* (as the film's first title indicates, the shorter cut had none of the Miami footage).

Neither the 36- or 45-minute edit has been officially released. When Apple Corp. later bought the rights to the film, they incorporated the Maysles' footage in their own documentary, *The First US Visit*, first released on video in 1991. *The First US Visit* also included the Beatles' performances on *The Ed Sullivan Show* and the Washington, D.C., concert.

Albert Maysles (David died of a stroke in 1987) wasn't entirely happy with the new edit, in part because of what was lost. Unable to film the Beatles during their first *Ed Sullivan* appearance due to union regulations, the Maysles wandered into a nearby apartment building and ended up filming a family watching the show, the two teenage girls focusing intently on the TV screen; it's a moment that nicely conveys the impact the Beatles were having on the average person.

What's Happening is occasionally screened at film festivals. *The First US Visit* was released on DVD in 2004, and that's the version to get, as it includes a "making of" feature with additional footage. The Maysles went on to film *Gimme Shelter*, the documentary about the Rolling Stones' 1969 tour that culminated in the Altamont concert (capturing the moment when a man in the audience was stabbed to death), and the cult favorite *Grey Gardens*, about the eccentric aunt and cousin of Jackie Onassis. In 2011, Albert Maysles released *The Love We Make*, a documentary about Paul's involvement in The Concert for New York, held in the wake of the September 11 attacks.

64 The Debut of the Fab Four Lineup

The day Pete Best was dismissed from the Beatles, August 16, 1962, the band had a show scheduled that evening in Chester. Though he'd just been fired, Pete was asked to remain with the group until Ringo's arrival, and he initially agreed. But once the shock of being sacked had worn off, he unsurprisingly declined to help out his former bandmates and didn't turn up for any of the gigs scheduled on August 16 and 17. Instead, Johnny Hutchinson, a drummer with Liverpool band the Big Three, sat in on drums for these dates.

Ringo had been finishing up the week with Rory Storm and the Hurricanes at a Butlin's holiday camp in Skegness, on England's Lincolnshire coast, and finally arrived on August 18 to play his first official date with the Beatles at a Horticultural Society Dance held at Hulme Hall in the village of Port Sunlight. The Beatles would ultimately play four shows at the venue, drawing crowds of around 500.

The band's last appearance at Hulme Hall, on October 27, 1962, was also the occasion for another first—the Beatles' first radio interview. Before their show that evening, the band recorded a short interview for *Sunday Spin*, a program broadcast via closed-circuit radio for the patients at the Cleaver and Clatterbridge hospitals, two facilities in the area. The seven-minute interview later appeared on a bonus flexi-disc provided with first-edition copies of Mark Lewisohn's *The Beatles Live!*

I Want to Tell You: George's Songwriting

It wasn't easy for an aspiring songwriter to work in the shadow of the Lennon/McCartney team. But George persevered, and eventually wrote a few classics of his own.

George was initially happy to leave the songwriting to John and Paul; after all, he still got to do his share of singing. But once the Beatles became recording artists, George thought he would try his hand at songwriting as well. His status as "the quiet Beatle" seemed to be confirmed by the title of his first song to appear on

The Tribute Single

Since John's murder, numerous artists have recorded songs in tribute to him. George was one of the first to release a tribute song, the only record that would have the involvement of all the other Beatles.

"All Those Years Ago" was originally written by George for Ringo, and an early version was recorded, with Ringo on drums and vocals, at George's home studio at Friar Park in November 1980. But Ringo was unhappy with the track, and it wasn't used. After John's death, George decided to rework the song as a tribute to his former bandmate, and recorded a new vocal. Paul and his wife Linda then added backing vocals to the track, also recorded at Friar Park.

The up-tempo number dropped in numerous references to John's songs, and labeled his killer as "the devil's best friend." The reaction to "All Those Years Ago" was mixed—some found the tune improbably upbeat for a tribute song—but fans loved the accompanying video, which featured an array of Beatles-related film clips, which were exciting to see in those pre-YouTube days. The single was released on May 11, 1981, in the US, where it just missed the top spot, peaking at No. 2. The UK release came on May 15, with the single only reaching No. 13. The song was also included on George's album *Somewhere in England*.

George smokes a cigarette before going on stage at the Finsbury Park Astoria in London. (AP Images)

a record, "Don't Bother Me," which was on *With The Beatles*. He wouldn't make another songwriting contribution to an album until *Help!*, which featured "I Need You" and "You Like Me Too Much" (though he always sang lead on at least one track on each Beatles album). His work really began to blossom on *Rubber Soul*, as he gradually revealed himself to be a thoughtful, if occasionally pessimistic, songwriter. Songs like "Think For Yourself" (*Rubber Soul*), "Taxman" (*Revolver*), and "Piggies" (*The Beatles*) each evinced no small measure of bitterness, and his views on love were often just as cynical ("If I Needed Someone" from *Rubber Soul*, "I Want to Tell You" from *Revolver*). Making it all the more interesting that one of his all-time classic songs is the decidedly romantic "Something," which appeared on *Abbey Road*; his other most notable Beatles composition, "Here Comes the Sun," is on the same album.

George's interest in Eastern music also had an impact on Lennon/McCartney songs as well as his own. He played the sitar on John's "Norwegian Wood" (*Rubber Soul*), thus introducing the instrument to rock music. And the use of Eastern instruments on George's songs like "Love You To," "Within You Without You," and "The Inner Light" added a distinctive flavor to the Beatles' music. That George's first post-Beatles solo album, 1970's *All Things Must Pass*, was a triple-album set makes the case that his songwriting talents were rather underutilized during the Beatle era.

The King

Lonnie Donegan's music influenced the Beatles to pick up instruments and start their own bands. But it was Elvis Presley who made them determined to play rock 'n' roll. As John famously put it, "Before Elvis, there was nothing."

Though Elvis made his first recordings in 1954 for Sun Records, those releases weren't readily available in Britain. It wasn't until Elvis had signed with a major label, RCA, and released "Heartbreak Hotel" in 1956 that the Beatles discovered him.

At first, they weren't sure what to expect. "'Heartbreak Hotel' seemed a corny title," said John. "But then, when I heard it, it was the end for me." Paul recalled being knocked out simply by seeing a picture of Presley in an ad. "Elvis looked so great," he said. "'That's him, that's him—the Messiah has arrived.' Elvis made a huge impression on us."

From the days of the Quarrymen on, there were always Elvis songs in the set, "Blue Moon of Kentucky," "All Shook Up," "Hound Dog," and "Jailhouse Rock" among them. The Beatles were primarily fans of Elvis' '50s rock 'n' roll, prior to his enlisting in the army in 1958. "I went off Elvis after he left the army," Paul said. "I felt they tamed him too much." John was typically blunt after Elvis' death in 1977, stating, "Elvis died when he went in the army." But according to Mark Lewisohn's *The Beatles Live*, they still performed some of Elvis' post-army songs: "Wooden Heart" and "Wild in the Country." They never recorded an Elvis song for one of their albums, but did perform two Elvis songs during their radio appearances, "That's All Right" and "I'm Gonna Sit Right Down and Cry (Over You)" (both appear on *Live at the BBC*).

When the Beatles made their first appearance on *The Ed Sullivan Show* in 1964, they were welcomed by a telegram sent by Elvis and his manager. They hoped to meet Elvis during their first US tour that summer, but the closest they came was when Paul spoke with Elvis over the phone. A meeting was finally set up the following year during the Beatles' second American tour, when they would be staying in Los Angeles for a few days. After intense negotiations, it was arranged that the Beatles would come to Elvis' home in Bel Air on the night of August 27, 1965.

George later admitted they got stoned on the way over, in part because of nerves; "We were nervous as hell," John agreed. But after some initial awkwardness on finally coming face to face with their idol, everyone relaxed, with John and Paul spending the most time talking to Elvis, Ringo playing pool with Elvis' friends, and George sharing a joint with another of Elvis' entourage outside by the swimming pool. There are different accounts as to whether the Beatles and Elvis jammed together. John says they did, but the other Beatles say no.

In the *Anthology* documentary, the Beatles still sound impressed by the encounter, recalling small details like seeing the remote control Elvis had for his TV, a device they'd never seen before. But no lasting bond formed between the two acts. For all their admiration, the Beatles found the atmosphere around Elvis somewhat strange; Ringo described Elvis as being surrounded by "sycophants." For his part, Elvis later described the Beatles as "kind of anti-American" during his impromptu meeting with President Richard Nixon on December 21, 1970 (evidently unaware that the Beatles had broken up the previous April).

Ringo and George later saw Elvis perform live during the '70s, by which time he'd added Beatles songs to his set, including "Something" and a medley of "Yesterday" and "Hey Jude." And if the Beatles didn't record any of Elvis' songs, the solo Beatles did. Ringo recorded "Blue Christmas" for *I Wanna Be Santa Claus* (1999). Paul recorded many Elvis songs: "That's All Right" and "Just Because" for *Choba B CCCP* (1988); "It's Now or Never" for *The Last Temptation of Elvis* (1990); "All Shook Up," "I Got Stung," and "Party" for *Run Devil Run* (1999); and "That's All Right" for the documentary *Good Rockin' Tonight: The Legacy of Sun Records* (2000), recording with Elvis' original side musicians, Scotty Moore and DJ Fontana.

And Elvis and the Beatles did play together in one sense. Paul's wife Linda had given him a very special present, a bass guitar previously owned by Bill Black, another of Elvis' side musicians. Paul played the bass on the Beatles' reunion singles, "Free as a Bird" and "Real Love."

67 Bob and the Beatles

The Beatles' early musical influences were easy to spot—British skiffle performers like Lonnie Donegan, American rock 'n' rollers like Elvis and Little Richard, and Motown and girl group acts as well. But they continued to absorb influences throughout their career, and in the 1960s their most important influence was Bob Dylan.

Mike McCartney takes credit for introducing his brother Paul to Bob's music; the other Beatles first heard him while they were in Paris in January 1964, after they picked up a copy of *The Freewheelin' Bob Dylan*; "We all went potty about Dylan," John recalled. Bob was likewise intrigued by their music, and during the Beatles' first American tour, journalist Al Aronowitz facilitated a meeting between the two, bringing Bob to the Beatles' hotel suite to meet them on August 28, 1964. It's been said Bob introduced the group to marijuana that night, though in fact the Beatles had tried it before. Bob even thought "I Want to Hold Your Hand" was a drug song, mishearing the line "I can't hide" as "I get high."

After that, the Beatles regularly gave Bob a plug in their interviews. The British music paper *New Musical Express* even credits them with boosting Bob's career in Britain, writing, "It was from the lips of John, George, Paul and Ringo that most of those who are now his fans learned his name."

You can hear the influence of Bob's folky, introspective style on such songs as "I'm a Loser," "You've Got to Hide Your Love Away," and "Norwegian Wood"; John was also thinking of Bob's penchant for obscure wordplay when he wrote the lyrics of "I Am the Walrus." Bob's wardrobe soon revealed a British influence, as he began to wear the kind of clothes found in such "Swinging London" fashion districts as Carnaby Street, and he even wore the same kind of pointy boots the Beatles had made popular. But the greater influence was musical; his increasing interest in rock music, spurred in part by the Beatles, led Bob to "go electric" on his 1965 album *Bringing It All Back Home*. As John put it, "Our tastes in music, though not the same, cross somewhere—you can tell that if you listen to his latest single 'Subterranean Homesick Blues.'"

During Bob's visit to the UK in 1966, he was filmed riding in the back of a limo with John, shot by D.A. Pennebaker, who'd also filmed Bob's first UK tour in 1965 for the documentary *Dont Look Back*. The 1966 footage was for a new documentary called *Eat the Document*, which was never officially released, though the film has circulated on bootleg. In their scene, Bob and John appear to be under the influence of some kind of substance, given their rambling conversation; John later admitted being "nervous as shit" during the filming.

The Beatle that Bob would become closest to was George. The two co-wrote the song "I'd Have You Anytime," which appeared on George's album, *All Things Must Pass*; the album also included his cover of Bob's song "If Not For You." Bob was a guest performer at the Concert for Bangladesh benefit shows George organized that were held August 1, 1971, at Madison Square Garden. Bob had largely stopped doing personal appearances during this period, and though he'd turned up at rehearsal, up to the last minute George wasn't sure if he'd appear during the actual show. Bob's five-song set was considered a highlight of both concerts.

In 1988, Bob joined the Traveling Wilburys, the name George gave to the group of musicians he worked with in recording a B-side for his single "This Is Love," the other members being Jeff Lynne, Roy Orbison, and Tom Petty. The group had so much fun working together they decided to record an album, and *Traveling Wilburys Vol. 1* was released in October 1988. After Orbison's death, the remaining Wilburys recorded a second album, *Traveling Wilburys Vol. 3*, released in 1990.

John had a somewhat more contentious relationship with Bob. He name-checked Bob in a few of his songs, like the Beatles' "Yer Blues" and "God," the closing track on his 1970 *John Lennon/Plastic Ono Band* album where he lists the people and things he no longer believes in (including the Beatles), referring to Bob as "Zimmerman," his real last name. And when Bob became a born-again Christian in the late '70s, John satirized Bob's "You Gotta Serve Somebody" in the stinging rebuke "Serve Yourself" (released on the 1998 set *John Lennon Anthology*). Bob's 2012 album *Tempest* features the more measured tribute, "Roll On John."

68 Raw Meat

The so-called "butcher cover" for the Beatles' *Yesterday and Today* album is one of the most valuable US Beatles albums. A mint-condition stereo copy is worth $12,000. The reason for its rarity is that the cover photo of the Beatles holding broken dolls and slabs of raw meat provoked a controversy that led to the sleeve being withdrawn.

On March 25, 1966, the Beatles walked into the studio of photographer Robert Whitaker. Whitaker, born in the UK, was living in Australia when he met the Beatles during their tour of the country in 1964. Brian Epstein offered him a job, and Whitaker subsequently moved to the UK, photographing the Beatles and other acts that Epstein managed. Whitaker also toured with the Beatles and got to know them well.

For the March session, Whitaker wanted to do something different. He planned a triptych of photographs that would be his "personal comment on the mass adulation of the group and the illusory nature of stardom" entitled "A Somnambulant Adventure." The first photo, representing their "birth," had the Beatles holding a string of sausages in front of a young woman, the sausages symbolizing an umbilical cord. The third photo showed George hammering nails into the head of a smiling John, meant to emphasize the fact that the Beatles were flesh and blood, like anyone else.

But it was the photo that was meant to be the second in the series that would get the widest dissemination. This shot had the Beatles in white butcher's smocks, with broken dolls draped on their shoulders and hunks of meat in their laps, all four Beatles smiling, not looking at all like the jolly Mop Tops they'd once been.

John in particular liked the shot for that very reason: "I especially pushed for it to be an album cover, just to break the image," he said. Conversely, George said he thought it was "gross, and I also thought it was stupid." Whitaker himself hadn't wanted the "butcher" shot to be used out of context. But the shot was pulled out for special use nonetheless, and first appeared in ads in the UK music papers *New Musical Express* and *Disc and Music Echo*. *Disc* readers wrote in to complain about the photo, but that was nothing compared to what happened when the shot was chosen for the cover of *Yesterday and Today*, one of Capitol's hodgepodge albums that featured tracks from *Rubber Soul*, *Revolver*, and the single "Day

Tripper"/"We Can Work It Out." After 750,000 copies were sent out, reports from Capitol's sales team came back to headquarters: the cover was unacceptable.

An immediate recall went into effect, and Capitol's president issued a statement that read: "The original cover, created in England, was intended as a 'pop art' satire. However a sampling of public opinion in the United States indicates that the cover design is subject to misinterpretation. For this reason, and to avoid any possible controversy or undeserved harm to the Beatles' image or reputation, Capitol has chosen to withdraw the LP and substitute a more generally acceptable design." Once recalled, the original covers were destroyed, and new covers were prepared with an innocuous picture of the Beatles posed around a steamer trunk. To save time, in some cases the new picture was simply pasted over the butcher cover.

It's not known how many butcher covers escaped destruction, but pristine originals now command high prices on the collector's market. When it was realized that in some cases the steamer trunk shot was pasted over the butcher cover, people tried to peel their albums to reveal the butcher shot underneath; these covers are also valuable, though not as much as an original, or "first state," cover. John always defended the cover. When asked about it in an interview during the Beatles' summer tour of America in 1966 he called it "as relevant as Vietnam. If the public can accept something as cruel as the war, they can accept this cover."

Further reading: *The Beatles' Story on Capitol Records Part Two: The Albums* (Bruce Spizer), *The Unseen Beatles* (Bob Whitaker)

69 Happy Holidays!

Members of the Official Beatles Fan Club were especially excited when Christmas rolled around. Because during the holidays, each member received an exclusive recording by the Beatles made just for them.

As membership in the fan club began to climb in the fall of 1963, the Beatles' staff became overwhelmed with applications. Soon, complaints began coming in from people who had sent in their money but had yet to receive anything. Beatles publicist Tony Barrow suggested that sending everyone a special Christmas record would help make amends, serving as "a damage limitation job," in his words. Brian Epstein didn't agree, so Tony shrewdly took the idea to the Beatles, who found it a good suggestion, and they insisted to Brian that they do it.

The first Christmas record was recorded at the end of a recording session on October 17, 1963. Tony gave the Beatles a basic script, but the Beatles ad-libbed freely. The final, five-minute recording started out with a jokey version of "Good King Wenceslas," with each Beatle then delivering a short message thanking fans for their support, and wishing them a Happy Christmas (or "Happy Crimble" in Beatle-speak) before closing with an equally jokey version of "Rudolph the Red-Nosed Reindeer." The recording was pressed on a thin flexi-disc and sent out to fan club members; there was a first run of 30,000 copies, with a second pressing of 35,000.

The record was extremely popular, so the fan club sent out Christmas records for the next six years. The second record was recorded October 26, 1964, and followed a similar format as the previous year, opening and closing with a song, with each member delivering a short message in between; at four minutes, this was the shortest Christmas disc. The third record, recorded on November 8, 1965, was the last to have the song-message-song format, this time opening with an off-key rendition of "Yesterday." Over the six-and-a-half minute recording, there were frequent snatches of made-up songs, which gave John in particular the chance to show off his many goofy voices. There was also a send-up of protest music with a verse of "Auld Lang Syne" delivered in the fashion of Barry McGuire's hit of that year, "Eve of Destruction."

Now the Beatles began to get more elaborate with their Christmas records. The 1966 record, recorded on November 25, 1966, in the office of the Beatles' music publisher, Dick James, had a theme song, "Everywhere It's Christmas," with a series of skits showing how Christmas was being celebrated around the world. The record ran just over six-and-a-half minutes, and was packaged in a sleeve with a cover illustration provided by Paul. It was also the first two-sided fan club record.

The 1967 record, recorded on November 28, 1967, is my favorite. There's another theme song, "Christmas Time Is Here Again" (a version of the song appeared as a bonus track on the "Free as a Bird" single). Over the next six minutes was a sound collage that mixed in parodies of game shows, news programs, radio dramas, sing-alongs, and a special guest appearance by actor Victor Spinetti, who was heard tap dancing. The cover art was also a collage of portraits put together by John, Ringo, and John's son Julian.

It was the last Christmas record the Beatles worked on together. For the next two years, each Beatle recorded his section for the Christmas record separately. The 1968 record ran nearly eight minutes. Paul wrote a special song. John read an acerbic story about two balloons named "Jock and Yono," a thinly-veiled attack at the hostility John had received from some of his "beast friends" about his new relationship with Yoko. Ringo gave a brief greeting at the beginning and appeared in a short skit. George delivered a heartfelt message, introduced Beatle aide Mal Evans, and had special guest Tiny Tim sing a bit of "Nowhere Man."

The 1969 Christmas record ran over seven-and-a-half minutes and was mostly devoted to John and Yoko conversing together while walking around their home, Tittenhurst Park, in Ascot. Paul sings a short song, as does Ringo, who also manages to get in a plug for his latest film, *The Magic Christian.* George's message is only a few seconds. Bringing things full circle, during one of the John and Yoko sequences, John sings a short bit of "Good King Wenceslas," the song heard on the very first fan club record. The cover photograph was provided by Ringo; his son Zak drew the back-cover illustration.

The British fan club had released all seven of the Christmas records. In America, the fan club records were mailed out from 1964 to 1969 (though the record mailed out in 1964 to US fans actually featured the recording made for the 1963 UK fan club record). In 1970, all seven records were compiled on an album and mailed to fan club members; the UK version simply reproduced the sleeve of the first Christmas record on its cover, but the US version put together a great cover with individual pictures of each Beatle from 1963 to 1969.

The records are great fun to listen to, prime examples of the Beatles' playful and clever humor. But they have yet to be re-released officially.

Further reading: *The Beatles Christmas Book: Everywhere It's Christmas* (Scott "Belmo" Belmer, Garry Marsh)

70 Beatles For Sale: Marking Time

The first comment people generally make about this album is how tired and world-weary the Beatles look on the cover. Well, they certainly had reason to look that way. *Beatles For Sale* was released at the end of one of the most hectic years in the Beatles' careers: they'd toured nine countries, including two trips to America; made their first feature film; made numerous radio and TV appearances; and released a steady stream of records.

No wonder the well had run a bit dry. Though the *Hard Day's Night* album had featured all original material, on *Beatles For Sale* the group returned to the formula of their first two records, presenting a mix of originals and cover songs. The bleak mood of the cover shot initially continues on the record, as can be seen in the titles of the first three songs: "No Reply," "I'm a Loser," "Baby's in Black"—all primarily John's songs, and all indicative of how he was increasingly drawing on his own feelings in his songwriting. The album also has some of the band's most inspired covers, especially John's sizzling take on Chuck Berry's "Rock 'n' Roll Music," and Paul in his best Little Richard mode on "Kansas City" (which adds a bit of Richard's song "Hey Hey Hey Hey!" at the end); there are also some gorgeous harmonies on the cover of Dr. Feelgood's "Mr. Moonlight." Carl Perkins gets two nods; Ringo takes on "Honey Don't," while George gets to close the album with "Everybody's Trying to Be My Baby." Of the other originals, "Eight Days a Week" is the kind of pure pop the Beatles were doing effortlessly by 1964 (it became a No. 1 single in America), while Paul's lovely, delicate "I'll Follow the Sun" was written back in his pre-Beatle days. Not every track succeeds—"Every Little Thing" is rather labored—but there's more than enough good stuff here.

Beatles For Sale was released on December 4, 1964, and topped the charts. Despite that, it's become one of the more overlooked Beatles albums—which has probably less to do with the quality of the songs on the album, and more to do with the remarkable work the Beatles did on their subsequent albums.

71 The First Solo Releases

Paul was the first Beatle to work on an outside musical project, writing music for the British film *The Family Way*. Paul wrote two musical themes, and the tunes were then arranged by George Martin, who also produced the soundtrack, working with a group of studio musicians dubbed "The George Martin Orchestra." Paul's work was first released on a UK single, "Love in the Open Air"/"Theme from *The Family Way*," released on December 23, 1966 (the US single was released April 24, 1967, with a non-soundtrack recording on the B-side). The soundtrack, noting Paul's involvement prominently on the front cover, was released on January 6, 1967, in the UK, and June 12 in the US, but failed to chart. Paul himself did not appear on the recording, though he won an Ivor Novello award for Best Instrumental Theme.

John made a very brief appearance on the UK single "How I Won the War," released October 13, 1967, as a tie-in with the film of the same name, credited to "Musketeer Gripweed [John's character in the film] and the Third Troop." Aside from his spoken-word contribution, John didn't play on the record, or write the music.

So the first Beatle to release a true solo record was George, with *Wonderwall Music*, the soundtrack of the film *Wonderwall*, released on November 1, 1968, in the UK, December 2 in the US; it didn't chart in the UK, but did reach No. 49 in the US. The record was immediately overshadowed by John's first solo album, *Unfinished Music No. 1: Two Virgins*, released on November 11, 1968, in the UK, November 29 in the US. It failed to chart in either country, but became notorious for the cover's front and rear shots of John and Yoko Ono in the nude. John's first non-Beatles single was the exuberant chant "Give Peace a Chance," released on July 4, 1969, in the UK, reaching No. 2, and July 7 in the US, reaching No. 14. The single was credited to the Plastic Ono Band.

George's first solo single was "My Sweet Lord," released on November 23, 1970, in the US, and January 15, 1971, in the UK. The song was George's first solo No. 1, but he would eventually be sued for the song's musical similarity to the tune of "He's So Fine," by the Chiffons; George was ultimately found guilty of "subconscious plagiarism."

Ringo entered the solo realm in 1970 with *Sentimental Journey*, released in 1970 on March 27 in the UK, reaching No. 7, April 24 in the US, reaching No. 22. The album was a collection of standards Ringo recorded "for my mum," including such well-known tunes as "Night and Day," "Bye Bye Blackbird," and "Love Is a Many Splendored Thing," not to mention the title track. Ringo's first solo single was "Beaucoups of Blues," the title track of his second album, a collection of country songs recorded in Nashville. The single was released, in the US only, on October 5, 1970, reaching No. 87; the album reached No. 65 in the US, and failed to chart in the UK. Ringo's first single to be released in both the US and UK was "It Don't Come Easy" (written by Ringo, with help from George), which was released on April 9, 1971, in the UK, April 16 in the US, reaching No. 4 in both countries. The B-side, "Early 1970," is especially interesting as it reflects Ringo's feelings about the Beatles' breakup.

Paul's first true solo release came in 1970 with the *McCartney* album, released April 17 in the UK, reaching No. 2, April 20 in the US, where it topped the charts. The homespun album featured Paul playing all the instruments, with some help on backup vocals from his wife Linda. It was decidedly low key in comparison to the layered production on *Abbey Road*, but it did feature Paul's first solo classic, "Maybe I'm Amazed," which oddly wasn't released as a single (a live version was later released as a single in 1977). So Paul's first non-Beatle single was the light pop song "Another Day," released on February 19, 1971, in the UK, reaching No. 2, and February 22 in the US, reaching No. 5.

The Loyal Aides

There were two men who were always to be found by the Beatles' sides for most of their career: Neil Aspinall and Mal Evans.

Neil Aspinall was born in 1941 in Wales, where his mother had moved for the duration of World War II, after which the family moved back to Liverpool. He met Paul and George when they were all students at the Liverpool Institute high school. He later recounted his first meeting with George came when they shared a cigarette—ironic, considering both of them would later die of lung cancer.

When he left school, Neil studied to be an accountant, lodging at Pete Best's family home. Eventually, the Beatles asked if he would be their road manager, and he bought a used van for the purpose, charging the Beatles a pound a gig. When Pete was fired from the group, Neil vowed to quit too, but Pete generously told him he shouldn't; he knew the Beatles were going places. But there was an additional complication. Neil had become romantically involved with Pete's mother, and that same summer of 1962 she'd given birth to their son, Vincent "Roag" Best. It was agreed that if Neil continued to work for the Beatles it would be easier if he moved out of the Best's home.

As the Beatles' career began to take off, there was too much work for Neil to handle on his own, so Mal Evans was hired to help out. Mal was born in 1935 and worked as a telephone engineer. He'd wandered into the Cavern on his lunch breaks, and quickly became a regular. The Cavern's owner eventually asked the 6'6" Mal if he'd be interested in working at the club as a bouncer; Mal agreed. It was his size that helped him land the job with the Beatles; not only was he strong enough to haul gear, he could also serve as a bodyguard.

Both men became the Beatles' most trusted aides. They traveled with them on tour, were with them in the studio, and were more or less permanently on call in case a Beatle needed anything. In the studio, they made occasional contributions to different recordings. Neil played tamboura on "Within You Without You" and harmonica on "Being for the Benefit of Mr. Kite"; Mal played keyboards on "You Won't See Me" and harmonica on "Mr. Kite." He set off the alarm clock you hear going on in "A Day In the Life," and can be seen banging on an anvil during "Maxwell's Silver Hammer" in the film *Let It Be.* He also had a small part in *Help!* as a channel swimmer and briefly appeared in *Magical Mystery Tour.*

Both men also worked at Apple Corp. Neil was general manager; Mal was briefly head of Apple Records before being replaced by Ron Kass, and continued to work at Apple as a personal assistant to the Beatles. Mal also brought the Iveys (later renamed Badfinger) to the label and produced some of their records; he also produced Apple artist Jackie Lomax.

Allen Klein tried to have Neil and Mal fired during his cost-cutting regime at Apple, but the Beatles refused; they simply couldn't do without them. After the breakup, Neil stayed on at Apple, eventually becoming managing director. Mal continued working for the Beatles as solo artists, co-writing "You and Me (Babe)" with George for Ringo's 1973 album *Ringo*, and co-writing "Lonely Man" for Splinter, who recorded for George's label Dark Horse. He'd separated from his wife, and at the end of 1975 was living in Los Angeles, preparing to produce Natural Gas (formed by Joey Molland of Badfinger). But on the night of January 5, 1976, Mal became intoxicated and began waving a gun around, leading to his girlfriend calling the police, who ended up shooting him dead.

Neil's life was much less dramatic, though the stress of working for the Beatles did lead to his having more than one heart attack. Once the Beatles' business problems cleared up, he oversaw release of the group's albums on CD in the '90s and into the 21st century, as well as the reissue of the Apple catalogue and other film projects. His long-planned documentary on the Beatles, *The Long and Winding Road*, ultimately led to the *Anthology* project. The last major Beatles project he worked on was the Cirque de Soleil *Love* show, which he executive produced. He retired from Apple in 2007. He died the following year of lung cancer on March 24, 2008.

Neil proved to be the Beatles' best secret keeper, rarely giving interviews, and one of the very few Beatles associates to not write a book about them. Though it's a shame that after his retirement he couldn't have committed a few of his memories to print.

73 The Turning Point

George was the first Beatle to arrive back in England from the Beatles' first engagement in Hamburg in 1960, having been deported in mid-November. Paul and Pete Best were deported at the beginning of December, with John following on about a week and a half later. Stuart Sutcliffe didn't return until the next year, choosing to stay with Astrid Kirchherr. Everyone was discouraged at how the trip had ended; neither John, Paul, or Pete even contacted George to let him know they were back in town.

Eventually, everyone got back in touch, and tried to get the band going again. While hanging out at the Jacaranda coffee bar one day, they met Bob Wooler, who worked as an emcee and DJ at local shows. Wooler spoke to a local promoter, Brian Kelly, on their behalf and managed to get them a booking at a show Kelly was promoting at Litherland Town Hall, a north Liverpool suburb, on December 27, 1960.

Though the band had played two shows in the previous week, with Chas Newby (whom Pete knew from his previous group, the Blackjacks) on bass, this was the show that really opened Liverpool's eyes to what an impressive band the Beatles had become. The endless hours they'd spent on stage in Hamburg had transformed them into a powerhouse act. When the Beatles opened their set with Little Richard's "Long Tall Sally," the attendees spontaneously rushed to the stage. "You had this mass of boys and girls just standing there watching the act, shouting and screaming for more," Pete later recalled. The Beatles were loud, raucous, and wild; instead of emulating British bands like the Shadows, who wore matching suits and neatly stepped from side to side in synchronization while they played, the Beatles wore leather suits and worked up a fierce sweat as they rocked through their numbers. Those lucky enough to be there were mesmerized and enthralled.

It was the show that changed everything for the Beatles. After their set, Brian Kelly placed a bouncer at their dressing room door, so that he could book them for future shows before any other promoter could get to them. In 1960, they'd played less than a month's worth of shows in Liverpool; now they were playing shows on a near daily basis. The Litherland Town Hall show was a true turning point for the band. From this moment on, the Beatles began their ascendancy to worldwide fame.

74. A Passage to India

The Beatles' interest in all things Indian led to sitars and other Eastern instruments being used in rock music. And when they took up meditation, they helped popularize the practice in the West.

George was the Beatle who first looked east. He was fascinated by the Indian instruments the musicians played in a restaurant scene in the film *Help!*, one of which was a sitar. He was soon trying to figure out how to play the instrument himself, and used it to provide some sophisticated accents to "Norwegian Wood" (which appeared on *Rubber Soul*). It was the first Western pop song to make use of the instrument, after which other musicians began adding sitar to their songs, most notably Brian Jones on the Rolling Stones' 1966 hit "Paint It Black." A number—but not all—of George's subsequent Beatles songs also used Indian instruments. In the fall of 1966, he traveled to India to take sitar lessons from renowned musician Ravi Shankar.

During location shooting in the Bahamas for *Help!*, a man George later learned was Swami Vishnu Devananda approached the Beatles and gave them each a copy of his book *The Illustrated Book of Yoga*. The time George and his wife Pattie spent in India also introduced them to Eastern philosophies, and Pattie joined the Spiritual Regeneration movement in Britain as a result. It was she who told George about an appearance the group's leader, the Maharishi Mahesh Yogi, was going to make in London at the Park Lane Hilton on August 24, 1967; George promptly contacted the other Beatles and urged them to attend. They were all impressed enough to head off to Wales the next day to attend a seminar the Maharishi was holding in Bangor, though their stay was interrupted when Brian Epstein's death was announced on August 27. By then they'd already given press conferences stating their allegiance to the Maharishi and announced they were giving up hallucinogenic drugs.

The following February, the Beatles and their wives (and in Paul's case, his girlfriend) went to the Maharishi's ashram in Rishikesh, on the banks of the Ganges River, to take a training course in meditation. They spent their days alternately meditating and attending lectures. It was a relaxing period, and the Beatles wrote a number of songs while in India, many of which ended up on their next album, including "Ob-La-Di, Ob-La-Da," "I Will," "The Continuing Story of Bungalow Bill" (loosely based on a fellow student who was also a big-game hunter), and "Dear Prudence," written for another fellow student, Mia Farrow's sister (Mike Love of the Beach Boys and Donovan were also students at the ashram). Oddly, despite the relaxed environment, John also wrote two of his more agonized songs in India, "Yer Blues" and "I'm So Tired."

Ringo, whose stomach was sensitive to spicy foods, only stayed at the ashram 10 days before deciding to go home. Paul returned to London at the end of March. And John and George left on April

George Harrison, Maharishi Mahesh Yogi, and John Lennon at a UNICEF gala in Paris in December 1967.

12, amid some controversy. A rumor spread that the Maharishi was trying to take sexual liberties with female students, which John in particular took as a sign of the guru's hypocrisy. But George later claimed he'd been planning to leave at that time anyway, as he didn't wish to go to Kashmir for the second part of the training course; he also dismissed the rumors about the Maharishi as the result of other people's jealousy. In any event, the two men left. John wrote an angry song about the experience that he planned to call "Maharishi," but George persuaded him he was going too far, and John rewrote the song as "Sexy Sadie."

What Happened To: George?

George's post-Beatles career started on a high note with *All Things Must Pass* (1970), a No. 1 hit on both sides of the Atlantic, and the accompanying No. 1 single "My Sweet Lord." Nine months later he organized two charity concerts for war-torn Bangladesh held on August 1, 1971. His album *Living in the Material World* (1973) also reached No. 1 in the US and No. 2 in the UK.

Then things went south. George strained his voice while recording *Dark Horse* (1974), and the subsequent tour suffered as a result. His marriage ended. Most embarrassingly, he was found guilty of "subconscious plagiarism" when the melody of "My Sweet Lord" was determined to be too close to that of the Chiffons' 1962 hit "He's So Fine." *Somewhere in England* (1981) enjoyed some sales in the wake of John's murder, but *Gone Troppo* (1982) failed to chart.

But there were positive developments too. After his marriage broke up, he began seeing Olivia Arias, who worked at A&M Records in the US; the couple had a son, Dhani Harrison, on August 1, 1978, and got married on September 2, 1978. He also co-founded a film production company, HandMade Films; the company's first release was *Monty Python's Life of Brian*.

In 1987, George was back on the charts with *Cloud Nine* (1987), which reached No. 8 US, No. 10 UK, and the accompanying single "Got My Mind Set On You" (No. 1 US, No. 2 UK). He formed the "supergroup" the Traveling Wilburys, and *Traveling Wilburys Vol. 1* (1988) and *Vol. 3* (1990) did well in the US, reaching No. 3 and No. 11 respectively (and No. 16 and No. 14 in the UK). In December 1991, he played a short tour of Japan with Eric Clapton.

George sold HandMade in 1994 after learning that his business partner had been financially cheating him. In 1997, he was diagnosed with throat cancer, which eventually moved to his lungs. He next suffered a knife attack when an intruder broke into his home on December 30, 1999. George died of cancer on November 29, 2001. His last album, *Brainwashed*, was released in 2002.

Interviews at the time made it sound as if the Beatles had broken with the Maharishi completely, which wasn't entirely true. George in particular remained a follower of Eastern faiths. On April 6, 1992, he played a benefit concert at London's Albert

Hall in support of the British branch of the Natural Law Party, which was founded by the Maharishi. In an interview about the event he said he still meditated regularly, and, asked about the guru's influence on the Beatles, added, "Maharishi only ever did good for us, and although I have not been with him physically, I never left him." Paul and Ringo have also said they continue to meditate, and on April 4, 2009, they both performed at a benefit concert at Radio City Music Hall for the David Lynch Foundation, an organization that promotes meditation around the world.

Further reading: *The Beatles in Rishikesh* (Paul Saltzman)

75 Getting *Naked*

Let It Be…Naked is one of the more curious releases in the Beatles' catalogue. It was something of a vanity project for Paul, who had been unhappy with the production on the original *Let It Be* album, particularly the overdubbing work done on his songs.

The production team that worked on *Let It Be…Naked* (Paul Hicks, Guy Massey, and Allan Rouse) was determined to get back to basics in a way that the original *Let It Be* album never had. The new album features many of the same versions of songs that appeared on the original album; this is the case with "Dig a Pony," "For You Blue," "I Me Mine," "Two of Us," "One After 909," "Across the Universe," "Let It Be," and the single version of "Get Back." "The Long and Winding Road" is a completely different take, done on the last day of the sessions, and featuring a slightly different lyric. And both "I've Got a Feeling" and "Don't Let Me Down" are composite versions, each song edited together from two different performances from the January 30, 1969, rooftop concert, thus fudging the "naked" concept somewhat.

Every track was remixed, giving the music a greater clarity. The biggest difference is that all of Phil Spector's orchestral over-dubs were completely removed, making "Across the Universe," "I Me Mine," "Let It Be," and "The Long and Winding Road" sound quite different. All the between-songs studio chat, the short song excerpts ("Dig It," "Maggie May"), as well as the snatches of conversation heard before and after the live songs, was cut as well. And the final running order is different. All of which makes *Let It Be...Naked* a very different experience from *Let It Be*—and perhaps making it a bit unfair to compare the two. While the new album does have excellent sound—the version of "Across the Universe" in particular is quite lovely—it doesn't have the warmth of the original album, not to mention the fly-on-the-wall feeling gener-ated by the between-songs chat and the short linking tracks. On the other hand, it does give you an idea of what the album might have sounded like had the Beatles stuck to the back-to-basic approach back in 1970. The *Let It Be...Naked* package also featured a second CD (entitled "Fly on the Wall"), with 22 minutes of additional dia-logue and song excerpts from the sessions; there was more dialogue presented in the CD's booklet.

Let It Be...Naked was released on November 17, 2003, in the UK, reaching No. 7, and November 18 in the US, reaching No. 5. It received mixed reviews; as Anthony DeCurtis noted in *Rolling Stone*: "Casual fans...will wonder what all the fuss was about; novices should still get the original." Hardcore fans, of course, will want both.

The First Beatles Single

On October 5, 1962, the first single solely credited to the Beatles was released: "Love Me Do"/"P.S. I Love You," on Parlophone in the UK. Both songs were Lennon/McCartney originals, and had been in the group's repertoire for some time.

"Love Me Do" dated back to the Quarrymen days, when John and Paul first started writing together, though their memories differ somewhat, Paul saying it was "completely co-written," while John felt his only contribution was adding to the song's bridge (what the Beatles liked to call "the middle eight"). The simplicity of the lyric and melody clearly shows that it was an early composition. John and Paul's vocal harmonizing, along with John's harmonica line, brightens up the performance.

"P.S. I Love You" was primarily Paul's song, with another simple narrative; the lyric is a letter home to a loved one. "There are certain themes that are easier than others to hang a song on," Paul explained, "and a letter is one of them." The Latinesque beat gives the number an upbeat feel.

"Love Me Do" almost didn't make the cut as the Beatles' first single. The band first recorded it (along with "P.S. I Love You") on June 6, 1962, when Pete Best was still in the band. Producer George Martin had already suggested boosting the tempo, but the song still dragged (this version can be heard on *Anthology 1*). The version recorded on September 4, with Ringo on drums, was an improvement, but George Martin still wasn't convinced. He'd wanted the group to record "How Do You Do It," a light pop number written by professional songwriter Mitch Murray. John and Paul balked at the suggestion, as they were anxious to record their own material from the beginning, but George Martin insisted, as he didn't feel the Beatles' original songs were strong enough. So the group complied, laying down a capable, if unenthusiastic, version of the song at the same September 4 session (also available on *Anthology 1*).

Martin eventually agreed to release "Love Me Do" and "P.S. I Love You," but still wasn't satisfied with the recordings the group had done, so he scheduled another session for September 11. When the band arrived they were surprised to find that Martin had booked session drummer Andy White to play the drums. Ringo was especially disappointed; having been in the group less than a month, he feared they were "doing a Pete Best" on him. White's versions do have a brightness missing on the September 4 version; to mollify Ringo, he was allowed to play tambourine on "Love Me Do," and shook the maracas on "P.S. I Love You." Ultimately, Ringo's version of "Love Me Do" was used on initial pressings of the UK single; White's version appeared on later pressings of the single and the *Please Please Me* album.

"Love Me Do" gave the Beatles their first No. 1—in Liverpool, where it unsurprisingly topped *Mersey Beat*'s chart. It peaked at No. 17 in *Record Retailer* and *New Record Mirror*, and slightly lower on England's other national charts; if not a huge success, it was nonetheless a respectable placing for a first release by a largely unknown group. The single wasn't released in the US until April 27, 1964, on Tollie, a subsidiary of Vee-Jay, featuring the Andy White version of "Love Me Do." With Beatlemania in full swing, "Love Me Do" quickly topped the charts, and "P.S. I Love You" also charted, reaching No. 10. Ringo's version of "Love Me Do" was first released in the US on Capitol's 1980 *Rarities* album; it's now available on *Past Masters*.

77 The Last Beatles Recording Session

John, Paul, George, and Ringo first entered the recording studio together on September 4, 1962. And it was just under seven years later, on August 20, 1969, that the last session which all of the Fab Four attended was held. The session began at 2:30 PM at Abbey Road Studios, with final mixing and editing done on John's song "I Want You (She's So Heavy)," which continued until 6:00 PM. After that, the group worked on the final running order of the *Abbey Road* album, a task that kept the group busy until 1:15 AM. The original running order had been: Side One—"Here Comes the Sun," "Because," "You Never Give Me Your Money," "Sun King," "Mean Mr. Mustard," "Polythene Pam," "She Came In Through the Bathroom Window," "Golden Slumbers," "Carry That Weight," "The End"; Side Two—"Come Together," "Something," "Maxwell's Silver Hammer," "Octopus's Garden," "Oh! Darling," "I Want You (She's So Heavy)." The final running order swapped Side One and Side Two, so that the album now ended with Paul's "love you make/love you take" couplet instead of the abrupt cut-off ending of "She's So Heavy." "Octopus's Garden" and "Oh! Darling" were also switched around in the final running order. Paul's ending gives the album a more satisfying conclusion (with his jokey hidden track "Her Majesty" providing a final surprise) to what was to be the final album the Beatles worked on, so it was time very well spent.

But August 20 wasn't the last Beatles session. Work on *Abbey Road* was completed on August 25. The rest of the year saw a few mixing sessions. What author Mark Lewisohn considers the last session of the Beatles "as a band" came on January 4, 1970, at Abbey Road Studios, when George, Paul, and Ringo recorded numerous overdubs for the song "Let It Be," the session beginning at 2:30 PM and continuing until 4:00 AM. The very last session that a Beatle attended was on April 1, 1970, when Ringo came to Abbey Road Studios to overdub drum parts on "Across the Universe," "The Long and Winding Road," and "I Me Mine." The session, which began at 7:00 PM, was produced by Phil Spector, who gave the musicians (a total of 50, including Ringo) and studio staff an increasingly hard time over the course of the long evening, until Ringo finally told him to back off.

The very last Beatles session came the following day, when Phil Spector returned to Abbey Road Studios to remix the songs recorded on April 1. None of the Beatles attended. It was also the last session of work on the *Let It Be* album, which would be released the following month.

78 Finally Hitting the Road

On May 10, 1960, the Beatles showed up for an audition in front of the biggest manager in British pop, Larry Parnes. They ended up landing a job that sent them out on their first-ever tour.

Liverpool promoter Allan Williams had co-promoted a few shows with the London-based Parnes. Parnes was looking for a band to back one of the stars in his stable, Billy Fury (who was originally from Liverpool), and asked Williams for help. Williams invited a number of Liverpool groups to audition for the position, which was held at a new club he'd just purchased, then called the Wyvern Social Club, which Williams would later reopen as the Blue Angel.

The Beatles—or the Silver Beetles, as they were then—were thrilled to audition in the company of some of Liverpool's top acts:

The First Song With a Beatle Lyric

The first record to feature an original number by the Beatles was the *My Bonnie* EP released in Germany in 1961, which featured the instrumental "Cry For a Shadow," written by John and George (though the record was credited to Tony Sheridan and the Beat Brothers).

But the first song released with a lyric by the Beatles wasn't "Love Me Do," but "I've Just Fallen For Someone." When the Beatles were supporting Johnny Gentle on his 1960 tour of Scotland, Gentle played John a song he was working on during the tour. "I couldn't work out a middle eight and John came up with something that seemed to fit," Gentle explained about the four lines John ended up contributing to the song. "It flowed well, but I thought he was out of order because I'd been writing songs for a year. I recorded it for Parlophone under the name of Darren Young, but there was no question of him getting a songwriting credit as we all helped each other in those days."

It was Adam Faith who actually released the song first, on his 1961 album *Adam Faith*. The Johnny Gentle/Darren Young single was released in July 1962.

Cass and the Cassanovas, Derry and the Seniors, Gerry and the Pacemakers, and Cliff Roberts and the Rockers. John also made sure to get Billy Fury's autograph at the audition. John, Paul, George, and Stuart Sutcliffe had just taken on a new drummer, Tommy Moore, who had been recommended to Williams by Brian Cassar; "Cass" in Cass and the Cassanovas. Tommy was late for the audition, so Johnny Hutchinson of the Cassanovas sat in until he turned up.

There are some great shots of the audition in the book *How They Became The Beatles*, showing the group attired in dark shirts and trousers and natty two-tone shoes, John and Paul giving their all (in one shot John strikes a perfect Elvis pose), with Hutchinson looking extremely bored at having to play with a group he clearly considers beneath him. There are conflicting accounts of what happened next; Williams says Parnes liked the Silver Beetles but not their bassist; Parnes later insisted it was the final drummer, Tommy Moore (who finally showed up), that he didn't like. In any case, the Silver Beetles weren't chosen to back Billy Fury, but were instead asked to back another performer in Parnes' stable, Johnny Gentle, who was heading out on a short tour of Scotland set to begin May 20.

The Silver Beetles were excited about the chance to tour like real musicians. Three of them even took on stage names, as they imagined "real" stars did: Paul became Paul Ramon, a name that conjures up the smoky romanticism of Rudolph Valentino; George became Carl Harrison, after rockabilly star Carl Perkins; and Stuart became Stuart de Staël, after the Russian artist Nicolas de Staël. "It sort of proved you did a real act if you had a stage name," Paul explained to biographer Hunter Davies.

From May 20 to 28, the Silver Beetles played seven shows. Audiences were small, but Paul enthusiastically sent a postcard home saying he'd been asked for his autograph. While driving to a gig in Fraserburgh on May 23, Gentle, then driving the tour van, got into an accident and Tommy Moore was seriously injured, losing some teeth and requiring stiches. He was not pleased to be hauled from his hospital bed to continue the tour.

They came home with little money in their pockets; cash had been so tight on the tour they'd had to skip out on one of their hotel bills. Tommy Moore hadn't enjoyed playing with the Silver Beetles at all, and he would leave the group by mid-June. But Gentle had liked the band; when he was next in Liverpool, he went to see the group on a July 2, 1960, date at the Grosvenor Ballroom and sat in with them for a few numbers. He also recommended them to Larry Parnes. But Parnes wasn't interested: "Maybe it sounds silly, but I just didn't want the worry of a five-piece group," he told author Philip Norman.

Further reading: *Johnny Gentle & The Beatles: First Ever Tour Scotland 1960* (Johnny Gentle, Ian Forsyth)

79 Unreleased Tracks

There are literally hundreds of unreleased Beatles recordings in the vaults. What are the chances of getting to hear them?

To get an idea of what's available, check out Richie Unterberger's book *The Unreleased Beatles*, which provides extensive information about unreleased material. And books like John C. Winn's *Way Beyond Compare* and *That Magic Feeling* not only list all known Beatles tracks and interviews, they also list what releases—legitimate or otherwise—contain the material.

There are several different categories of unreleased tracks. There are home demos and rehearsals dating back to 1960, when John, Paul, George, and Stu sat around Paul's home jamming together. Eventually, each of the Beatles had their own recording equipment at home, and could make their own demos. Not much of this material has been officially released, though a number of tracks from John's archives were aired on the radio series *The Lost Lennon Tapes*.

There are also the BBC radio sessions. Out of the 275 songs the Beatles recorded between 1962 and 1965, only 73 have been officially released. Then there are live performances, going back to the 1957 Quarrymen show where Paul met John. Not every Beatle performance over the years was recorded, but a number of them were. Nonetheless, not a single complete Beatles concert has been officially released to date. The same can be said of the group's live television appearances, with a few exceptions, such as *The Ed Sullivan Show* DVD set that includes the complete broadcasts of the 1964 and 1965 programs the Beatles appeared on. But it's the studio sessions that have barely seen the official light of day. The *Anthology* CDs, related singles and DVDs, and the *Let It Be...*

Naked and *Love* CDs are the only official releases with previously unreleased studio material.

Of course you can find a great deal of this material on the collector's circuit. Bootleg CDs and DVDs are still being sold, though they've increasingly been replaced by online file sharing. Sites like YouTube also stream unreleased material. But most fans would prefer to buy official releases, both for the superior sound quality, and because the money spent on such releases will actually go to the Beatles.

Deciding what to release from such a vast catalogue can be a daunting prospect. But there are some releases that would be very easy to put together. The complete Decca Records audition for example, or the complete Christmas fan club recordings. A proper compilation of all the live Hamburg recordings would be an invaluable historical document, and the Hollywood Bowl and Shea Stadium concerts are ready to go. Given the multi-disc box-set treatment other artists receive, a box set with all the BBC recordings would be a nice high-end item (bootleg label Great Dane put out a nice nine-CD box of the BBC sessions, complete with a professionally printed booklet).

Certainly, the Beatles' studio recordings would take more time to sort through. Often a "take" of a song isn't complete, but only a partial version. And there are "edit pieces," which might only contain a short guitar overdub. There are fans that want to hear everything, but your average listener would probably find the bootleg of the Beatles' March 5, 1963, recording session, with its 13 takes and edit pieces of "From Me to You," something of a challenge to listen to. Or consider the bootleg series *The Complete "Get Back" Sessions*, which captures most of the action during the tense January 1969 sessions and runs to 38 volumes (each volume a two-CD set, for a total of 76 CDs). There are undoubtedly some hardened fans who might want to listen to every minute, but commercial prospects for such a set are slim.

But the Internet has changed the way music is shared and listened to. It's not hard to imagine an official website offering made-to-order CDs or DVDs, instant downloads, and streaming of the entire Beatles catalogue. The Beatles probably won't go as far as making everything available. But there's certainly the potential to put out more than a few releases with unreleased material.

80 Some People Do Go Both Ways

There have long been rumors that John had some kind of sexual relationship with the band's manager, Brian Epstein. Most accounts limit that relationship to what happened during a two-week holiday John and Brian spent in Spain, in April and May of 1963, though Albert Goldman, in *The Lives of John Lennon*, claims the relationship lasted until Epstein's death in 1967. The allegations have been repeated in nearly every Lennon biography since his death, and many Beatles histories as well; the Spanish trip was also the subject of the 1991 fictional film short *The Hours and Times*.

John's trip with Brian did raise eyebrows at the time, not only because Brian was a known homosexual who had an interest in John, but also because John's wife Cynthia had just given birth to their son, Julian. On the surface, it seemed strange that when he had a break in his schedule, John wouldn't want to spend that time with his wife and newborn child. But for someone with a decided ambivalence about being married, the trip was likely a chance to escape the increasing responsibilities of his personal life. As John told *Rolling Stone*, "I wasn't going to break the holiday for a baby. I just thought what a bastard I was and went."

While the two were on holiday, they did relax and open up to each other, Brian finally able to talk freely about being homosexual without fear of censure. John also felt free to question Brian about the subject in a way he wouldn't have back at home. He later recalled sitting at cafés with his manager, watching as young men walked by and asking, "Do you like this one, do you like that one?" "I was rather enjoying the experience," he later told *Playboy*, "thinking like a writer all the time: 'I am experiencing this.'"

But what was the extent of that experience? Soon after the trip, at Paul's 21st birthday party in Liverpool that June, Cavern DJ Bob Wooler made an insinuating remark to John about his trip with Brian, and John promptly beat up the hapless DJ (he later offered a public apology and gave Wooler £200 to cover his medical expenses). But in a calmer state of mind, John told his good friend Pete Shotton (as recorded in Shotton's memoir *John Lennon: In My Life*), that he allowed Brian to masturbate him; a similar account was given in *The Love You Make*, a memoir by Brian's friend and aide Peter Brown (co-written with Stephen Gaines). And in Hunter Davies' 1985 edition of *The Beatles* he said John had told him he'd had a one-night stand with Brian, a story Davies dismissed: "I didn't really believe it, though John was daft enough to try anything once." But in Philip Norman's *John Lennon*, he has Yoko saying John told her nothing happened between him and Brian, and that he'd only let people think so "so that everyone would believe his power over Brian to be absolute"—a rather improbable explanation.

John himself was rather oblique about the matter in his interviews. Here's how he described his relationship with Brian in his 1980 *Playboy* interview: "It was almost a love affair, but not quite. It was not consummated. But it was a pretty intense relationship." Which still leaves the door open for something happening, if not "consummation." But it seems unlikely that John and Brian were physically involved at all after their trip.

81 Early Beatles Recordings

The Beatles made their first professional recordings in Hamburg. But they also made a few private recordings, to hear what they sounded like.

Soon after George had joined the Quarrymen in 1958, he told the group that he'd heard about a man named Percy Phillips, who ran P.F. Phillips' Professional Tape and Disc Recording Service out of the back room of the converted house at 38 Kensington in Liverpool where he ran an electrical shop. The band decided to book a session, which was held later that year; the exact date is unknown. Phillips' setup was rudimentary—a tape recorder, a disc cutting machine, a four-way mixer, and microphones—but the Quarrymen were nonetheless pleased to be making a record.

The lineup was John, Paul, George, pianist John "Duff" Lowe, and drummer Colin Hanton. The first song they recorded was Buddy Holly's "That'll Be the Day," with John on lead and Paul providing the harmonies. It's an engaging performance, especially in comparison with the amateur recording of the Quarrymen done the previous year, on the day John met Paul. The second song recorded was a joint composition by Paul and George (though Paul has said George's contribution was limited to the guitar solo), a slow number entitled "In Spite of All the Danger." The doo-wop influenced number again has John on lead, and has some similarities to the feel of Elvis Presley's "Trying to Get to You."

Phillips' standard practice was to record to tape, then, if the client liked the result, cut to disc. Lowe said the Quarrymen couldn't afford that option, so they recorded straight to disc, meaning they couldn't correct the slight errors (though Phillips said they did record to tape, and the tape was later erased for reuse on the next session). Even so, they still didn't have enough money on them to cover the final cost of 17 shillings and six pence, and had to return to Phillips' studio later to pay the balance and pick up the record, a 10-inch shellac disc that played at 78 rpm. Each member of the group took it in turn to borrow the disc. The record had a public airing when Colin Hanton had it, as he loaned it to a friend, who took it to work and played it over the company's PA system.

Lowe was the last to borrow the disc, and never passed it on to anyone else. In 1981, he put it up for auction, but was soon contacted by Paul's lawyers, who purchased the record from him for an undisclosed sum. Paul then had a limited number of copies made as both a 10-inch 78 rpm disc, and a 7-inch 45 rpm disc, which he gave out to friends as a gift. The songs were eventually officially released on *Anthology 1*, though "In Spite of the All the Danger" has unfortunately been edited from its original 3:30 running time to 2:27.

During their first stint in Hamburg, the Beatles made a similar recording at another cut-your-own-record facility called Akustik Studio. On this recording, John, Paul, and George joined with Ringo in backing Lu Walters, singer and bassist in Rory Story and the Hurricanes, the band Ringo was in at the time. It's said this lineup recorded "Fever," and the standards "Summertime" and "September Song." The recording marks the first time that John, Paul, George, and Ringo recorded together, though unfortunately no copies of the disc have surfaced to date.

The Beatles also made home recordings of themselves practicing, using a reel-to-reel tape recorder. About two hours of material, said to have been recorded in 1960 at Paul's home, have surfaced, mostly available on the collector's circuit, though three songs, "Hallelujah, I Love Her So" (recorded by Ray Charles and Eddie Cochran), "You'll Be Mine" (a Lennon/McCartney composition), and "Cayenne" (an instrumental written by Paul) were officially released on *Anthology 1*. The recordings feature John, Paul, George, and Stuart Stucliffe (the only recordings of

Sutcliffe on bass); Paul has said his brother, Mike, may also have contributed some percussive beats.

82 Literary Lennon

John became known as "The Writing Beatle" with the publication of his first book in 1964, *In His Own Write*.

John had been writing absurdist verse and short stories since childhood. While at Quarry Bank High School he created pages for a mock newspaper he called *The Daily Howl* that he shared with his friends, and also contributed writing to Bill Harry's music paper *Mersey Beat*. Once the Beatles' career had taken off, someone passed on samples of John's writing to British publisher Jonathan Cape, who commissioned a book. John drew on older works, and also wrote new pieces for the book, which was eventually titled *In His Own Write*. The slim volume ran to 79 pages, and featured short stories, poetry, and illustrations; Paul also wrote a short introduction. The book was published in March 1964 and was an immediate hit. Highbrow critics enjoyed John's pe nchant for wordplay (such as "dancing with wild abdomen" and "drinking and making melly") and saw him as the natural successor to other British authors like Edward Lear, Lewis Carroll, and especially James Joyce; as *The Times Literary Supplement* wrote, "Worth the attention of anyone who fears for the impoverishment of the English language and the British imagination." John had always had a fondness for Lewis Carroll, but later admitted he'd never read James Joyce.

Another volume of similar length (93 pages) with an equally punning title, *A Spaniard in the Works*, followed in June 1965. The book didn't generate quite the same acclaim, but was successful enough that John was asked to write another book. But his previous writing had been freer and spontaneous and he resisted writing to a schedule. "Once it became, 'We want another book from you, Mr. Lennon,' I could only loosen up to it with a bottle of Johnnie Walker," he told *Playboy*. "And I thought, if it takes a bottle every night to get me to write…. That's why I didn't write anymore." But the two books were later adapted for the theater, initially in a show called *Scene Three Act One*, which debuted at London's Old Vic Theatre on December 7, 1967; the show was then reworked and renamed *In His Own Write*, and debuted in London on June 18, 1968, again at the Old Vic. Both productions were directed by Victor Spinetti, the actor who appeared in three of the Beatles' movies.

After John's death, another volume of his writings was published in 1986, *Skywriting By Word of Mouth*, drawn from pieces he'd written from the mid- to late '70s. John dismissed it as "mad stuff…. some of it's funny, but it's not right enough." The pieces were similar in style to his early books (as the title of piece, "Lucy in the Scarf with Diabetes" reveals), but, also like his earlier work, the stories tended to taper off when he got bored with whatever he was writing.

Further reading: *The Art & Music of John Lennon* (Peter Doggett)

83 The Beatles' First Manager

Allan Williams was a club owner and small-time entrepreneur in Liverpool when the Beatles first met him. He would prove instrumental in giving the fledgling band a much-needed boost at a time when they were on the verge of falling apart.

Allan first came to know John, Paul, George, and Stuart Sutcliffe as patrons of the Jacaranda coffee bar that he owned, describing them

The Beatles with Gene Vincent at the Star Club in Hamburg in spring 1962. Lennon and ex-drummer Pete Best playfully hold knives to Vincent's throat.

as "a right load of layabouts." But he developed a soft spot for them and occasionally gave them little jobs to do, including painting the bathrooms at the Jac and building floats for one of his outside promotions, an arts ball fashioned after the annual Chelsea Arts Ball in London. In 1960, Allan moved into music promotion, co-promoting a May 3 rock show with London impresario Larry Parnes, with Gene Vincent topping a bill that featured numerous Liverpool acts. Parnes was impressed with this untapped pool of Liverpool talent and asked Allan to set up an audition of local bands that he might be interested in adding to his stable.

The Beatles had asked to be added to the bill of the May 3 show, but Allan turned them down, thinking they weren't strong enough. But he invited them to the audition, which was held May 10 at a new nightclub Allan had just acquired, which he would remodel and later open as the Blue Angel. Parnes liked the group well enough that he offered them a support slot on a Scottish tour with one of his acts, Johnny Gentle. Following the tour, Allan arranged a few other bookings for the group. His biggest coup was in setting up their first residency in Hamburg. But it was then that Allan began to have a run of bad luck. He opened a rock club called the Top Ten in Liverpool in December 1960, but it was destroyed by fire 10 days after it opened. And though he helped the Beatles gain re-entry into Germany for another Hamburg season in 1961, contacting the German consulate in Liverpool on their behalf, the group later informed him they wouldn't be paying him any commission, since they had set up the actual club booking themselves. Allan wrote an angry letter in response, but took no further action. When Brian Epstein approached Allan the following year, saying he wished to manage the group and wanted to know if Allan still had any mana- gerial ties with them, Allan said no and advised Brian, "Don't touch them with a fucking bargepole," thus becoming the self-styled "man who gave the Beatles away"—the title of his 1975 memoir. A musical based on the memoir opened in Dublin in 2002.

Allan was later involved in producing the first Beatles conven- tions held in Liverpool, and regularly attends events during Beatle Week.

Further reading: *The Man Who Gave The Beatles Away* (Allan Williams, William Marshall)

84 Don't Pass Him By: Ringo's Songwriting

Ringo was primarily known as the Beatles' drummer and occasional singer. But he notched up a few songwriting credits during his Beatle days as well.

What Happened To: Ringo?

Ringo's first post-Beatles releases were decidedly idiosyncratic: *Sentimental Journey* (1970) was an album of standards, and *Beaucoups of Blues* (1970) was a country album recorded in Nashville. Then came the hits: "It Don't Come Easy," "Back Off Boogaloo," and especially the 1973 album *Ringo*, with its hit singles "Photograph" and "You're Sixteen," all of which reached the Top 10 in the US and UK. He also continued acting, generally taking on supporting roles; his performance in *That'll Be the Day* (1973), where he played the friend of a rising rock 'n' roller in '50s-era Britain, is considered his best.

His marriage ended in 1975. In 1980, he met Barbara Bach, who co-starred with him in the film *Caveman*, the two married on April 27, 1981. By then, his recording career was in a slump; *Goodnight Vienna* (1974) was his last Top 10 album to date. He did find success as the narrator of the British children's television show *Thomas the Tank Engine and Friends*, as well as the US version, *Shining Time Station*.

In 1988, he and his wife entered a rehab clinic in Arizona to treat their alcoholism. A revived clean-and-sober Ringo went on his first-ever tour the following year, billed as Ringo Starr and His All-Starr Band. Ringo has toured in the All-Starr setup ever since; the band is made up of musicians who've had their own hits (Peter Frampton, Billy Preston, and Sheila E. are among those who have played in different All-Starr lineups), and everyone sings a few songs.

Though he hasn't had a major hit in years, Ringo continues to release new albums, and has made dozens of guest appearances on other artists' records. He's the only Beatle to have played on records by all the other Beatles (John only appeared on Ringo's records; George appeared on Ringo's and John's; Paul appeared on Ringo's and George's). In between All-Starrs tours, he also makes occasional live appearances. Like Paul, he's a vegetarian. And his trademark phrase is "Peace and love."

Ringo's early songwriting efforts were dismissed because he had a tendency to simply rewrite other people's songs, to the other Beatles' amusement. And when he finally did come up with an original idea for a song called "Don't Pass Me By," it sat on the shelf for a few years before the Beatles did anything with it.

Ringo's songwriting debut finally came on *Rubber Soul*, with the country-flavored "What Goes On" (co-written with help from John and Paul). He received a joint credit with the other Beatles for the instrumental "Flying," which appeared on *Magical Mystery Tour*, and "Don't Pass Me By" finally made its appearance on *The Beatles*, this time solely credited to "Richard Starkey." He also received sole credit for the charming "Octopus's Garden," another aquatic-themed number in the vein of "Yellow Submarine," that appeared on *Abbey Road*. And he received joint credit for two of the jams on *Let It Be*: "Dig It" and "Maggie Mae."

These days, Ringo is a confident enough songwriter to write nearly all the songs for his albums, aside from the covers he chooses to do.

85 The Only Authorized Beatles Biography

In 1966, journalist Hunter Davies interviewed Paul for the "Atticus" gossip column in the *Sunday Times*. He'd got on well with Paul, and later approached him about providing music for a film he was writing the script for, *Here We Go Round the Mulberry Bush*. That project came to nothing, but during their talks, Davies suggested that he write a serious book about the Beatles. Paul agreed and helped Davies set up an appointment with Brian Epstein, who also agreed to the venture. A contract was signed giving Davies two-thirds of the proceeds, and the Beatles one-third. Thus, the book that became *The Beatles*, first published in 1968, was a fully authorized publication—the only authorized book in which all four Beatles cooperated.

This caused Davies some problems after he finished the book. The Beatles had a few minor corrections they asked for, but in a new introduction in the 1985 edition of the book, Davies recounts that the Beatles' family members and associates had asked for many more changes. John's aunt Mimi was particularly outspoken in insisting that stories that showed John in a less-than-flattering light be removed (she insisted that John never swore as a child, for example). John agreed that his aunt should be mollified. So Hunter was quite irritated when years later John described the book as a "whitewash," as he'd only done what John requested him to do.

Hunter was able to be a fly on the wall during one of the most productive phases of the Beatles' careers, providing eyewitness accounts in his book of songwriting sessions for *Sgt. Pepper* as well as recording sessions for the album. Because the book came out before the Beatles broke up, there's none of the revisionism that comes when a story has been told too often over the years, and facts have become muddy, or forgotten. And there's a freshness about the main text that makes *The Beatles* one of the best books on the group to this day.

The Beatles was a best seller when it was first published. Though Davies never wrote a sequel, revised editions published in 1985, 2002, and 2009 have extensive introductions and epilogues that feature new material. Hunter also wrote *The Quarrymen* (2001), an interesting book on the non-famous members of the band.

86 Tony Sheridan: The Teacher

It was recording as Tony Sheridan's backing group that led to the Beatles making the record that brought them to the attention of Brian Epstein. But who was Tony Sheridan?

Sheridan was born Anthony Esmond Sheridan McGinnity on May 21, 1940, in Norwich, England. His first instrument was the violin, "But then I heard my first electric guitar sounds," he told me. "It was probably something like skiffle, Lonnie Donegan or something. And that just told me straight away, 'This is what I'm going to do, nothing else.'" At age 15 he began hitchhiking into London, where he played at the 2i's Coffee Bar in Soho. By 18, he'd been signed up as a regular on the UK music TV show *Oh Boy!*, when he dropped the "McGinnity" part of his name and became Tony Sheridan. "I was the first guy to be allowed to play electric guitar live on British television," he said. "It's a dubious honor, but it's true!"

Sheridan was eventually fired from *Oh Boy!* for being unreliable ("I had a reputation for being a bit wild"), but he soon found work as a session musician in the studio and a backing musician on the road; he shared the bill with Eddie Cochran and Gene Vincent on their British tour in 1960, where Cochran was killed in a car accident (and Vincent seriously wounded). Back at the 2i's, he was approached by Bruno Koschmider, the German club owner who was looking for English musicians to play his Kaiserkeller club in Hamburg. Sheridan had no regular band, but got together a group of musicians willing to go to Germany. It was due to the success of Sheridan's band that Koschmider continued to book English groups for his clubs, eventually including the Beatles. The Beatles frequently played with Sheridan both on and offstage, John and George in particular studying his guitar technique and nicknaming him "The Teacher."

Sheridan wasn't initially impressed with the Beatles' first records. "I think they sold out, at the beginning," he said. "'Please Please Me' and 'Love Me Do' and that stuff, I thought, ah, they've sold their soul. They've forgotten the reason they wanted to play; ambition got the better of them. The music they were getting into in the Hamburg days was much more rhythm & blues, it was black music. It wasn't this bubblegum stuff that they

The Live Hamburg Recordings

At the end of December 1962, the sound manager of the Star-Club, Adrian Barber (previously a member of Liverpool groups Cass and the Casanovas and the Big Three), recorded several sets by the Beatles in order to test the club's sound system. These tapes, which ran about four hours, were the first extensive live recordings ever made of the Beatles.

The tapes eventually ended up with Ted "Kingsize" Taylor, lead singer with another Liverpool group, Kingsize Taylor and the Dominos. He later offered the tapes to Brian Epstein, who turned him down, and in the '70s, working with Allan Williams, approached the Beatles directly, and was again turned down. A deal was finally made with an independent label, Lingasong, after which the Beatles sued to prevent the release of the recordings. But their efforts failed, and the double-album set *Live! At the Star-Club In Hamburg, Germany; 1962* was released on May 2, 1977, in the UK, June 13 in the US, each version having different songs.

Though rougher, in many ways it's more interesting than *Live at the Hollywood Bowl*, not least because of the variety of songs. But the album only reached No. 111 in the US. There have been innumerable permutations of the 30 total songs released over the years—until 1998, when Apple Corp. finally blocked further distribution of the recordings. Since then, they have yet to be officially released.

came out with, which was basically just pop, wasn't it?" But he was pleased to note his influence on their later work. "One of the nicest things for me was to hear sometimes a particular chord or harmony that I'd taught George, who was very keen on learning anything he could," he said. "I was slightly older, I knew a bit more. And I was into weird chords and things. And to hear these suddenly coming through one of the Beatles tracks from the late '60s, that was quite gratifying to hear that, 'cause I know where he got certain things."

Sheridan remained in Hamburg until 1967, recording for Polydor, and enjoying some residual popularity for his recordings with the Beatles when their career took off. In 1967, he went to Vietnam to play for the US troops and ended up staying two years. He eventually toured in most of Europe, as well as Israel and Australia; in 1978, he moved to Los Angeles, where he lived for a year and recorded the album *Worlds Apart* with members of Elvis Presley's 1970s touring band.

Sheridan lived in northern Germany with his wife Anna, continuing to record and perform, and sometimes making appearances at Beatles conventions. And though he never reached the heights of his one-time bandmates, he was happy about what he achieved. "I'm one of these persons who's never tried to 'make it,'" he said. "Success is something I'm not after and never have been after. So I'm doing what I always have been doing; music and writing and making the occasional record as the chance comes along without really having to beg for it, as most people have to do. And in that respect, I've been pretty lucky. The reason I started playing music hasn't really changed. It's just because I enjoy it. I love doing it, that's all."

Sheridan died on February 16, 2013, in Hamburg, at age 72, after a long illness.

87 At the Top of the Charts

Calculating the first No. 1 hits the Beatles had in America is easy; the first No. 1 single was "I Want to Hold Your Hand" and the first No. 1 album was *Meet The Beatles.*

It's a little more complicated on the other side of the Atlantic, at least regarding the band's singles. "Love Me Do" was the band's first-ever No. 1 in Britain, but only in the pages of Liverpool's music paper, *Mersey Beat;* it never got higher than No. 17 in any of the national charts. There were a number of national charts in the UK at the time, which is where the confusion results over the band's next single, "Please Please Me." In *Melody Maker,* the *New Musical Express, Disc,* and the BBC's own chart, the single reached No. 1. But in *Record Retailer,* the single peaked at No. 2 (Frank Ifield's "I Remember You" held down the top spot). Today, the charts *Record Retailer* compiled are seen as being the most consistent, so it's their charts that are regarded as the "official" British chart listings. Thus, pick up a book like *The Complete Book of the British Charts* and you'll find "Please Please Me" peaking at No. 2, not No. 1 (which also explains why the song is not on the *1* album). The Beatles' third single, "From Me to You," was an across-the-board No. 1 hit.

Twist and Shout, the Beatles' first EP, topped *Record Retailer's* EP chart. In fact, *Record Retailer* was the only publication with an EP chart; in other publications, *Twist and Shout* was treated like a single (in *Melody Maker's* singles chart, *Twist and Shout* peaked at an impressive No. 2). The *Please Please Me* album was another across-the-board No. 1 hit in all the UK album charts.

88 Fabs On Film No. 7: Non-Beatles Movies That Featured a Beatle

Aside from the four films the Beatles made (*A Hard Day's Night, Help!, Yellow Submarine,* and *Let It Be*), and the TV film *Magical Mystery Tour,* the Beatles were involved in a number of other film projects as well.

John was the first Beatle to make a solo film appearance, in Richard Lester's 1967 anti-war film *How I Won the War,* based on the novel by Patrick Ryan. The "war" of the title is World War II, and the absurdist storyline follows the exploits of a hapless army regiment wandering around Africa with plans to set up a cricket pitch behind enemy lines. Most chilling is the scene when John's character, "Musketeer Gripweed," is killed. After being wounded, John looks straight into the camera and says, "I knew this would happen. You knew it would happen, didn't you?"

But John would be most famous—or infamous—for the arty films he made with Yoko. Between 1968 and 1970, the two worked on nine films together: *Smile* (1968), a 50-minute film of John's face breaking into a smile (filmed at high-speed, so that when projected at normal speed the smile took quite a while to fully develop); *Two Virgins* (1968), a 21-minute film of John and Yoko's images merging together; *Honeymoon* (1969), featuring footage from the couple's bed-in in Amsterdam following their wedding; *Self Portrait* (1969), another slow film, 15 minutes in length, showing John's penis achieving a partial erection; *Apotheosis* (1969), a 16-minute film of a helium balloon rising into the air, which actually had a sequel, *Apotheosis 2* (1969); *Up Your Legs Forever* (1970), a study of people's legs in the fashion of Yoko's *Bottoms*; and *Fly* (1970), originally a 50-minute film, later cut to 20 minutes, following a fly crawling over the body of a naked woman. Most striking was the film *Rape*, shot in 1968. The "rape" is not sexual, but metaphorical, as a camera crew begins by following an attractive woman around London. At first amused by the attention, the woman becomes increasingly annoyed, and then frightened, as the camera refuses to let her alone. She eventually breaks down in tears—without her having been physically touched at all. It's a work that's even more resonant today, in the era of reality TV.

Ringo had been singled out for his performances in *A Hard Day's Night* and *Help!*, so it was natural that he ended up making the most feature films. During the Beatle years, he had a small

Former boxing champion Sugar Ray Robinson along with Ringo on the set of Candy *in 1968.* (AP Images)

Hits to Spare

From 1963 to 1965, the Beatles released two albums and at least three singles a year, which kept John and Paul very busy as songwriters. But they were still able to provide songs for other acts in Brian Epstein's stable, songs that the Beatles never ended up releasing themselves.

Cilla Black was a fellow Liverpudlian who launched her career with Lennon/McCartney's "Love of the Loved," a moderate hit in the UK (the Beatles recorded the song at their Decca audition). "It's For You" and "Step Inside Love," both primarily written by Paul, did better; the latter tune was also the theme song of her first television series.

Billy J. Kramer was another Liverpudlian who fronted the Manchester-based group the Dakotas. A number of his singles were Lennon/McCartney numbers not recorded by the Beatles: "Bad to Me," "I'll Keep You Satisfied," and "From a Window" (a B-side, "I'll Be on My Way," was another song the Beatles only performed at a BBC session).

Other Lennon/McCartney originals recorded at the Decca audition were also given to other artists. "Like Dreamers Do" was recorded by the Applejacks, who had a moderate UK hit with it. "Hello Little Girl," recorded by the Fourmost, reached the UK Top 10; they also recorded the Lennon/McCartney song, "I'm in Love."

Peter & Gordon were Peter Asher (Jane Asher's brother) and Gordon Waller, who had a big success with Lennon and McCartney's "World Without Love," which topped the charts in the US and UK. They had further hits with "Nobody I Know," "I Don't Want to See You Again," and "Woman."

The Beatles tried recording "That Means a Lot," but never completed a satisfactory version of it (it was later released on *Anthology 2*). So the song was given to P.J. Proby, a Texan based in England; it reached the UK Top 30.

Not every Lennon/McCartney number was a hit: the Chris Barber Band's "Cat Call" (a rewrite of the Beatles' instrumental "Catswalk"), the Strangers' "One and One Is Two," and Tommy Quickly's "Tip of My Tongue" fared poorly in the charts. Most of the songs mentioned here were released on the compilation *The Songs Lennon and McCartney Gave Away*, but it's now out of print.

role in the 1968 film *Candy*, based on Terry Southern's satirical novel of the same name (Southern's most notable credit was co-writing the screenplay for *Dr. Strangelove: Or, How I Learned to Stop Worrying and Love the Bomb*). The film follows the amorous exploits of Candy, the title character; Ringo played a gardener, one of Candy's many amours. His next role was in another film based on a Terry Southern novel, *The Magic Christian* (1969), where he played the adopted son of Peter Sellers, a rich eccentric out to prove people will do anything for money. The film's theme song, "Come and Get It," was written by Paul, and performed by the group Badfinger.

Paul and George made the fewest film outings during the Beatle era. George wrote and performed music for the 1968 film *Wonderwall*, about a lonely man (played by Jack MacGowran, who co-starred with John in *How I Won the War*) who becomes obsessed with his beautiful next-door neighbor and spies on her through a hole in the wall. Paul wrote music for the film *The Family Way* (1966), a comedy about a young couple unable to consummate their marriage.

89 Lonnie Donegan: The Man Who Launched a Thousand Skiffle Groups

Lonnie Donegan's success in Britain in 1956 sparked an interest in skiffle music that led to teenagers across the country taking up music, including the young Beatles.

Donegan was born Anthony James Donegan in 1931, and played guitar and banjo in various jazz bands, including his own group, the Tony Donegan Band (after which he changed his first name to Lonnie). In 1954, Donegan was playing with the Chris

Barber Jazz Band. During a Barber recording session, Donegan was able to record some songs as a trio, playing guitar, Barber playing double bass, and Beryl Barden playing washboard. The first song to be released, in 1955, was "Rock Island Line," credited to Lonnie Donegan and His Skiffle Group. The single rose to No. 8 in the UK charts and created a sensation among British youth. For the rest of the decade, and into the early '60s, Donegan had hits with such songs as: "Cumberland Gap," "Puttin' on the Style," "My Old Man's a Dustman" (all of which topped the UK charts), "Tom Dooley," and "Does Your Chewing Gum Lose Its Flavor (On the Bedpost Overnight)" (which both reached No. 3).

Donegan didn't enjoy the same success in America; "Rock Island Line" and "Chewing Gum" were the only songs to reach the Top 10. But to the British, Donegan was the "King of Skiffle," and his group played a large role in encouraging music fans that they could make music too. As Rod Davis, the Quarrymen's banjo player, told me in an interview, "All you have to do is talk to a rock 'n' roller whose age is on the wrong side of 70 and they will say, 'Oh yeah, it was 'Rock Island Line' that did it for me. And it had that effect on everybody [in Britain] really. It was such a contrast from the music that had gone on before. And this was music that was within reach; you didn't have to be classically trained to play it."

The simplicity of the music was key to skiffle's appeal. For while John, Paul, George, and Ringo were all excited by rock 'n' roll, skiffle was a simpler music to play, especially as some of the instruments could even be fashioned at home. A rudimentary bass was made by using a washtub or tea chest turned upside down, with a piece of rope attached to a broom handle fitted on top; the family washboard could be used as a percussion instrument, played by thimble-capped fingers. All the Beatles played skiffle music before progressing to rock 'n' roll, and all of them have acknowledged Donegan's influence.

Ringo later played drums on Donegan's 1978 album *Puttin' on the Style*, which featured re-recordings of Donegan's early hits. And at time of writing, John's copy of "Rock Island Line" is on display at the British Music Experience museum in London. John had sold the record to Rod Davis in 1957 for two shillings and six pence; Davis subsequently had it autographed by all the musicians on the record. "So one day when I'm short of a few bob, as we say in England, I may have to sell it," he joked.

Further reading: *Puttin' on the Style: The Lonnie Donegan Story* (Spencer Leigh)

The Hollywood Bowl Shows

The Beatles made their first appearance at the Hollywood Bowl on August 23, 1964. It was the sixth show of their first major US tour in August and September, and drew a sellout crowd of over 18,000. Over the course of 35 minutes, the band performed 12 songs: an abbreviated "Twist and Shout," "You Can't Do That," "All My Loving," "She Loves You," "Things We Said Today," "Roll Over Beethoven," "Can't Buy Me Love," "If I Fell," "I Want to Hold Your Hand," "Boys," "A Hard Day's Night," and "Long Tall Sally." The show was recorded by Capitol Records for a possible live album, and acetates of the performance were made for the Beatles to listen to. But the band, and producer George Martin, felt that the overall sound quality was poor, and that the recording had been further marred by the constant screaming of the fans. So no album was released, though Capitol did use an excerpt of "Twist and Shout" on the album *The Beatles' Story*.

Undeterred, Capitol recorded the next two Hollywood Bowl shows the Beatles played, on August 29 and 30, 1965. They played the same set both nights: "Twist and Shout," "She's a Woman," "I Feel Fine," "Dizzy Miss Lizzy," "Ticket to Ride," "Everybody's Trying to Be My Baby," "Can't Buy Me Love," "Baby's In Black," "I Wanna Be Your Man," "A Hard Day's Night," "Help," and "I'm Down." The Beatles again vetoed the idea of releasing a live album, though the August 30 performance of "Twist and Shout" was used in the overdubbing of *The Beatles at Shea Stadium* television special. Capitol approached the group again in 1966, suggesting a release of the 1964 performance as a Christmas release, and were met with another refusal.

After the Beatles broke up, Capitol once again brought up the subject of releasing the Hollywood Bowl shows in 1971, but were again turned down. Then, in 1976, the Beatles' contract with EMI expired, meaning the company was now free to reissue material however they wished. Initial plans were to release a double-album set. In 1977, George Martin was brought in to work on the project, cleaning up the tapes, and it was decided to release a single album, editing together a composite performance that drew on all three shows: "Twist and Shout" (August 30, 1965), "She's a Woman" (August 30, 1965), "Dizzy Miss Lizzy" (an edit of the August 29 and 30, 1965, performances), "Ticket to Ride" (August 29, 1965), "Can't Buy Me Love" (August 30, 1965), "Things We Said Today" (August 23, 1964), "Roll Over Beethoven" (August 23, 1964), "Boys" (August 23, 1964), "A Hard Day's Night" (August 30, 1965), "Help" (August 29, 1965), "All My Loving" (August 23, 1964), "She Loves You" (August 23, 1964), and "Long Tall Sally" (August 23, 1964).

The Beatles Live at the Hollywood Bowl became the first official live album the group released, and certainly captures the frenzy of the American shows. It was released on May 4, 1977, in the US, reaching No. 2, and on May 6 in the UK, going all the way to No. 1. But despite its popularity (selling over a million copies in the US), the album has never been released on CD. Though of course,

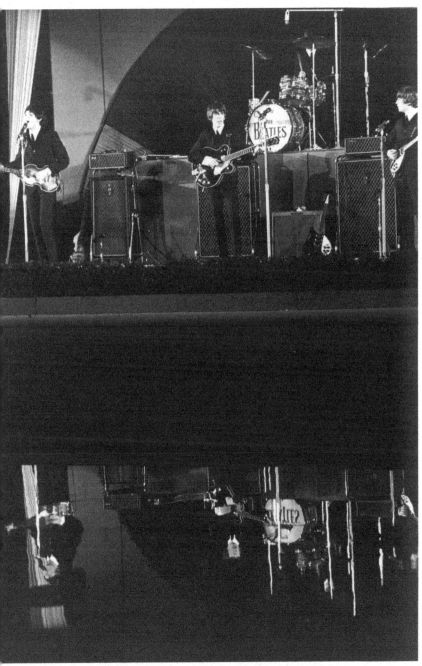

The Beatles playing at the Hollywood Bowl on August 23, 1964.

one would rather have an official release of all three shows with the songs in their proper order, and not the incomplete *Live at the Hollywood Bowl* lineup.

Further reading: *The Beatles Swan Song: "She Loves You" & Other Records* (Bruce Spizer)

91
The Man Who Got Brian Epstein Interested In The Beatles

Raymond Jones has gone down in rock history as the man who tipped off Brian Epstein about the existence of the Beatles. Over the years, some have tried to say he didn't exist. Epstein's assistant (and future Beatles aide) Alistair Taylor claimed that he was Jones, saying he wrote the name himself in NEMS' order book to ensure that the shop order the "My Bonnie" single (orders were only fulfilled if there was a written request in the order book). And Liverpool promoter Sam Leach claimed he told Epstein about the Beatles' popularity, but that Brian, not wanting to give credit to someone else, made up the story about Raymond Jones.

But Raymond Jones does exist. I interviewed him after being introduced to him via Beatles historian Spencer Leigh, who had in turn tracked down Raymond with help from Cavern DJ Bob Wooler, who knew Raymond when he was a music-mad fan who was a regular at Liverpool's music clubs. And he's understandably irritated at stories about his non-existence: "I've listened to people who are pretending to be me and it's just not true!" he says. "I don't know why people try to pretend to be something that they're not."

In 1961, Raymond worked at a printer's shop a short distance from the Cavern, where he first saw the Beatles during a lunchtime session. He was immediately impressed by the band and made a point of seeing as many of their shows as he could: "I just followed them wherever they went," he says. "I used to adore them. I just loved what they were doing."

When a friend told Raymond about the "My Bonnie" single, he went into NEMS to order it; history says the date was October 28, 1961. "I didn't know they'd made a record with Tony Sheridan," he says. "I thought they'd made a record themselves, so I went and asked for it, and that's how it came about." The man who took his order happened to be Brian Epstein, who asked Raymond to tell him more about this local group. "He said to me, 'Where do they play?'" Raymond recalls. "And I said, 'Just up the road.' Epstein's shop was about five minutes away from the Cavern."

Brian told Raymond he'd track down the record, and when two young women came into the store the same day requesting "My Bonnie," he became even more interested. Though Brian had possibly seen the Beatles' name in the *Mersey Beat* music paper, he hadn't bothered to find out more about them before. It was Raymond's request that motivated Brian to learn more about the Beatles, and arrange to see them at the Cavern. After he met them, he also realized he'd seen them hanging around in his shop, chatting to the clerks and playing records.

Raymond later received an autographed copy of Brian's autobiography, *A Cellar Full of Noise*, as a thank you. But over subsequent years, he largely stayed out of the limelight. He appeared at one of the first Beatles conventions in Liverpool in 1977, but didn't enjoy the experience much and was content to stay in the background. "I've been told I could've capitalized on the whole thing," he says. "Didn't want to. One guy said to me, 'Have you made any money out of the Beatles?' And I said, 'No, why should I? I had all my enjoyment from them in Liverpool.'"

Since Taylor and Leach began circulating their stories, Raymond has done a few more interviews, reconfirming his role in the Beatles story. Though he's quick to not take any credit for their success. "People ask me, 'Would the Beatles have got where they are if you hadn't of gone into the NEMS?' I thought they would've made it anyway! It's just a thing that happened. I know my name may go down in history, but that means nothing to me. It was just one of those things. I just happened to be the guy who went in and asked Brian Epstein for the record. And nobody can take that away from me."

92 The Official Beatles Magazine

In August 1963, the first issue of *The Beatles Book Monthly* was published in Britain. It was not your typical fan club newsletter; it was a stand-alone publication, printed on glossy paper, with plenty of photos, both black and white and, later, color. Because it was an official publication, the magazine's writers and photographers got exclusive access to the group, and the magazine chronicled the Beatles' career for most of the '60s.

The magazine was conceived by publisher/editor Sean O'Mahony, whose first encounter with the Beatles came in September 1962, when he arranged for a writer to do a story on the group for his magazine *Pop Weekly*. He was then probably the first publisher to put the Beatles on the cover of a national magazine when he ran a June 1963 cover story on the group in his new publication, *Beat Monthly*. He next approached Brian Epstein about putting out a magazine that just focused on the Beatles. Brian arranged for Sean to meet the band, and they agreed to the proposal. As editor, O'Mahony adopted the pseudonym "Johnny Dean."

The issues are great fun to read, as you can watch the Beatles' career unfold via first-person accounts. There was a regular column with official fan club news, a monthly "Beatle Song," news items, articles and reviews, letters from readers, and plenty of pictures. The print run of the first issue was 110,000 copies; at its height, the magazine's circulation was 350,000. O'Mahony tried to launch the magazine in America, but it never received wide distribution. At first, O'Mahony was told there was no interest in the Beatles in the states; later, larger publishing houses viewed the magazine as competition, and O'Mahony was unable to break into the market.

Over time, the Beatles grew less enamored with the magazine and made themselves less available for interviews and photo sessions. There was a major blowup between the group and the publisher, when, having not been able to get new shots of the group, fake moustaches were drawn on the magazine's photographs to match their current bewhiskered appearance. Once that was worked through, the magazine continued until December 1969, ceasing publication with its 77th issue. O'Mahony wrote something of a rebuke to the group in that last issue, especially criticizing their use of drugs.

But that wasn't the end of *The Beatles Book*. In May 1976, O'Mahony decided to republish the original 77 issues, with the magazine reprint placed inside four to eight pages of new material. When the reprints ended in September 1982, the magazine continued in a new format for just over 20 years, finally ceasing publication in January 2003 when O'Mahony decided to retire. Meaning the magazine's second incarnation had lasted over three times as long as its original run!

What did the latter-day *Beatles Book* cover? Well, there were always new releases to write about: Beatles reissues, solo albums, live shows, film projects, books about the group. There were also in-depth articles on Beatles history, interviews with people who knew or worked with the group (and occasionally an interview with an actual Beatle as well), as well as articles on collecting. There was also news about the Beatles' personal lives: marriages, divorces, the arrival of a new child—or grandchild. The writing was also more "adult," and not afraid of being critical; the original magazine, geared toward teenage fans, was unabashedly positive.

Original issues of the magazine are now collector's items, and the reprints are rising in value as well. A number of noted Beatle authors began their career at the magazine, including Mark Lewisohn and Peter Doggett.

Further reading: *The Best of the Beatles Book* (Johnny Dean)

93 Get Back to School

You can attend classes in the same building where Paul and George (and Neil Aspinall) went to school. And no, it doesn't mean going back to high school.

Both Paul and George attended the Liverpool Institute for the UK equivalent of junior high and high school, located in the city center on Mount Street. George was an indifferent student and eventually dropped out. Paul stayed on, but his education ended when the Beatles left for Germany in August 1960. At the time that Paul and George attended the "Inny," John was right next door as a student at the Liverpool College of Art; Paul and George would frequently go over to the college to join John for impromptu practice sessions.

The Institute closed in 1985, and the building fell into disrepair. Paul toured his former school while working on his album *Liverpool Oratorio* and decided to see what he could do to preserve the building. George Martin introduced him to Mark Featherstone-Witty, who was interested in establishing a performing arts school. Paul persuaded him to use the Liverpool Institute building for the

What Happened To: Paul?

Paul has had the most commercially successful career of any of the Beatles. After the release of *McCartney* (1970) and *Ram* (1971), Paul formed the band Wings. The group's first albums were moderate successes, but *Band on the Run* (1973) was an unqualified smash. There was a triumphant tour of the US in 1976, and hits like "My Love," "Listen to What the Man Said," and "Silly Love Songs."

The 1980s began with another No. 1 UK album, *McCartney II* (No. 3 in the US), and the hit single "Coming Up" (No. 1 US, No. 2 UK). But when Wings arrived in Japan on January 16, 1980, Paul was busted for marijuana and promptly arrested; he was deported on January 25. It was the end of Wings and the end of touring for a while. Paul's *Tug of War* (1982) was a No. 1 US and UK hit, but his 1984 film *Give My Regards to Broad Street* was widely panned. Though the film's soundtrack still topped the charts in the UK, Paul's album sales began to slump.

In 1989, Paul returned to touring, adding a substantial number of Beatles songs to the setlist. Though his chart placings remain erratic (in the US, 2001's *Driving Rain* reached No. 26, while 2007's *Memory Almost Full* reached No. 3), Paul's concerts are guaranteed sellouts. He's also written classical music (*Liverpool Oratorio, Ecce Cor Meum*, and *Ocean's Kingdom*, a score for a ballet, to name a few), and his side projects would fill a book of their own. His publishing company owns many valuable song catalogues (including Buddy Holly's), though ironically he doesn't own most of his own Beatles songs; he and John lost the Beatles' catalogue at the end of the '60s.

After Linda died in 1998, Paul married Heather Mills on June 11, 2002. Their turbulent relationship ended in divorce in 2008, but did have one happy result, Paul's daughter Beatrice Milly McCartney, born October 28, 2003. On October 9, 2011, he married American Nancy Shevell.

school, and after a period of fundraising, the Liverpool Institute for the Performing Arts opened in 1996. LIPA offers BAs in acting, dance, music, and behind-the-scenes performing arts skills as well (such as management and sound design). There are now programs for younger students too, through the LIPA 4:19 Part-Time Academy (for students 4 to 19 years old).

But you needn't be a student to visit LIPA. The school hosts public performances throughout the year (check www.lipa.ac.uk for info). Public events are also held at the venue during International Beatle Week.

Further reading: *Optimistic, Even Then: The Creation of Two Performing Arts Institutes* (Mark Featherstone-Witty)

94 The Pre-Fab Four

The Rutles: All You Need Is Cash is the best Beatles parody, bar none.

This hilarious take on the Beatles story began as a one-off sketch on the British TV comedy show *Rutland Weekend Television*. The show's star and chief writer was Eric Idle, of the *Monty Python* comedy troupe, while Neil Innes, formerly of the Bonzo Dog Doo-Dah Band (who appeared in *Magical Mystery Tour*), wrote most of the musical numbers. One of the show's sketches featured an ersatz Beatles band called the Rutles, seen performing the poppy, Beatlesque number "I Must Be In Love," and shot in a style reminiscent of the *cinema verité* of *A Hard Day's Night*. The Rutles clip was later broadcast on *Saturday Night Live* when Idle hosted the program on October 2, 1976. It received a good response, so *SNL* producer Lorne Michaels put up the money for a TV special.

The special, *The Rutles: All You Need Is Cash*, written by Idle, aired on US television in 1978. All the most well-known aspects of the Beatles story were sent up brilliantly. The story of Ron Nasty (Neil Innes), Dirk McQuickly (Eric Idle), Stig O'Hara (Ricky

Fataar), and Barry Wom (John Halsey) is chronicled from their humble beginnings at the Cavern; to their astonishing rise to fame that led to legendary appearances before royalty, on *The Ed Sullivan Show*, and at "Che Stadium"; the creation of their landmark films *A Hard Day's Rut*, *Ouch!*, *Yellow Submarine Sandwich*, and *Let It Rot*; their flirtation with that mind-altering substance, tea; and the lawsuits that brought the group to an end, though they remain a legend. A legend that will last a lunchtime.

All You Need Is Cash captured the Beatles' visual appearance to an uncanny degree, using the same costumes, sets, and camera angles; footage of actual Beatles coverage also blurred the line between fact and fiction. Several *SNL* regulars were featured in the cast, including John Belushi as fierce business manager "Ron Decline" and Dan Aykroyd as "Brian Thigh," the record executive who turned down the Rutles. Mick Jagger and Paul Simon good-naturedly played themselves, and George himself turned up, playing a news reporter. Neil Innes' songs were clever pastiches of the Beatles' own songs: "With a Girl Like You" ("If I Fell"), "Doubleback Alley" ("Penny Lane"), "Piggy in the Middle" ("I Am the Walrus"), and "Cheese and Onions" ("A Day In the Life"). Unfortunately for Innes, they were a bit too clever; ATV, who then owned the Beatles' songs, sued and eventually won 50 percent of the copyright.

There was an accompanying soundtrack, and the film was later released on video and DVD. Three of the Rutles (Nasty, Stig, and Barry) reunited in 1996 to release the album *Archaeology*. In 2002, Idle put together a sequel, *The Rutles 2: Can't Buy Me Lunch*; it featured no new contributions from the other Rutles, and wasn't nearly as well received as the first Rutles film.

In addition to being a terrific satire of the Beatles story, *All You Need Is Cash* was also an early "mockumentary," inspiring future films like *This Is Spinal Tap*.

95 Beatles vs. Stones? Not Really

There's sometimes a great rivalry between Beatles fans and Rolling Stones fans. But the Beatles and Rolling Stones themselves were friends, meeting up at clubs and occasionally working together.

The Beatles even had a hand in getting the Stones a record deal. On May 10, 1963, Dick Rowe, head of A&R for Decca Records, was judging the Lancashire and Cheshire Beat Group Contest held in Liverpool. To his embarrassment, George Harrison was also a judge—embarrassing because Rowe was still trying to live down the ignominy of being branded "the man who turned down the Beatles," as he'd failed to sign them after they auditioned for Decca in 1962. But George held no grudges, and while talking together told Rowe about a great new group he'd recently seen in London: the Rolling Stones. Rowe wasted no time, and signed the Stones within a week.

Four months later, on September 10, 1963, John and Paul had just left an awards luncheon for the Variety Club of Great Britain (where they'd picked up an award as Vocal Group of the Year), when they ran into the Stones' manager, Andrew Loog Oldham. The Stones were having trouble coming up with a second single, and Andrew wondered if John and Paul could help out. They agreed and went off with Andrew to the Stones' rehearsal space, where they played them a then-unfinished song, "I Wanna Be Your Man." The Stones liked it, and as they watched in astonishment, John and Paul went into another room and quickly finished it off. "Right in front of their eyes we did it," John later explained. "It was a throwaway.... We weren't going to give them anything *great*, right?" The Beatles recorded the song, with Ringo on lead, as an album track for *With The Beatles*. The Stones released their version as a single on November 1, 1963, and it became their first Top 20 hit in the UK.

John and Paul later provided backing vocals on the Stones' 1967 single "We Love You," while Brian Jones played sax on "You Know My Name (Look Up the Number)," the B-side of "Let It Be." And John appeared on *The Rolling Stones' Rock 'n' Roll Circus* TV special, taped in December 1968, but not released until 1996.

96 Beatles *Love* Show

You don't have to be a Beatles fan to enjoy the Cirque du Soleil *Love* show (aka *The Beatles Love*) in Las Vegas. But it sure helps!

Cirque du Soleil ("Circus of the Sun") is a Canadian-based performance troupe who've gained international recognition for their elaborate shows where the only animals used are human beings. Cirque's artists perform dazzling acrobatic feats during their shows—they're generally in the air at least half of the time during a performance—the color, lights, sound, and costumes all create a dazzling experience.

George became a fan of the troupe, and eventually a friend of one of Cirque's founders, Guy Laliberté. In 2000, George suggested that the Cirque produce a Beatles show; Guy liked the idea, the other Beatles agreed, and negotiations began. Cirque has a number of shows running in Las Vegas, and it was decided to stage the Beatles show at the Mirage casino and hotel, in the same theater that had been used for Siegfried and Roy's long-running show. That production, which had the two magicians interacting with white tigers, closed in 2003 when one of the tigers injured Roy Horn. The theater was completely redesigned for the Beatles show, becoming a theater-in-the-round, with each seat equipped with three speakers.

The show's storyline is loosely based on the Beatles' own story, though it's not a literal biography; there are no characters playing the Beatles. Instead, the show draws on elements of their life and times; the World War II environment they grew up in, the psychedelic age, the rise of the '60s protest movement. The show ends with two big sing-alongs: "Hey Jude" and, during the curtain call, "All You Need Is Love," when confetti cascades on the audience.

The most remarkable work was done with the music. Instead of having live music, as most Cirque shows do, the score drew

The Beatles: Rock Band

If you're not a musician, you can still get some idea of what it's like to play a Beatles song via the music video game *The Beatles: Rock Band*. As in other games of this ilk, you're provided with instruments—in this case, guitar, bass guitar, and drums—to "play" by holding down buttons on the guitars or hitting the drums in time with the screen display; microphones are provided for singers. The instruments, called "peripherals," were specifically designed to emulate the Beatles' own instruments, such as Paul's trademark Hofner violin bass. Playing a song correctly earns points, allowing players, and the band, to move up a level.

George Harrison's son, Dhani, was instrumental in getting the Beatles involved with *Rock Band*, enthusiastically bringing the idea to Apple Corp. Giles Martin, George Martin's son, was brought in to produce the music, creating the musical "stems" needed for each instrumental track. The game's imagery drew on the wealth of archive material available, and re-creates settings like the Cavern, the *Ed Sullivan* appearances, Shea Stadium, and Abbey Road Studios. The game uses a total of 45 Beatles songs.

The Beatles: Rock Band was released on September 9, 2009, as a tie-in with the reissuing of the Beatles' catalogue on CD the same day. It's currently sold over 3 million units, less than expected, but still deemed "respectable" sales.

on the Beatles' own catalogue, with George Martin and his son Giles creating medleys that "mashed up" music from one song with another. In "Get Back," one of the opening songs, you'll also hear the classic opening guitar chord from "A Hard Day's Night," the orchestral crescendo from "A Day In the Life," and the drum and guitar solos from "The End." While there are 26 songs on the soundtrack, they utilize parts from 120 songs. The different musical lines fit together surprisingly well, and if you already know the Beatles music by heart, it's great fun recognizing which songs all the various parts come from. The soundtrack won two Grammys, for Best Compilation Soundtrack for Motion Picture, Television, or Other Visual Media, and Best Surround Sound Album.

Love finally opened on June 30, 2006, with Paul, Ringo, Olivia Harrison (representing George), and Yoko Ono (representing John) all in attendance. The show received rave reviews, and at time of writing is still running—and probably will be for some time to come. It's certainly the most remarkable use of the Beatles music in a stage show and is definitely worth seeing at least once. Though there's so much to take in, don't be surprised if you find yourself wanting to see it again—and again. If you can't make it to Vegas, the "making of" DVD, *The Beatles Love: All Together Now* (which won a Grammy for Best Long Form Music Video), will give you some idea of what you're missing; and if you have seen the show, it makes a nice souvenir.

97 A Beatle For a Day

We think of the Beatles as being John, Paul, George, and Ringo. More knowledgeable fans will also know Pete Best was once in the lineup, as well as Stuart Sutcliffe. But there were other musicians who can also boast about being "former Beatles."

The group had dropped the "Quarrymen" name by the end of 1959. In 1960, they became known variously as the Silver Beetles, the Silver Beats, and finally the Beatles. The group's first proper drummer of 1960 was Tommy Moore, who'd been recommended by Brian Cassar, leader of Liverpool band Cass and the Cassanovas. At age 36, Moore was considerably older than the rest of the group but agreed to join them. When the group auditioned for promoter/manager Larry Parnes in May 1960, Johnny Hutchinson, of the group the Big Three, sat in on drums for a few songs when Tommy was late, giving him the right to the claim "I played with the Beatles"—at least for a few minutes. He later played two shows with the band after Pete Best was fired and before Ringo had arrived.

Tommy Moore left the band the following month, and on at least one occasion, John asked the audience at a show if there were any drummers that fancied sitting in with the group for the evening. A large, dangerous looking youth only remembered as "Ronnie" took up the challenge, bashing away at the drum kit with such force the Beatles were careful to never make such a careless offer again. Soon after, the Beatles heard a drummer named Norman Chapman rehearsing in a room near Allen Williams' Jacaranda club. After tracking him down and enthusing about his playing, Chapman agreed to join the band, but was only able to play a few shows until being drafted.

It was then that Pete Best joined, and the Beatles went off to Hamburg. That trip had ended in disarray, and when the Beatles slowly regrouped to play shows back in Liverpool in December 1960, Stuart Sutcliffe was still in Germany. Another friend, Chas Newby, was brought in to play bass. But Newby was only able to play a few shows with the group before returning to college. With Stuart still in Germany, a new bassist was still needed, and Paul eventually agreed to make the switch when John and George stead-fastly refused to take up the instrument. Stuart rejoined the group briefly on bass when he finally returned to Liverpool, but after the band's second season in Hamburg they were down to a foursome: John, Paul, George, and Pete.

In August 1962, Ringo replaced Pete Best. There were no more changes to the lineup until 1964, when Ringo became ill right before the Beatles were to start a world tour. Session drummer Jimmy Nicol was brought in to fill in for Ringo from June 4 to 13, when the Beatles played 10 shows in Denmark, the Netherlands, Hong Kong, and Australia.

98 All Those Books

There are thousands of Beatles books in print. There are probably more being written even as you read this. You could go through your entire life reading nothing but books about the Beatles. How do you know where to start?

The Beatles themselves have told their own story in books, most notably in *The Beatles Anthology*. John never wrote a book about his life, but *Lennon Remembers* (his 1970 interview with *Rolling Stone*) and *All We Are Saying: The Last Major Interview with John Lennon and Yoko Ono* (his 1980 interview with *Playboy*) serve as de facto autobiographies; in the latter he even goes through the Beatles catalogue song by song, saying who wrote what.

Paul has published books of his artwork (*Paul McCartney: Paintings*), his poetry (*Blackbird Singing: Poems and Lyrics 1965-2001*), and even a children's book (*High in the Clouds*). He hasn't written an autobiography, but he did collaborate extensively with

Barry Miles on *Paul McCartney: Many Years From Now*, which covers his life through the breakup of the Beatles.

George worked with UK-based Genesis Publications on a number of lavishly produced limited edition books. *I Me Mine* was the first, which primarily featured facsimile reproductions of his handwritten lyrics, but did have a short interview section; the book was eventually published in a cheaper edition. The same publisher also put out two volumes of *Songs by George Harrison*. Genesis also did a book by Ringo, *Postcards From the Boys*, a collection of postcards he'd received from the other Beatles; a cheaper edition of this book was again later published.

Beyond that, as far as reading, it depends on what particular aspect of the Beatles' career you're most interested in. The best

The First Book About The Beatles

The True Story of The Beatles was the world's very first biography of the Fab Four. The book was by Billy Shepherd, and was first published in England in 1964 by Beat Books, run by Beat Publications, the same company that produced *The Beatles Book* magazine. "Billy Shepherd" was a pseudonym for writer Peter Jones, an editor at UK music magazine *Record Mirror*; he also wrote articles for *The Beatles Book* under the Billy Shepherd name.

As the 224-page book was written for the group's teenage fans, it emphasizes the positive and downplays anything potentially controversial; nothing about their drug use in Germany or John marrying Cynthia because she got pregnant (though it does talk about the time the Beatles backed a stripper at one of Allan Williams' clubs). The breathless tone of the writing is also amusing: "'I couldn't believe my eyes when I first saw this scruffy lot,' Brian [Epstein] has said, of his first glimpse of the sensations-to-be. Now millions cannot feast their eyes enough on the fringed four."

But as an artifact of its time, it's genuinely fun to read. The book was later published in America by Bantam Books and at time of writing could be picked up reasonably inexpensively online for around $10. The UK edition of the book goes for a higher price.

overall biographies are Hunter Davies' *The Beatles* and Philip Norman's *Shout! The Beatles in Their Generation* (the 2005 edition is updated and expanded). Norman also wrote the best John biography, *John Lennon*. Jon Wiener's *Come Together: John Lennon In His Time* looks at John's life from a political perspective, and Peter Doggett's *The Art and Music of John Lennon* is an insightful look at the subject. The best Paul biography is Howard Sounes' *Fab: An Intimate Life of Paul McCartney*, and brother Mike's book *Thank U Very Much: Mike McCartney's Family Album* has lots of pictures and good stories. Olivia Harrison's *George Harrison: Living in the Material World* is a lavish coffee-table book with rare photos and commentary from George and his friends; *Harrison*, compiled by the editors of *Rolling Stone*, is another richly detailed compendium. There's only one biography of Ringo, Alan Clayson's *Ringo Starr* (get the second edition, published in 2001).

You can't write about Beatles books without mentioning Mark Lewisohn. The former *Beatles Book* contributor set the bar high with his first book, *The Beatles Live!*, the first book to document every verifiable live show. He then got the chance of a lifetime, being able to listen to all the Beatles' officially recorded work, resulting in the book *The Beatles Recording Sessions*, an amazing look inside the Beatle vaults. *The Complete Beatles Chronicle* is a comprehensive day-by-day history, and he's also co-author of the definitive guide to London Beatles sites, *The Beatles London* (be sure to get the 2008 expanded edition). He's since been working on a three-volume Beatles biography, which will undoubtedly provide new revelations. At time of writing, the first volume was set for publication in 2013.

Here's a few more: *Love Me Do: The Beatles Progress* (Michael Braun), an excellent look at the early years; *You Never Give Me Your Money: The Beatles After the Breakup* (Peter Doggett); *A Hard Day's Write: The Stories Behind Every Beatles Song* (Steve Turner); *The Beatles: 10 Years That Shook the World*, compiled by the editors of

Mojo magazine. Not to mention the numerous books by Spencer Leigh and Bruce Spizer, and the other books I've mentioned throughout the text. Check the bibliography as well. And that's still only the tip of the iceberg.

One Last Time...

The last Beatles photo session was on August 22, 1969, at John Lennon's home, Tittenhurst Park, located in Ascot (photos from the session first appeared on the cover of the US album *Hey Jude*). The last time the group played live together was on January 30, 1969, on the roof of the Apple Corp. headquarters. And the last Beatles recording session was April 1, 1970, at EMI Recording, though only one Beatle was in attendance: Ringo. But when was the last time all four Beatles were in the same room together?

It turns out—at a business meeting less than a month after that final photo session. With the completion of the *Abbey Road* album, there were no new Beatles projects in the works, and, as Peter Doggett notes in *You Never Give Me Your Money*, "There was no reason for the Beatles to meet except business." Doggett further writes that John Eastman flew to London on September 15, 1969, to meet with the Beatles to discuss their buying the Lennon/McCartney publishing catalogue, Northern Songs. Eastman, Allen Klein, and the four Beatles met "a day or two later," meaning some time between September 16 and 18 (on September 19, George returned to Liverpool to see his mother, who was ill). The meeting was most likely held at Apple Corp., where the group would've sat around a table, trying yet again to hash out their business differences, issues that had seemingly become insurmountable. As

The Beatles at their last public performance, an impromptu concert from the rooftop of the Apple Corp. building on January 30, 1969.

Doggett puts it, "A saga that had begun in passionate commitment to rock 'n' roll music ended in a life-draining argument about the consequences of that passion."

Their initial meetings had been so simple. John and Paul had met at a church fête. Paul and George had met on the bus. Ringo had run into the others when they were all struggling musicians in Liverpool. Who would've guessed that the last meeting between all four Beatles would find them so at odds with each other—right after they'd made an album that many consider the best of their career? Of course, as the business issues became resolved over the years, the four would spend more and more time together throughout the '70s: hanging out at each other's homes, attending the same parties, dropping in on each other's recording sessions, making guest appearances at each other's shows, or simply going out to dinner together like friends do. People had often talked about the powerful force that seemed to be around the four Beatles whenever they were all together. But after that meeting in September, no one would ever experience such a sensation again.

100 Here Come the Sons

In addition to seeing solo Beatles (Paul, Ringo), former Beatles (Pete Best), and pre-Beatles (the Quarrymen), there are other performers you can see who have a very intimate connection to the Beatles—their offspring.

Julian Lennon (born John Charles Julian Lennon) is John's son with his first wife, Cynthia. He made his recording debut on John's 1974 album *Walls and Bridges*, playing drums on a brief cover of Lee Dorsey's "Ya Ya." His first solo album was *Valotte* (1984), his most commercially successful recording to date (reaching the Top 20 in the US and UK), and producing the hit singles "Too Late for Goodbyes" and the title track. He's released five albums since, occasionally supporting their release by touring. He's also made occasional film and TV appearances. In 2010, the Morrison Hotel Gallery in New York City hosted an exhibition of his photographs.

Sean Taro Ono Lennon, John's son with his second wife, Yoko, made his recording debut with a short spoken-word recitation on *Season of Glass*, the 1981 album Yoko made in the wake of

John's death. He didn't launch his own solo career immediately, first touring and recording with Cibo Matto. His first solo album, *Into the Sun*, was released in 1998. His second solo album wasn't released until 2006, though he'd kept busy during the intervening years, playing with a variety of other artists live and in the studio, including Rufus Wainwright, Ben Lee, and Marianne Faithfull. In 2008, he formed the band Ghost of a Saber Tooth Tiger with his girlfriend Charlotte Kemp Muhl. He's toured to support all his releases, and has toured with Yoko as well. He also started a record label, Chimera Music, which releases his own music, music by his mother, and other artists.

Paul's son, James Louis McCartney, also took his time striking out as a solo performer. He made his recording debut playing guitar on the track "Heaven on a Sunday" on his father's 1997 album *Flaming Pie*; he also appeared on Paul's 2001 album *Driving Rain*, and his mother Linda's posthumous album, 1998's *Wide Prairie*. He finally released his first EP, *Available Light*, in 2010. A second EP soon followed, and when the two EPs were packaged in one set (2011's *The Complete EP Collection*), he supported the release by touring in the US.

George's son, Dhani (pronounced like "Danny") Harrison, provided guitar and backing vocals on his father's 2002 posthumous album *Brainwashed*. In 2006, he started electronica/trip-hop band thenewno2, taking the name from a character in the cult British TV series *The Prisoner*. The band released their first EP that same year, with an album, *You Are Here*, released in 2008. A second album followed in 2012; both releases were promoted by touring in the US. In between thenewno2 albums, Dhani started a second band, the folk-rock trio Fistful of Mercy, with Ben Harper and Joseph Arthur. The band's album, *As I Call You Down*, was released in 2010, followed by a US tour.

You can see Ringo's first son, Zak Richard Starkey, in a variety of bands—though he's always behind the drum kit, not

Imitation Beatles

It's not possible to see the Beatles in concert anymore. But for those who want to do more than just watch archive footage of the group, there is another option—impersonators.

There's a tribute act for every possible taste. The early Beatles. The *Sgt. Pepper*-era Beatles. The solo Beatles. Groups that dress and sound like the Beatles. Groups that exclusively play Beatles songs but aren't strict impersonators.

The first big Beatle tribute act was the show *Beatlemania*, which opened on Broadway in 1977, and featured the group playing songs from "I Want to Hold Your Hand" to "Let It Be." The Broadway show closed in 1979, and there have been several touring companies since. A film version of the show was released in 1981, though it was poorly received and has never been released on DVD.

Veterans of the show later joined other Beatle tribute acts, like Rain in the US and the Bootleg Beatles in the UK. Rain started out as the group Reign, a Southern California band who incorporated Beatles numbers into their show. They were then asked to provide the music for the 1979 film *The Birth of the Beatles*, after which they became a full-time tribute act, which is when *Beatlemania* cast members began joining the group.

If you live in or near a large city, an Internet search will probably turn up a tribute band (or two) in your area. If you go to a Beatles convention, like the one in Liverpool during International Beatle Week or the US-based Fest for Beatle Fans, you can experience a wide variety of tribute bands.

down front. The first name band he worked with was a reformed Spencer Davis Group. His first album was *The Wind in the Willows*, a musical based on the classic children's book of the same name, co-written with Eddie Hardin and released in 1985. He's alternated between playing in his own bands and serving as drummer for the Who, Oasis, and several editions of his father's touring All-Starr Band.

Ringo's second son, Jason, also became a drummer. He's played in numerous UK-based bands, including Musty Jack Sponge and the Exploding Nudists (which also featured his brother Zak), Buddy Curtis and the Grasshoppers, the People's Friend, and the Empire of Sponge.

James provoked a flurry of excitement when he told the BBC that he'd be "up for" a musical collaboration with the other Beatle sons. When the media jumped all over the quote as if such a venture was a done deal, he hastily issued a statement saying his comment had been blown way out of proportion: "I was just thinking out loud about playing with Beatles family friends, nothing more." It was nonetheless a sign of how much the Beatles still mean to people. And their musical legacy lives on; both in their own music and in the music they've inspired subsequent generations to create.

Sources

Axelrod, Mitch. *Beatletoons: The Real Story Behind the Cartoon Beatles*. Pickens, South Carolina: Wynn Publishing, 1999.

Badman, Keith. *The Beatles Diary Volume 2: After the Break-Up 1970-2001*. London: Omnibus Press, 2001.

Beatles, The. *The Beatles Anthology*. San Francisco: Chronicle Books, 2000.

Bedford, David. *Liddypool: Birthplace of the Beatles*. Deerfield, Illinois: Dalton Watson Fine Books Ltd., 2011.

Belmer, Scott "Belmo" and Garry Marsh. *The Beatles Christmas Book: Everywhere It's Christmas*. Ft. Mitchell, Kentucky: Belmo Publishing, 2008.

Carr, Roy. *Beatles at the Movies*. New York: HarperPerennial, 1996.

Castleman, Harry and Walter J. Podrazik. *All Together Now: The First Complete Beatles Discography 1961-1975*. New York: Ballantine Books, 1975.

Clayson, Alan and Spencer Leigh. *The Walrus Was Ringo: 101 Beatles Myths Debunked*. Surrey, England: Chrome Dreams, 2003.

Clayson, Alan and Pauline Sutcliffe. *Backbeat: Stuart Sutcliffe: The Lost Beatle*. London: Pan Books, 1994.

Cox, Perry and Frank Daniels. *Price Guide For The Beatles American Records, 6th Edition*. New Orleans: 498 Productions, 2007.

Davies, Hunter. *The Beatles*. New York: McGraw-Hill, 1985.

Davies, Hunter. *The Quarrymen*. London: Omnibus Press, 2001.

Dean, Johnny, ed. *The Best of The Beatles Book*. London: Beat Publications, Ltd., 2005.

Doggett, Peter. *Lennon*. London: Omnibus Press, 1995.

Doggett, Peter. *Classic Rock Albums: Let It Be/Abbey Road*. New York: Schirmer Books, 1996.

Doggett, Peter. *The Art & Music of John Lennon.* London: Omnibus Press, 2005.

Doggett, Peter. *You Never Give Me Your Money: The Beatles After the Breakup.* New York: HarperCollins, 2009.

Howlett, Kevin. *The Beatles at the Beeb: The Story of Their Radio Career 1962-65.* London: BBC Publications, 1982.

Ingham, Chris. *The Rough Guide to The Beatles.* London: Rough Guides Ltd., 2009.

Jones, Ron. *The Beatles Liverpool: The Complete Guide.* Liverpool: Ron Jones Assoc. Ltd., 2006.

Leigh, Spencer. *Drummed Out! The Sacking of Pete Best.* Bordon, England: Northdown Publishing Ltd., 1998.

Leigh, Spencer. *The Cavern: The Most Famous Club in the World.* London: SAF Publishing Ltd., 2008.

Leigh, Spencer. *The Beatles In Hamburg.* Chicago: Chicago Review Press, 2011.

Leigh, Spencer. *The Beatles In Liverpool.* Chicago: Chicago Review Press, 2012.

Lewisohn, Mark. *The Beatles Live!* London: Pavilion Books, Ltd., 1986.

Lewisohn, Mark. *The Beatles Recording Sessions.* New York: Harmony Books, 1988.

Lewisohn, Mark. *The Complete Beatles Chronicle.* New York: Harmony Books, 1992.

Madinger, Chip and Mark Easter. *Eight Arms to Hold You: The Solo Beatles Compendium.* Chesterfield, Missouri: 44.1 Productions, LP, 2000.

Maguire, James. *Impresario: The Life and Times of Ed Sullivan.* New York: Billboard Books, 2006.

Miles, Barry. *Paul McCartney: Many Years From Now.* New York: Henry Holt, 1997.

Miles, Barry. *The Beatles Diary Volume 1: The Beatles Years.* London: Omnibus Press, 2001.

Norman, Philip. *Shout! The Beatles In Their Generation*. New York: Fireside, 2003.

Norman, Philip. *John Lennon: The Life*. New York: Ecco, 2008.

Reeve, Andru J. *Turn Me On, Dead Man: The Beatles and the 'Paul-Is-Dead' Hoax."* Author House, 2004.

Robertson, John. *The Complete Guide to the Music of The Beatles*. London: Omnibus Press, 1994.

Sheff, David. *All We Are Saying: The Last Major Interview with John Lennon and Yoko Ono*. New York: St. Martins' Griffin, 2000.

Sounes, Howard. *Fab: An Intimate Life of Paul McCartney*. Cambridge, Massachusetts: Da Capo, 2010.

Spizer, Bruce. *The Beatles Records On Vee-Jay*. New Orleans: 498 Productions, 1998.

Spizer, Bruce. *The Beatles' Story On Capitol Records Part One*. New Orleans: 498 Productions, 2000.

Spizer, Bruce. *The Beatles' Story On Capitol Records Part Two*. New Orleans: 498 Productions, 2000.

Spizer, Bruce. *The Beatles on Apple Records*. New Orleans: 498 Productions, 2003.

Spizer, Bruce. *The Beatles Are Coming! The Birth of Beatlemania In America*. New Orleans: 498 Productions, 2003.

Spizer, Bruce. *The Beatles Swan Song*. New Orleans: 498 Productions, 2007.

Spizer, Bruce and Frank Daniels. *Beatles For Sale On Parlophone Records*. New Orleans: 498 Productions, 2011.

Thomson, Elizabeth and David Gutman. *The Lennon Companion: Twenty-Five Years of Comment*. New York: Schirmer Books, 1988.

Trynka, Paul, ed. *The Beatles: Ten Years That Shook the World*. New York: Dorling Kindersley, 2004.

Unterberger, Richie. *The Unreleased Beatles*. San Francisco: Backbeat Books, 2006.

Warwick, Neil and Jon Kutner, Tony Brown. *The Complete Book of the British Charts*. London: Omnibus Press, 2004.

Wenner, Jann S. *Lennon Remembers*. New York: Verso, 2000.

Whitburn, Joel. *Top Pop Albums*. Menomonee Falls, Wisconsin: Record Research, Inc., 2010.

Whitburn, Joel. *Top Pop Singles 1955-2010*. Menomonee Falls, Wisconsin: Record Research, Inc., 2011.

Whitaker, Bob. *The Unseen Beatles*. San Francisco: Collins Publishers, 1991.

Winn, John C. *Way Beyond Compare: The Beatles' Recorded Legacy Volume One*. New York: Three Rivers Press, 2008.

Winn, John C. *That Magic Feeling: The Beatles' Recorded Legacy Volume Two*. New York: Three Rivers Press, 2009.